BLACK BRITISH WRITING

Black British Writing

By
R. Victoria Arana and Lauri Ramey

BLACK BRITISH WRITING
Copyright © R.Victoria Arana and Lauri Ramey, 2004

All rights reserved.

First published in hardcover in 2004 by
PALGRAVE MACMILLAN®
in the United States - a division of St. Martin's Press LLC,
175 Fifth Avenue, New York, NY 10010.

Where this book is distributed in the UK, Europe and the rest of the world,
this is by Palgrave Macmillan, a division of Macmillan Publishers Limited,
registered in England, company number 785998, of Houndmills,
Basingstoke, Hampshire RG21 6XS.

Palgrave Macmillan is the global academic imprint of the above companies
and has companies and representatives throughout the world.

Palgrave® and Macmillan® are registered trademarks in the United States,
the United Kingdom, Europe and other countries.

ISBN-13: 978–0–230–61705–6 paperback

Library of Congress Cataloging-in-Publication Data

Black British writing / edited by R.Victoria Arana and Lauri Ramey.
p. cm.
Includes bibliographical references and index.
ISBN 0–230–61705–0
1. English literature—Black authors—History and criticism.
2. Blacks—Great Britain—Intellectual life. 3. Race relations in literature.
4. Blacks in literature. 5. Race in literature. I. Arana, R. Victoria.
II. Ramey, Lauri.

PR120.B55B58 2004
820.9'896041—dc22   2004044431

A catalogue record of the book is available from the British Library.

Design by Newgen Imaging Systems (P) Ltd., Chennai, India.

First PALGRAVE MACMILLAN paperback edition: May 2009

10 9 8 7 6 5 4 3 2 1

Printed in the United States of America.

Transferred to Digital Printing in 2009

This book is dedicated with love to our families—Marty, Nate, Ryan, Marit, Howard, and Brandon—who have shown patience and eagerness for us to finish

CONTENTS

PREFACE

R. Victoria Arana & Lauri Ramey

Black British literature is a relatively new field of study and one that is experiencing extraordinarily rapid development across the globe. It is in this burgeoning context that *Black British Writing* has been hailed by highly esteemed scholars as the ideal place to begin the study of black British authors and their writing.[1]

Black British Writing is intended for students as well as teachers, for novices as well as fans, and this paperback edition comes as a response to widespread demand for a readable, reliable, and affordable scholarly introduction to this important field.

Black British Writing opens a wide span of knowledge and covers a range of integrated topics. Its chapters, written in clear and concise style, identify important themes, provide historical background and bibliographical information, and suggest ways to incorporate black British writing in twenty-first-century programs of literary and cultural study. Chapters cover the history of the field, trends in fiction, poetic movements, diasporic and transatlantic links, critical issues, pedagogical strategies, and the influence of the writing on contemporary British and world cultures. The book's generous scholarly apparatus will save readers much time and trouble as they deepen their acquaintance with those black British theorists, critics, and creative writers—past and present—whose works have generated so much current interest in black Britain's literary achievements.

Black British Writing already has appeared on countless graduate and undergraduate course syllabi, graduate reading lists, and bibliographies of books and articles. Its pioneering essays have stimulated the pursuit of new and related research projects and inspired various noteworthy publications, including *Contemporary Black British Writers*, Vol. 347 of the *Dictionary of Literary Biography* (Columbia, S.C.: Bruccoli, Clark & Layman, 2009); *Before Windrush: Recovering an Asian and Black Literary Heritage within Britain*, edited by Pallavi Rastogi and Jocelyn Fenton Stitt (Newcastle: Cambridge Scholars Publishing, 2008); *'Black' British Aesthetics Today*, edited by R. Victoria Arana (Newcastle: Cambridge Scholars Publishing,

2007); *A Black British Canon?*, edited by Gail Low and Marion Wynne-Davies (Houndmills, UK, and New York: Palgrave Macmillan, 2006), and *Write Black, Write British: From Post Colonial to Black British Literature*, edited by Kadija Sesay (London: Hansib, 2005).

We thank the students, colleagues, scholars, and critics around the world who have praised *Black British Writing*. They have been urging us for some time to publish a paperback edition that students can afford to buy for their personal libraries. We are glad that the time has come for a wider dissemination of this classic introductory text.

Note

1. Vincent B. Leitch, in Living with Theory (Oxford: Blackwell, 2008), notes that "an online Google search of 'Black British literature' turned up 2 million items on February 21, 2007"; in that context, the one book Leitch recommends as an introduction to this fast-growing field is Black British Writing (p.163). See also Winston Napier's laudatory review essay in Modern Language Studies 35.2 (Fall 2005) which calls Black British Writing a canonical text in Black British literary culture and "an important reference for further study of Black intellectual culture" (pp. 119-120).

INTRODUCTION

R. Victoria Arana and Lauri Ramey

T. S. Eliot wrote, in the 1920s, that the newest literary works entering a canon do not merely tack themselves onto the end of it, but in fact reconfigure the very essence of that canon, transforming the present sense of its historical past and of its literary traditions. The validity of Eliot's insight is unassailable—if ironic, given the fact that Eliot, like the black British writers we discuss in this volume, was an immigrant to Britain from a former colony—a poet and critic who assimilated himself into the British literary canon as the very embodiment of Britishness and who helped through his critical exertions to define a British literary canon that became even more arcane, classicist, royalist, and selective than it had been before. Today, we learn that Benjamin Zephaniah—the Birmingham-born black poet, writer, actor, and presenter—has just turned down the honorific O.B.E. (Order of the British Empire), for which Eliot would have groveled. Eliot might even have been opposed to the Queen's offer to Zephaniah in the first place, for, in his "Tradition and the Individual Talent," Eliot certainly did not propose to let just anyone into the literary parlor. Such historical twists and turns remind us of the about-face that followed the arrival in England of the *Windrush* generation. Britain opened the door to the Empire, but certainly did not expect the colonials to come, to stay, and to expect the same life that the Anglo-Saxons themselves enjoyed. There is a good chance that the wide-ranging manifestation of present-day black British writing will have an equivalent, if not exactly ironic, sort of impact on our future sense of British literary history. This collection of essays lays out some of the ways that such revisions have already begun to take place. Mike Phillips predicted in 1998 that changes were indeed "irresistible" and inevitable.[1]

Today, the United Kingdom has embarked on a nationwide conversation dedicated to the venture of "Re-inventing Britain" itself. It may be that the motives for this ferment are fundamentally political and economic, a normal response to a changing culture—the closure of mines, Britain's difficulty competing in the world's markets. No one is blithely affirming that Britons in great numbers actually believe in the need for cultural reinvention and are going about the process willingly and happily, except perhaps for Britain's newest citizens. All the same, whatever their ethnic origins, most Britons are concerned about the survival of their distinctive cultures and traditions and are looking for ways to preserve lifestyles they fear will die otherwise. Simultaneously, new writing by an extremely eclectic avant-garde of egalitarian young black Britons is sweeping the British Isles. This neo-millennial movement is more than merely *popular*;[2] it has taken the arts and political establishments by storm. Backed by the British Council, the London Arts Council, and other English, Welsh, and Scottish civic and cultural organizations, members of this avant-garde are performing their poetry, producing their plays, and reading their fiction across the United Kingdom and throughout the world. Indeed, the "Re-inventing Britain" campaign, contextualized in R. Victoria Arana's essay in this collection, constitutes a nationwide public response to the compelling nature of the millennial theme sounded by the new black British writers and their supporters, the latest generation of successful black British cultural activists. One trait of this generation is that its members do undeniably consider themselves a vanguard, use the term *cultural activists* as much as *writers* or *artists* to define themselves, and are in many cases very much involved in popular culture, ranging from performance and hip hop to music and film.

There is no doubt that both the avant-garde and the "Re-inventing Britain" campaign have been driven spiritually and practically by the boom in postcolonial critical theory that has infused the academy in recent decades. The boom has also sprung in part from the explosion of easily accessible and inexpensive community-based creative writing courses, such as Spread the Word and The CityLit, where classes are often taught by the very same young and dynamic black British writers. However, the neo-millennial avant-garde artists are clear about wishing to distinguish their voices from those of the preceding ("postcolonial") generation and very explicit about differentiating their neo-millennial aspirations from the old (colonialist and imperialist) ethos of Great Britain. In her essay, Maria Helena Lima looks at the contradiction between the social marginalization and cultural centeredness of young blacks in Britain and, focusing on their creative writings, foresees a spanking new English way of life where "the 'brown man's burden' will be to make everyone comfortably black *and* British."[3] Susan Yearwood finds in the fiction of Buchi Emecheta paradigms that figure forth multiracial Britain's "irresistible rise" as a "contentious" process that in many cases is emotionally destructive, particularly to black women— but one that, for all the madness of it, is indeed inevitable. Kadija George Sesay outlines three key ways in which the newest black British writers distinguish their own worldview from those of their immediate antecedents and of non–British-born fellow black writers: their treatments of identity, language, and imagery. The neo-millennial generation of black British writers is, on the face of it, less embattled than their postcolonial parents and grandparents; and they are more sophisticated. Born in England or Scotland or Wales, often to racially mixed families, they do not write about their *staying power*[4] because they are not the ones who migrated. Britain, they affirm, *is* their country. They are now rewriting Britain's literary history as well as drafting its future.

Among the throng of voices representative of this new wave are those of Kwame Dawes, Rasheed Araeen, Susheila Nasta, and Bernardine Evaristo. Dawes, himself a member of this new generation (and the author of a collection of poems entitled *Shook Foil*, published in 1999), explains that the earlier generation "preferred to be associated with the nationalism inherent in the shaping of a West Indian, African or Indian aesthetic and tradition, and the British had no other way of speaking of these writers but as immigrant voices that belonged to that place from whence they came and not to the place to which they come."[5] Dawes draws a generational distinction along those lines. Nevertheless, some of the contributors to this volume of essays do discern that a sense of abiding alien-ness still emerges in numerous fairly recent literary works, from Evaristo's *Lara* to Jackie Kay's poem "In My Country" (1993)— along with the corollary perspective that, if one is perceived to come from elsewhere, one is not really fixed, and a removal to that place could be imminent. While that viewpoint is dealt with by the new cultural activists as, in the main, an inheritance from older generations more than as something directly felt, this most-British generation does not neglect to register the arrivants' distresses when apposite. The youngest writers among them, we are told, reject altogether the resentments that accompany "an identity of 'otherness' " and—feeling a strong social and cultural context shared with one another—"quite arrogantly (if understandably), and, perhaps foolishly, assert a new invention: the black British voice."[6] Rasheed Araeen, the founding editor of *Third Text: Third World Perspectives on Contemporary Art & Culture*, has written extensively on distinctions between postcolonial aesthetics and what is now astir[7]—as have Alison Donnell, editor of a groundbreaking tool for research in black British writing and culture,[8] and Susheila Nasta, the editor of the distinguished literary journal *Wasafiri*.[9] Evaristo—after publishing her uproariously anachronistic *The Emperor's Babe* (2001)— politely pooh-poohed Homi Bhabha's theoretical nostrums about an "in-between" space for non-white writers, but affirmed that she *could* connect with "some of" what Bhabha has said about "the post-modern cocktail made up of mixing literary genres, nations and cultures, and the dynamic that ensues when this happens."[10] Evaristo had (in *The Emperor's Babe*) just flounced past the philosophical pitfalls of identity politics by taking on "nations" and "cultures" as just so much subject matter to conjure with in a trendy book-length narrative poem about a Latin-chatting Nubian in Londinium during the early days of the Roman Imperium. Another critic, Raimund Schäffner, not so long ago summarized the stance of the new black British avant-garde this way:

> To them, identity formation is an open, dialectical and dynamic process of permanent renegotiation. It points to the future and is not merely a rediscovery of roots, the importance of which, however, is not underestimated. They plead for cultural diversity and deny the existence of rigid borders between different cultures, which are not self-contained but open to cross-influence.[11]

There is a considerable amount of "reconfiguring" and "re-inventing" going on in Britain at the moment. And, in a practical sense, this is what those of us who have contributed to this collection of essays—either as interdisciplinary writers or as scholars with an interest in British literature, culture, and tradition—have also been doing. We are "reconfiguring" and "re-inventing" our sense of how to represent not only contemporary British literature with its mother lode of black-authored works, but also everything that came before and was excluded and still is largely excluded from the canon of British literature.[12] Lauri Ramey's essay in this collection bears centrally on this issue in discussing the exclusions of canon-formation where black British poetry is concerned.[13] The essay by Chris Weedon approaches the topic from the vantage point of cultural and literary criticism through a close examination of identity and belonging in contemporary black British writing.

The works by contemporary black British writers present challenging starting points, not merely *because* they draw so variously on the British literature of the past,[14] but also because they incorporate a wealth of materials and methods from around the world. It is a point that Jude Chudi Okpala makes, with specific reference to the case of Ben Okri, in his essay in this volume. The capricious character of literary traditions—especially as these do still breathe and live for the contemporary black British writer—informs the essays (also collected here) by Judith Bryan, Ann Kelly, Alinda J. Sumers, and Tracey Walters. With that said, to appreciate fully the accomplishments of black British writers, today's novice readers of new British literature need lots of help, for black British writers do not form a school or share a style. Andrea Levy's novels *Every Light in the House Burnin'* (1994), *Never Far from Nowhere* (1996), and *Fruit of the Lemon* (1999) borrow narrative strategies from Virginia Woolf and Lawrence Durrell as well as from the Caribbean storyteller's art. Judith Bryan's fictional works—especially *Bernard and the Cloth Monkey* (1997)—possess psychological qualities reminiscent of D. H. Lawrence's best and most powerful short stories and allude as well to the *kehinde* (or ghost child) of African legend. Courttia Newland's novels—*The Scholar* (1997), *Society Within* (1999), and *Snakeskin* (2002)—probe West London neighborhoods with the same sort of narrative passion that Victorian novelists lavished on their fictional creatures, spaces, and places. And, like a modern Charles Dickens or William Thackeray or George Eliot, Newland captures an enormous range of registers of London English. Diran Adebayo's recent novel *My Once Upon a Time* (2000) weaves a rich and beguiling narrative tapestry of African diasporic stories about Eshu Elegba, materials culled from keen observation of London nightlife and its multicultural voices, and the sparkle of a freshly conceived cultural myth. As Patience Agbabi herself suggests by *signifyin'* on the Wife of Bath (with her own Wife of Bafa), her poetic sequences in *Transformatrix* (2000) are a twenty-first-century, hip-hop–like equivalent to Chaucer's *Canterbury Tales*. Lauri Ramey's essay (chapter 7) in this volume focuses closely on Agbabi's poetry and poetics, especially in the ways Agbabi connects with British literary traditions through her contemporary modes of mediation. Bernardine Evaristo's versified novel *The Emperor's Babe* can be compared to Spenser's *The Faerie Queene* inasmuch as it revels in an invented archaic language and nudges and winks all over the place to suggest that more is meant than meets the eye. Her versified semiautobiographical novel, *Lara* (1997), is epic in its generational reach, Wordsworthian in its self-conscious attributes, and Robert Browning–like in its evocation of different characters through individuating monologues. Jackie Kay's volumes of poetry and her novel *Trumpet* (1999) are triumphant Scottish celebrations of the capacity human beings have to create and to transform themselves—but cannot be fully appreciated without considerable knowledge of American blues and jazz music and musicians. This sort of call out could go on and on, but we think it begins to convey something of the challenge that black British writers pose, in terms of the range of works to which they can be related—indeed, to which they *actually refer*, and which form for them a sort of Eliotic "tradition" against which they playfully (but very seriously) signify. A different selection of focal texts would, of course, suggest still other connections and still other intertexts. Postmodern as this approach may seem, it does foreground a concern we may all harbor regarding which heretofore-canonical British literary texts are indispensably foundational, especially for an understanding of contemporary British literature, so richly multiethnic nowadays. By inviting a reconsideration of the subject matter of British literary history, the essays in *Black British Writing* make decisive inroads into what is sure to be a fruitful area of future literary and critical study.

Notes

1. Mike Phillips and Trevor Phillips, *Windrush: The Irresistible Rise of Multi-Racial Britain* (London: HarperCollins, 1998).
2. See R. Victoria Arana's essay "Black American Bodies in the Neo-Millennial Avant-Garde Black British Poetry," *Literature and Psychology: A Journal of Psychoanalytic and Cultural Criticism* 48, 4 (2002): 47–80.
3. Quoted from Maria Helena Lima's earlier version of this essay, "The Politics of Teaching Black *and* British," *BMa: The Sonia Sanchez Literary Review* 6, 2 (Spring 2001): 47. Following the historic Black British Writers Symposium held at Howard University in April 2000 (discussed in R. Victoria Arana's essay in this collection), *BMa* Founding Editor Frenzella Elaine DeLancey invited Lauri Ramey to guest edit a special issue of the journal called *Sea Change: Black British Writing*, with R. Victoria Arana as associate editor. Earlier versions of several articles that appear in this book were originally published in Volume 6 Number 2, which the editors of this collection wish to acknowledge.
4. See Peter Fryer's *Staying Power: The History of Black People in Britain* (London and Boulder, Colorado: Pluto Press, 1984), especially 386–399.
5. Kwame Dawes, "Negotiating the Ship on the Head: Black British Fiction," *Wasafiri* 29 (Spring 1999): 19.
6. Ibid.
7. See, e.g., Rasheed Araeen, "A Forum: Reinventing Britain," *Wasafiri* 29 (Spring 1999): 40–43, 46–47; and his "A New Beginning: Beyond Postcolonial Cultural Theory and Identity Politics," *Third Text: Third World Perspectives on Contemporary Art & Culture* 50 (Spring 2000): 3–20.
8. See Alison Donnell, "Nation and Contestation: Black British Writing," *Wasafiri* 36 (Summer 2002): 11–17; also her "Introduction" to *Companion to Contemporary Black British Culture* (London and New York: Routledge, 2002), xii–xvi.

9. See, e.g., Susheila Nasta's apposite editorial "Writing in Britain: Shifting Geographies," *Wasafiri* 36 (Summer 2002): 3–4, where she points out that it has been one of the principal objectives of her publication "to mark an important and influential presence and to open up alternative ways of reading and writing the 'nation.' "

10. Evaristo is quoted in "A Forum: Reinventing Britain," *Wasafiri* 29: 49.

11. See Raimund Schäffner's "Assimilation, Separatism and Multiculturalism in Mustapha Matura's *Welcome Home Jacko* and Caryl Phillips's *Strange Fruit*," *Wasafiri* 29 (Spring 1999): 70.

12. At the April 2002 meeting of the Pacific Coast Conference on British Studies, R. Victoria Arana, Thorell Tsomondo, and Ann Kelly shared designs for a number of new courses offered at Howard University, including the new undergraduate *British Literary Foundations* course and the sequel courses: *Early Modern British Literature, The Age of Revolution: British Literature 1660–1800, Victorian Life and Literature,* and *Modern and Post-Colonial British Literature,* as well as a number of graduate courses including *Post-Colonial British Literature, New Black British Writers, Contemporary Black British Travel Writing,* single-author graduate courses (e.g., *Buchi Emecheta and Her Literary Progeny*) and the year-long field-of-studies graduate course *20th- and 21st-Century British Literature.* The speakers had participated in the Black British Writers Symposium at Howard University in April 2000. Today, British literature syllabi around the world reflect a reconfigured sense of British literature— a major canonical revolution, owing at least in part to the contributions at the Howard University symposium by those authors whose essays are collected in this volume.

13. This topic was discussed by the speakers on the panel "Out of Print, Out of Mind: Canon Making" at the *Publishing the Black Experience* conference, held at The British Library, London, on November 1, 2003. The panel, moderated by Kadija George Sesay, featured anthologists Onyekachi Wambu, Melanie Abrahams, Lauri Ramey, and R. Victoria Arana.

14. In "Black American Bodies," R. Victoria Arana catalogues at some length the presence of a remarkable variety of traditional poetic forms, allusions to English literary characters of the past, and reworkings of canonical British works by contemporary black British poets (especially Patience Agbabi, SuAndi, Bernardine Evaristo, and Jackie Kay) as well as by a number of others featured in Courttia Newland's and Kadija George Sesay's *IC3: The Penguin Book of New Black Writing in Britain* (London: Penguin, 2000).

CHAPTER 1

NARRATING THE AFRICANIST PRESENCE IN THE EARLY MODERN SURVEY OF ENGLISH LITERATURE

Ann Kelly

In the undergraduate introductory survey of Early Modern English literature running from 800 to 1800 C.E., Volume I of *The Norton Anthology of English Literature* is the standard choice.[1] Unfortunately, the *Norton* generally projects the idea that English culture is self-contained, homogeneous, and defined primarily by the writings of upper-class High Church men. To counteract this view, I emphasize that England has been repeatedly colonized by ideas from cultures outside itself, that elite literary culture is only one of the literary cultures present at any given time, and that persons marginalized or absent from the canon represented by the *Norton* may have had more influence in shaping English culture than many of the practitioners of High Art included in its pages. Among the colonizing influences, I put particular emphasis on what Toni Morrison, in *Playing in the Dark: Whiteness and the Literary Imagination*, has called the "real or fabricated Africanist presence."[2] While Morrison argues that the "Africanist presence" is an essential catalyst in the formation of American culture, I believe the "Africanist presence" serves a similar function in the development of English culture as well. To highlight this thesis, I focus on representations by English writers of Africans and Africa as well as on the writings of Africans published in England at the end of the eighteenth century. Although the most recent edition of the *Norton*, has added short excerpts from two Afro-Britons—Ignatius Sancho and Olaudah Equiano—I still need other texts to fill in the gaps. At the moment, I am using Vincent Carretta's *Unchained Voices: An Anthology of Black Authors in the English Speaking World of the 18th Century*[3] as well as other verbal and visual materials.

By no means do I turn the course into a polemic on race, nor do I omit the important works that have traditionally been part of the Early Modern survey course. Rather, I try to demonstrate that a knowledge of cultural collisions gives us a fuller understanding of English literary production. The narrative of my Early Modern survey has an emancipatory plot, in which hegemonically controlled scribal culture gradually gives way to heteroglossic market-driven print culture. In print culture, the popularity of a publication, not the status of its author, is most important. Through print publication, nonprivileged individuals can rise to prominence and even change the world. In the late eighteenth century, the abolitionist movement, spearheaded by writers of African descent, was such a moment.

To specifics, now. The study of English literature generally begins with the Old English folk epic, *Beowulf*. The interpolations of the Christian monks as they recorded the tale in manuscript provide an opportunity to talk about the way the dominant culture appropriates and transmits texts, an insight that helps students understand the offerings of *The Norton Anthology*. I remind the students that the Anglo-Saxons colonized and essentially silenced the native Celts living in what is now England, the first of many cultural revolutions that shaped the hybrid or multicultural literature lumped under the rubric "English." Foreign influences from Africa invaded England and the rest of Northern Europe through extensive trade routes that connected medieval Europe to the rest of the world. The large numbers of African coins in Nordic treasure hordes, such as those mentioned in *Beowulf*,[4] the representation of one of the Magi as well as the Queen of Sheba as African in medieval art,[5] and the importation of Islamic motifs from North Africa into manuscript illumination[6] are just a few examples of the recurrent impacts of African culture. (I bring visual materials into the classroom to show the students.) Medieval English citizens routinely traveled to Jerusalem, where they were exposed to non-European, non-Christian civilizations that no doubt modified their view of their home country. The prevalent genres of the medieval period, however, did not encourage complex representations of these cultural encounters. For example, even though Chaucer's Knight and the Wife of Bath traveled many times to the Holy Land, as did Margery Kempe (*Book of Margery Kempe*), the texts of these personae do not represent the revelatory estrangement such an experience would produce. If such oral and scribal accounts did in fact exist, because of limited circulation, they could have had only a very minimal impact on the English culture as a whole.

Print technology, which ushered in the Renaissance, did much to increase the colonization of the collective English mind with paradigms from civilizations based on radically different premises. Translation and publication of classical texts, for example, put secular ideas and new genres into play. Accounts written by Greek and Roman scholars—such as Herodotus, Pliny, Diodorus Siculus, and Leo Africanus—as well as travel accounts written by contemporary English travelers broadly disseminated "real and fabricated" images of Africa and other far-flung places, often with the help of illustrations in the form of woodcuts and engravings. African villains, like Aaron in *Titus Andronicus*, or African heroes, like Othello, began appearing on the stage. During the early seventeenth century, the London Lord Mayor's parade was led by an African dressed in gold.[7] The Renaissance fascination with Africa stimulated aristocrats to hire young Africans as servants and dress them up in exotic attire. Portraits from the period often include these servants. While emphasizing the social superiority of the English aristocrat, the portraits do not demean the Africans but detail, instead, their individual beauties.

At this point in the course, I try to get the students to imagine a world where class rather than race determines identity—that is, a time before racism became an essential feature of national ideology, especially in the colonies that were to become the United States, where racial difference was embedded in social, political, and legal institutions. To illustrate the difference between the perspectives of England and America, past and present, I assign Ben Jonson's *Masque of Blacknesse*, which only recently was included in the *Norton Anthology*. The class is usually amazed that an English Queen and her ladies in waiting would dress up in blackface to enact a drama that argues the superiority of African beauty over European beauty. To supplement this reading, I bring in copies of Jonson's footnotes to his masque, which document the great respect the classical world had for the civilizations and people of Africa.

The English Civil War, in the middle of the seventeenth century, mirrored the growing schism between two literary cultures within England. On the one hand, there were university-educated Anglicans writing in classical forms and favoring scribal publication among their coterie. On the other hand, there were middle- or underclass dissenters (non-Anglican Protestants) writing in popular new genres and seeking a mass audience through print. With its enormous technological advantage, print culture and its values inevitably prevailed. By the end of the seventeenth century, most of the citizens of England gained their information and sense of their place in the world from print-published materials, primarily ephemera such as newspapers, pamphlets, and broadsides. Print circulated news, rumors, and information to readers throughout England and among those who were involved far from the metropolis in national and international affairs. This phenomenon marked the birth of public opinion as a political force. Print gave power to the people.

As a result of changes brought about by print culture, we start encountering the production of prose genres (political and religious tracts, biography, autobiography, the personal essay, the novel) written and read by people who did not necessarily have classical educations or any stake in preserving the status quo. Both John Bunyan's *Grace Abounding* and Aphra Behn's *Oroonoko* show how previously marginalized classes of writers (in this case, women and underclass dissenters) achieve fame and influence through print. Elite Augustan writers like John Dryden (in *MacFlecknoe*) and Alexander Pope (in *The Dunciad*) reveal their anxiety that popular prose genres would supplant neoclassical forms and the conservative paradigms they implied. I point out that such fears are realized as the novel, by the mid-eighteenth century, becomes the dominant literary form. In talking about the rise of the novel, I introduce the argument of Margaret Doody's convincing, but highly controversial book, *The True Story of the Novel*, that the novel originated not in England or France during the seventeenth or eighteenth centuries, but in Africa in classical times.[8]

Behn's *Oroonoko*, published about the same time as Milton's *Paradise Lost*, provides an introduction to popular prose fiction and underscores the public fascination with lifestyles outside the homeland. *Oroonoko* shows that colonial life was generally represented in the English printscape as lawless, degenerate, and morally compromised by the institution of chattel slavery, a concept alien to most English readers, who read accounts of it with horror, fascination, and ever-growing distaste. *Oroonoko* also illustrates the trumping of race by class in British culture of the late seventeenth century. The text offers the enslavement of a royal prince as yet another proof of the depravity of the colonists, even though they do give him special privileges because of his status. Regarding students' questions about Oroonoko's close relationship with the white woman narrator, I point out that in a subsequent version of the play by Thomas Southerne, Oroonoko's wife, Imoinda, is white. American students have trouble understanding that racially mixed marriages were not illegal or even remarked upon in England during this period. By the end of the seventeenth century, London had a sizable black community, where racial intermarriage was not uncommon. To illustrate social interactions between the races, I ask the students to download William Hogarth's engravings, which feature interracial crowds as well as scenes of black servants in the houses of the rich. Often using the black characters as moral norms, Hogarth's engravings show the increasing disapproval of libertine and ostentatious lifestyles, such as those enjoyed by aristocrats and colonial planters.[9]

The representation of a moral gap between England and her dissolute colonies found in Behn's *Oroonoko* is reiterated in various issues of *The Spectator*, in particular, the story of Inkle and Yarico, which I photocopy for students as a supplement to the entries in *The Norton Anthology*. Inkle is an English merchant shipwrecked in America, who is saved from certain death by an Indian princess, who takes him to a secret cave. There they live together in perfect love. He promises that if he is ever rescued he will take her back to England with him. One day, an English ship bound for Barbados appears, and the couple goes aboard. By the time Inkle reaches the Caribbean, he has thought better of his vows to Yarico and their unborn child. Upon arrival in Barbados, he sells them into bondage. The tale makes Mr. Spectator weep, evidence of his empathy, or *sensibility*, as the eighteenth century termed it. The frequent appropriations of the Inkle and Yarico story (most of which transform Yarico from Indian to black) illustrate the uneasiness of the English public about the moral impact of colonial culture on that of the home country and elicit the sympathies of a middle-class readership encouraged by *The Spectator* and other popular publications to think that an emotional response to suffering, not aristocratic birth, is the measure of true nobility.

Africa and slavery are themes represented in many of the prose writings of the eighteenth century, such as Jonathan Swift's *Gulliver's Travels*, Defoe's *Robinson Crusoe*, and Samuel Johnson's *Rasselas, Prince of Abyssinia*, all of which I either assign or discuss. Until the last quarter of the eighteenth century, though, the abolition of slavery and the slave trade was not a dominant concern in the print media. All that changed in 1772 with a high-profile court case, in which Judge Mansfield ruled that a colonial planter visiting London could not force his black slave to return with him to the colonies. The Mansfield decision opened the floodgates to publications concerning African slavery, as well as inspiring one of the most popular poems of the eighteenth century, "The Dying Negro," in which Thomas Day ventriloquizes the thoughts of a black slave who is about to commit suicide because his master is wresting him away from his English bride and forcing him to go back to the Caribbean. (This poem is now available on the Internet and I ask my class to download it.) The Mansfield Decision galvanized anti-slavery writers (comprising both English and Afro-Britons) to begin a concerted media campaign to rally public opinion. At the same time, the evangelical Protestant sects, in particular Methodists and Baptists, began enlisting black congregants and facilitating their literary production, many examples of which are contained in Vincent Carretta's collection, *Unchained Voices: An Anthology of Black Authors in the English-Speaking World of the 18th Century*, which becomes a major text in the last part of the course.

After reading neoclassical writers such as Milton, Pope, and Dryden as well as the poets of sensibility such as Gray, Cowper, and Goldsmith, we come to the poems of Phillis Wheatley in *Unchained Voices*. Students see how she blends sensibility and classicism into poems that assert her mastery of elite literary forms and that establish her as a public spokesperson or a bard with prophetic vision. By publishing an ode to George Whitefield, an internationally known Methodist preacher from England, Phillis Wheatley became famous worldwide through reprints in the Methodist press. Unable to get a volume of her collected poetry published in Boston, Wheatley traveled to London, where her efforts were assisted by the Countess of Huntingdon, a patron of several other black Methodist writers. While Wheatley was in London, she met with abolitionist leaders. Knowing that because of the Mansfield Decision she was free in England, she evidently made her manumission a condition of her return to Boston.[10] While derogated by Americans, such as the slave-holding Thomas Jefferson, Wheatley's talent was generally praised by English reviewers, most of whom noted how her accomplishment is a potent argument for abolition.

Another African writer, Quobna Ottobah Cugoano, also brilliantly dismantles the racist taxonomies promoted by so-called Enlightenment thinkers—but in a different way. His *Thoughts and Sentiments on the Evil and Wicked Traffic of Slavery* is an exhaustive and erudite rebuttal of all possible arguments for slavery. Following Cugoano, we read the conversion narratives of John Marrant (*A Narrative of the Lord's Wonderful Dealings with John Marrant*) and Ukawsaw Gronniosaw (*A Narrative of the Most Remarkable Particulars in the Life of James Albert Ukawsaw Gronniosaw, An African Prince, as related by himself*), both in contact with George Whitefield and the Countess of Huntingdon. Living in New York as a slave, Gronniosaw is freed upon his master's death, goes to England, preaches in Methodist chapels, and marries an English woman—all supposedly signs of God's Providence. Marrant, a free black is converted by Whitefield, goes to live among the Cherokee Indians, becomes a Methodist minister in Nova Scotia, where thousands of black British loyalists went after the American Revolution. Other similar accounts published in England by George Liele, David George, and Boston King provide windows into the lives of free black Britons living in America,

Canada, England, and Sierra Leone. These eighteenth-century pamphlets by Afro-British writers define them as participants in the national conversation mediated by print, thus explicitly and implicitly undermining the idea of racial difference upon which the institution of slavery rests.

As opposed to the seemingly artless conversion narratives of Africans published in the religious press, Ignatius Sancho and Olaudah Equiano took a self-consciously literary approach. (Although the *Norton* now has a few excerpts from both writers, I prefer the longer selections in *Unchained Voices*.) Through witty letters published in the newspapers and correspondence with prominent individuals, Sancho gained a national reputation as a social and literary pundit. Equiano also made the British reading public aware of him by publishing letters to the newspapers. These letters, which supported abolition, were often cosigned by the other self-styled "Sons of Africa." By the time his *Interesting Narrative* appeared, Equiano was already famous. Applying the techniques of Bunyan, Swift, Defoe, and Sterne, Equiano's *Interesting Narrative* tells the compelling story of his emancipation from slavery and makes the larger argument that no one should be enslaved. The literary efforts of Equiano and other black eighteenth-century writers had a direct effect on the abolition of the English slave trade in 1803.

As one can see, my approach to organizing the first part of the British Survey is heavily influenced by the methodologies of New Historicism, postcolonial criticism, and cultural studies, all of which are reflected in my emphasis on the multicultural influences on English literature, my incorporation of materials that liberal humanists might not recognize as "literary," and in my emphasis on the interrelationship between literary representation and political/social realities. At the same time, I try not to neglect important canonical authors, though I show how they are connected to the major narrative arc that organizes the course: the transition from a culture influenced by an Africanist presence fabricated by English authors, to a culture (in the late eighteenth century) in which the representations of Africans and Africa include those constructed by persons of African descent who, through print, constitute a real Africanist presence. Thus the course emphasizes that the "real or fabricated Africanist presence" has been an essential feature and shaping force in English literature and culture.

Notes

1. The other commonly used textbook is the *Longman Anthology of British Literature* (Volume I, edited by David Damrosch, New York: Longman, 1998). While this volume includes more popular literature and writings by

marginalized persons than it used to, it does little to illuminate the connections between Europe and Africa. Volume II of the *Longman* does include some of the abolitionist discourse at the turn of the nineteenth century, but as I demonstrate in this essay, the keen interest in the virtues and vicissitudes of the black African started well before 1800.

2. Toni Morrison, *Playing in the Dark: Whiteness and the Literary Imagination* (Cambridge, Massachusetts: Harvard University Press, 1992), 6.
3. Vincent Carretta, ed., *Unchained Voices: An Anthology of Black Authors in the English-Speaking World of the 18th Century* (Lexington: University of Kentucky Press, 1996).
4. David Wilson, ed., *The Northern World: The History and Heritage of Northern Europe* (New York: Harry N. Abrams, 1980), 144, 192.
5. See, e.g., illustrations in Jan Nederveen Pieterse, *White on Black: Images of Africa and Blacks in Western Popular Culture* (New Haven: Yale University Press, 1992), 25–26.
6. G. O. Simms, *The Books of Kells* (Dublin: Colin Smythe Publishers, in association with Trinity College, 1994), n.p.
7. Edward Scobie, *Black Britannia: A History of Blacks in Britain* (Chicago: Johnson Publishing, 1972), 6.
8. Margaret Anne Doody, *The True Story of the Novel* (New Brunswick, New Jersey: Rutgers University Press, 1996).
9. David Dabydeen, *Hogarth's Blacks: Images of Blacks in Eighteenth Century English Art* (Athens: University of Georgia Press, 1987).
10. Carretta, *Unchained Voices*, 68, note 1.

Works Cited

Carretta, Vincent, ed. *Unchained Voices: An Anthology of Black Authors in the English-Speaking World of the 18th Century.* Lexington: University of Kentucky Press, 1996.

Dabydeen, David. *Hogarth's Blacks: Images of Blacks in Eighteenth Century English Art.* Athens: University of Georgia Press, 1987.

Doody, Margaret Anne. *The True Story of the Novel.* New Brunswick, New Jersey: Rutgers University Press, 1996.

Morrison, Toni. *Playing in the Dark: Whiteness and the Literary Imagination.* Cambridge, Massachusetts: Harvard University Press, 1992.

Norton Anthology of English Literature. 7th edition. M. H. Abrams and Stephen Greenblatt, general editors. New York and London: Norton, 2000.

Pieterse, Jan Nederveen. *White on Black: Images of Africa and Blacks in Western Popular Culture.* New Haven: Yale University Press, 1992.

Scobie, Edward. *Black Britannia: A History of Blacks in Britain.* Chicago: Johnson Publishing, 1972.

Simms, G. O. *The Book of Kells.* Dublin: Colin Smythe Publishers, in association with Trinity College, 1994.

Wilson, David, ed. *The Northern World: The History and Heritage of Northern Europe.* New York: Harry N. Abrams, 1980.

Selected Supplemental Materials to Develop the Africanist
Presence in the Survey of Early Modern English
Literature, 800–1800 C.E.

Primary Texts

Behn, Aphra. *Oroonoko*. Edited by Catherine Gallagher. New York: Bedford/
St. Martin's, 2000. A Bedford Cultural edition that contains a wealth of
primary materials that illuminate the slave trade, the life in the Caribbean,
literary contexts, and adaptations of Behn's novel.

Behn, Aphra. *Oroonoko*. Edited by Joanna Lipking. New York: Norton, 1997.
Many short excerpts from contemporary discussions on the following topics:
colonizers and settlers, observers of slavery, noble Africans in Europe, opin-
ions on slavery, reactions to Behn's novel.

Carretta, Vincent, ed. *Unchained Voices: An Anthology of Black Authors in the
English-Speaking World of the 18th Century*. Lexington: University Press of
Kentucky, 1996. Contains full texts or excerpts from sixteen writers.

Cugoano, Quobna Ottobah. *Thoughts and Sentiments on the Evil of Slavery*.
Edited by Vincent Carretta. New York: Penguin Books, 1999.

Equiano, Olaudah. *The Interesting Narrative and Other Writings*. Edited by
Vincent Carretta. New York: Penguin, 1995. First publication of a collection
of Equiano's letters, most of which appeared in newspapers.

Eze, Emmanuel Chukwudi, ed. *Race and the Enlightenment: A Reader*. Oxford:
Blackwell, 1997. Contains a sampling of eighteenth-century discourse on
racial categorization, an Enlightenment era project.

Felsenstein, Frank, ed. *English Trader, Indian Maid: Representing Gender, Race,
and Slavery in the New World: An Inkle and Yarico Reader*. Baltimore: Johns
Hopkins University Press, 1999. A collection of adaptations of the Inkle and
Yarico story published primarily in the eighteenth century.

Ferguson, Moira. *The Hart Sisters: Early African Caribbean Writers, Evangelicals,
and Radicals*. Lincoln: University of Nebraska Press, 1993. Contains materials written by Anne Hart Gilbert and Elizabeth Hart Gilbert, women of
African descent who married English Methodist ministers and lived with
them in Antigua.

Hall, Kim. *Things of Darkness: Economies of Race and Gender in Early Modern
England*. Ithaca, New York: Cornell University Press, 1995. An appendix
contains twenty-eight poems featuring black personae or characters.

Krise, Thomas, ed. *Caribbeana: An Anthology of English Literature of the West
Indies 1657–1777*. Chicago: University of Chicago Press, 1999. Full texts by
twelve writers focusing on life in the Caribbean, which inexorably centered
on slavery.

Sancho, Ignatius. *The Letters of the Late Ignatius Sancho, An African*. Edited by
Vincent Carretta. New York: Penguin Books, 1998.

Stedman, John Gabriel. *Narrative of a Five Years Expedition against the Revolted
Negroes of Surinam*. Edited by Richard and Sally Price. Baltimore: Johns
Hopkins University Press, 1988. A magnificent, unbowdlerized edition,
complete with engravings by Blake. Focuses on maroon resistance.

Wheatley, Phillis. *Poems.* Edited by Julian Mason. Rev. and enlarged edition. Chapel Hill: University of North Carolina Press, 1989. Also contains Wheatley's correspondence.

Useful Secondary Material

Bolster, W. Jeffrey. *Black Jacks: African American Seamen in the Age of Sail.* Cambridge, Massachusetts: Harvard University Press, 1997.

Doody, Margaret Anne. *The True Story of the Novel.* New Brunswick, New Jersey: Rutgers University Press, 1996.

Dabydeen, David. *Hogarth's Blacks: Images of Blacks in Eighteenth-Century English Art.* Athens: University of Georgia Press, 1987.

———. *The Black Presence in English Literature.* Manchester: Manchester University Press, 1985.

Ferguson, Moira. *Subject to Others: British Women Writers and Colonial Slavery, 1670–1834.* New York and London: Routledge, 1992.

Gates, Henry Louis, Jr. "The Trope of the Talking Book," ch. 3. in *The Signifying Monkey: A Theory of African-American Literary Criticism.* New York: Oxford University Press, 1988, 127–169.

Gerzina, Gretchen. *Black London: Life Before Emancipation.* New Brunswick: Rutgers University Press, 1995.

Gilroy, Paul. *The Black Atlantic: Modernity and Double Consciousness.* Cambridge, Massachusetts: Harvard University Press, 1993.

Hall, Kim. *Things of Darkness: Economies of Race and Gender in Early Modern England.* Ithaca, New York: Cornell University Press, 1995.

Hendricks, Margo and Patricia Parker, eds. *Women, "Race" and Writing in the Early Modern Period.* London and New York: Routledge, 1994. A collection of essays.

Matar, Nabil. *Islam in Britain, 1558–1685.* Cambridge: Cambridge University Press, 1998.

Morrison, Toni. *Playing the Dark: Whiteness and the Literary Imagination.* Cambridge, Massachusetts: Harvard University Press, 1992.

Pieterse, Jan Nederveen. *White on Black: Images of Africa and Blacks in Western Popular Culture.* New Haven: Yale University Press, 1995.

Thornton, John. *Africa and Africans in the Making of the Atlantic World, 1400–1800.* 2nd edition. Cambridge: Cambridge University Press, 1998.

CHAPTER 2

SEA CHANGE: HISTORICIZING THE SCHOLARLY STUDY OF BLACK BRITISH WRITING

R. *Victoria Arana*

"Centered at Last"

Writing in 1987 of his own identity as a black Briton, Stuart Hall announced, with some amazement, his discovery that he was no longer in the margin: he had become "centered at last." The nascent reality to which as a cultural critic he was referring (the *centeredness* of black Britons) is what I am here calling the "sea change." What Hall went on to say about that *centeredness* bears repeating:

> I've been puzzled by the fact that young black people in London *today* are marginalized, fragmented, unenfranchized, disadvantaged, and dispersed. And yet, they look as if they own the territory. Somehow, they too, in spite of everything, are centered, in place: without much material support, it's true, but nevertheless, they occupy *a new kind of space* at the center. And I've wondered again and again: what is it about that long discovery-rediscovery of identity among blacks in this migrant situation which allows them to lay a kind of claim to certain parts of the earth which aren't theirs, with quite that certainty? I do feel a sense of—dare I say—envy surrounding them. Envy is a very funny thing for the British to feel *at this moment* in time—to want to be black! Yet I feel some of you surreptitiously moving toward that marginal identity.[1]

The second idea Hall expresses in this passage, that British *non-blacks* are moving "surreptitiously" and enviously toward a *black* identity, is an equally tantalizing one—and one that Professor Maria Lima appraises in her essay in this book. I, too, have seen some evidence of this motion. The recent official "Report on the State and Future of British Studies in

North America" (published by the North American Conference on British Studies [the NACBS] in 1999) addresses the reality that British prestige—even British *identity*—is getting a battering, not just in America, but around the world. The report proposes that its members scramble, pick up the pieces, and make the best of a bad situation.[2] Like the young black people in London, many of the scholars and teachers who make up the membership of the NACBS and who have been specializing in the culturally "safe," "mainstream" field of British studies (English cultural, military, economic, and political history; English literature; English constitutional law, and so on) may find themselves "marginalized, fragmented, unenfranchized, disadvantaged, and dispersed" as American institutions of higher education adapt to the times, put British Colonialism and the British Empire in scholarly perspective, and refashion their programs of study. Many members of this endangered species, *Scolasticus britannicorum*, wish they had been paying more attention to the *black* side of their subject area over the years and had been producing apposite lists of publications on *black* topics to legitimize their claims to prestige in today's pluralistic and egalitarian universe of ideas. In the United States, institutional and student interest in (Anglo-Saxon) English literature and history seems, particularly, to be declining.[3] From England, we learn that the English-English are suffering an identity crisis and "don't know who they are anymore"[4] while the black British are feeling "centered at last," as Stuart Hall put it.

Into this context come the youngest generation of black British writers, announcing, "We are here to expand and to redefine what it means to be British," and their nationwide effort seems to be working. Just as the NACBS is wondering what *pragmatic* thing to do about Britain's downsized power (and the impact of that decline on the lives of scholars who make their living studying things British), the young *black* Britons are deciding, also pragmatically, that it is no use crying about how Britain and their own ancestors got into this "pickle" (a postcolonial life in England itself) since, out of the postimperial crack up and disarray, another sort of order can emerge and, indeed, *is* emerging—and the future of Britain is, they now are saying, as much theirs to decide as anyone's. It is a birthright.

So, who are these young black British people who are expressing these convictions today? The essays of this book provide a cluster of interlocking and mutually elucidating responses. I have entitled my own contribution toward an answer "Sea Change" for a number of reasons: First, the arrival and official recognition of "a black presence" in British studies (what is recommended as an "opportunity" for British scholarship by the NACBS) represents one sort of *sea change*—a new and fairly sudden drive to expand and legitimize this specific field of study. Second, the *avant-garde spirit* that infuses the literary works produced by the very latest generation of black Britons represents a new paradigm, a *sea change*, from the thematic interests of earlier black British writers. And, perhaps even more important, as certain cultural critics—Stuart Hall, Homi Bhabha, Paul Gilroy, among them—have shown, the last few years have witnessed the birth of a new cultural and social movement that is *broader than merely academic* and *broader than specifically literary*: it is the multicultural and multiracial (Anglo-Indian, Anglo-Pakistani, Anglo-Caribbean, Anglo-African) mobilization that is proclaiming itself loudly from hundreds of platforms and stages around the British Isles and popularly and officially styling itself as nothing less magnificent than "*Re-inventing Britain.*"[5]

Re-inventing Britain, as Professor Ann Kelly points out in her essay, is not a new phenomenon. Britain, historians long have known, has refashioned itself at intervals, with an apparent precipitancy evocative of the sort of change a *sea change* brings. The British nation has re-invented itself each time it has absorbed another influx of people from outside Britain who have brought with them different customs, different languages, and new ideas. The Norman invasion and conquest of Britain proved, after all, to be eucatastrophes. What hasn't been noted with absolute clarity yet—especially in relation to the postcolonial influx of the mid-twentieth century—is that, invariably, those invaders who come to Britain to stay are the ones who call the shots on cultural change and adjust the British cultural landscape to suit themselves.

If, as Stuart Hall has postulated, "Identity is an invention,"[6] then two interesting and interwoven processes are emergent now: (a) the invention of a meaningful and acceptable black British identity and (b) the British nation's re-invention of its always-already-hybrid sense of self, a more complex process that will proceed in a way richly dependent on how black and Asian Britons as well as the white ones manage their *affiliative* self-actualizations. British-born black writer Andrea Levy put it bluntly: "If Englishness does not define me, redefine Englishness."[7] To "redefine Englishness" is also the objective of those black British writers who, like Caryl Phillips, reach back artistically into the European or British past to lay a proprietary claim on English history. In her essay "The Evolution of Black London" black British novelist Judith Bryan concurs: it is by laying claim artistically to British history that "today's black British writers have a unique opportunity to participate" in the remaking of Britain.

An Intellectual Sea Change

My own purpose in this essay is to historicize, not black British literature *per se*, but the scholarly study of it. In that effort, I must situate the Howard University symposium "Teaching 'Black British Writers'" in relation to that academic history. As teachers of literature—and especially as teachers of English literature—several of us at Howard University have been responding pedagogically since the late 1980s to intellectual currents that involve us ongoingly in research on the black presence in Britain and in British literature, in the redesign of our British literature courses, and in reconceptualizations of our departmental and college curricula. Resources that we could use for our classes were hard to come by: out of print, scattered, forgotten, or too new to have been picked up by academic and trade publishers. The "Teaching 'Black British Writers'" symposium held on April 15, 2000 at Howard University was the first fully fledged international conference to focus academic attention on black British writing as a scholarly discipline.[8] On that occasion, the speakers all delved to varying degrees into the specific experiences of studying as well as teaching black British literature. In their capacities as writers and teachers, the Howard symposium speakers all recognized that a sea change was occurring in British society, in current black British writing, and in the study of black British literature. This book broadens our collective, historical endeavor to introduce the richly promising new state of the art to others.

If we pay close attention to the published record concerning *studies* of black British literature and take note of certain concurrent events of domestic British history, we can actually see how, where, and when the sea change began to occur.

The Importance of 1981

Today, the British Council is not the only governmental entity that seems enthusiastic about the changing demography of the United Kingdom: the Corporation of London, The Arts Council/England, the Scottish and Welsh governments, and many other bodies today sponsor vibrant cultural activities. Their largesse annually supports countless events throughout the British Isles and around the world, events that with increasing frequency feature British poets and novelists, filmmakers and cultural commentators who happen to be black.[9] This is something new. And the year 1981 was decisive in marking this particular turn of events. If the British Council thinks it is to Britain's advantage to support and publicize her black authors, probably the British Establishment likes what today's young black writers are saying; either *that*, or the Council would rather put up with *discourse* than with force, its harsher alternative. In spring and summer 1981, a tumult of rioting, resistance, and rebellion against racist police violence hit London, Brixton, "Handsworth in Birmingham, Chapeltown in Leeds, Bolton, Luton, Leicester, Nottingham, Birkenhead, Hackney, Wood Green Walthamstow, Hull, High Wycombe, Southampton, Halifax, Bedford, Gloucester, Sheffield, Coventry, Portsmouth, Bristol, Edinburgh, Reading, Huddersfield, Blackburn, Preston, Ellesmere Port, Chester, Stoke, Shrewsbury, Wolverhampton, Newcastle, Knaresborough, Derby, Stockport, Maidstone, Aldershot, and dozens of other places, *black and white youth together* against the police."[10] This new generation's combative reaction against the increasingly brutal, racist policing in Great Britain prompted Margaret Thatcher almost immediately to propose a narrower, reactionary redefinition of British citizenship—and of residents' civil rights. Her initiative was promptly endorsed by her loyal followers (the Conservative Party and a xenophobic white citizenry) and enacted into law. The new law was a preemptive strike by the Thatcher government against the Establishment's feeling of total loss of civic control. The legislation Thatcher introduced (and that was adopted as the British Nationality Act of 1981) stated: "Only those whose parents had been born in the United Kingdom, or had been legally 'settled' there, would henceforth qualify for the newly created 'British citizenship.'"[11] The resultant shock was felt instantly.

The civil insurgence of 1981 (and the concomitant 1981 parliamentary legislation) prompted an intellectual reaction of outrage against the overt racism of the government's actions and an explosion of artistic responses by black British writers and artists, dramatists and filmmakers. Among the former were immediate journalistic responses by Salman Rushdie,[12] a landmark book by Paul Gilroy,[13] scholarly acts of recovery like those of Peter Fryer (whose *Staying Power: The History of Black People in Britain* first appeared in 1984), and a whole raft of reclamative literary scholarship.[14] The resolve behind the concurrent artistic developments was approximately equivalent to the spirit that motivated the American "Black Arts Movement" of the 1960s and 1970s. Enthusiasm snowballed. It took only a decade or so for scholarship regarding black Britons to arrive at the point of being able to produce, for instance, *Unchained Voices*, the distinguished anthology of eighteenth-century black British writers edited by Vincent Carretta,[15] and the influential anthology of criticism *Black British Cultural Studies*, edited by Houston

Baker, Manthia Diawara, and Ruth Lindeborg.[16] Dennis Walder's book-length study *Post-Colonial Literatures in English* provides an excellent selected bibliography of many of the key texts, creative and critical, that emerged following the riots of summer 1981.[17]

Strong Ideas and Willfulness

"Ring out the old, ring in the new!" cried Tennyson famously (but he didn't really mean it, for he loved the past). What he wanted gone was the pain of loss, and his elegiac *In Memoriam*, where he enunciated *that* feeling (in Part 106), has proved one of England's most popular long poems ever written. Just so. It would indeed be convenient if all the painful parts of the past just passed away. But that sort of "escape" is impossible; cultural change takes strong ideas and willfulness. This is what Stuart Hall was getting at in the paragraph on "that long discovery-rediscovery of identity among blacks in this migrant situation which allows them to lay a kind of claim to certain parts of the earth which aren't theirs" with which I began this essay. And even Stuart Hall admits, in that piece, that he is "carrying around" the old-time Jamaican family and the comprador culture he tried to escape by migrating to England—carrying them around, he says, "locked up somewhere in my head, from which there is no migration";[18] and he is "carrying [them] around" even though he feels "centered" as a new Briton. Something from the past must nevertheless come to rest—must stop—for that feeling of newness and possibility to occur. As Stuart Hall explains, "All the social movements which have tried to transform society and have required the constitution of new subjectivities have had to accept the necessarily fictional, but also the fictional necessity, of the arbitrary closure which is not the end, but which makes both politics and identity possible."[19] Closure of a sort must come; but we do also hear (from thinkers who have attended closely to the postcolonial world) that a total "dismantling" of the effects of imperialism "cannot be achieved . . . . [for it] is not possible to return to or to rediscover an absolute pre-colonial purity, nor is it possible to create national or regional formations entirely independent of their historical implication in the European colonial enterprise."[20] Nevertheless, the very fact that thoughtful, sensitive people have been moved to formulate such sentences surely means that something new is in the offing. And, as we hope this collection of essays shows, when a new wave of literature appears, it exemplifies new ways of feeling. In 1998, Mike Phillips and Trevor Phillips published an important book, *Windrush: The Irresistible Rise of Multi-Racial Britain*.[21]

It focuses on what followed upon the mass migration of blacks from the Caribbean to England beginning in 1948 and continuing through the next decade or so. Consider the blithe and buoyant tone of their title's diction: *multi-racial Britain* (suggesting a colorful, cosmopolitan sort of demesne), *rise* (with its connotation of nearly effortless elevation), *irresistible* (with its connotation of charm as well as strength). The spirit of the arrivants that the Phillipses describe is unquestionably a strong force.

The Mid-1980s

A quick scan of the world of literary scholarship reveals what a heap of what Stuart Hall calls the "dismantling" and reconstituting "of new subjectivities" has been taking place in the last twenty or so years! By the mid-1980s we saw the emergence of the by-now-familiar discourse of self-conscious identity-formations: the theorizing of *Negritude*, Homi Bhabha's ideas of nation and narration, the designation "Black literature" (the theoretical amalgam of non-white, post-African, African, Afro-American, Caribbean, East Indian, Arab, Pakistani, Near Eastern, and Aboriginal writing).[22]

In fact, in response to the intellectual ferment in theorizing cultural identity, Ivan Van Sertima published his groundbreaking historical study of Africans in Europe[23] and David Dabydeen published his pioneering critical anthology of essays on blacks in English literature, a collection of scholarship, impressively comprehensive for its day in its coverage of black writers and of black characters in British writing from the Renaissance to the late twentieth century.[24] The Dabydeen publication represented a major advance in the scholarly construction of a *literary* "Black British" identity. Several of the essays in his collection deserve careful, individual attention, not merely because they examine the works by and about blacks in their original historical contexts, but because they do so for very explicit and timely cultural purposes.

In his article "Reading the novels of empire . . .," Brian Street retheorizes the presence of blacks in the literature of Britain's colonialist era, making the perspicacious claim that

> To examine nineteenth-century representations of the "savage in literature" is not, then, a matter of merely antiquarian interest, irrelevant to modern-day "race relations"; it is, in fact, the crucial ground on which the symbols and myths of those [modern-day race] relations are most clearly exposed . . . .[25]

Writing in 1985 about the relationship of imperialist attitudes to the present, Street argued that the past was not dormant, nor had it gone away:

> Representations both of contemporary "Third World" societies and of "ethnic" groups within Britain draw to a large extent . . . on the same assumptions and beliefs and the same images that underlay [scientific and literary] representations of "primitive" society in the last century.[26]

The terms *primitive* and *savage*, Street wrote, have simply been replaced in the 1980s by "new coinages and euphemisms" like *ethnic tribalism* and *underdeveloped nations*. Street carefully constructed his analysis of 1985-style racism upon a historical study of the overlap between nineteenth-century Darwinian discourse, the science of its day, and the narrative discourse of such fabrications as Conan Doyle's *The Lost World*, John Buchan's *Prester John*, H. Rider Haggard's *Allan Quatermain*, Edgar Rice Burroughs's *Tarzan of the Apes*, R. M. Ballantyne's *Coral Island*, and G. A. Henty's *A Boy's Adventures around the World*. Street's objective ("to go beyond the simple identification of 'bias' or 'ethnocentricism' ")[27] was to emphasize what others writing in the 1980s—including James Donald and other scholars of linguistics and pedagogy[28]—were also saying about language and literature: that spoken words and published books are not simply nonviolent media of communication and coercion. They are the very foundations of cultural hegemony.

In short, the old racist texts of cultural construction were being rediscovered in the mid-1980s as *sites* of cultural contestation by academics of the "cultural critique" persuasion. That point is made specifically in Dabydeen's collection, not only by Brian Street (as I have pointed out), but also by David Daniell in his study of Buchan's imperialist fiction[29] and by Abena Busia in her piece on the cultural baggage in stories about contemporary buccaneers.[30] Writing about the most recent novels of then–best-selling contemporary authors (especially Frederick Forsyth, Paul Theroux, Laurence Sanders, and Tasman Beattie), Abena Busia laid it out: it's the same old, nineteenth-century imperialist, race-supremacist story in contemporary clothes. "It is [still] the African who must be suppressed," wrote Busia, "and as this [malignant] 'truth' too has become a constant factor within the literature [on Africa authored by whites], the texts themselves become elements of oppression." Mindful of the sorry state of literary affairs, Busia concluded emphatically: "A re-composition of the relations of power in that respect has not yet been undertaken."[31] In noting this *lack*, Busia was drawing attention to hegemonic strategies more calumniatory than those precipitating Thatcher's British Nationality Act of 1981: the ethnocentric, international power plays implicit in mainstream Anglophone publishing vogues.

In that same collection of essays, Kenneth Parker called for a new curriculum with an objective that is "not simply a matter of ensuring that 'the black presence' [be] expressed in the classroom, but more fundamentally, [to ensure that the new curriculum might make] a contribution to the project of destroying racism in contemporary Britain."[32]

The common property of the essays published in Dabydeen's 1985 collection is their precise identification of a *lackingness* and a *needfulness* in the wider British literary culture. The whole of the bibliography included in *The Empire Writes Back*[33] possesses the sort of period flavor to which I am referring here. It is too long to incorporate in this context, but too rich to ignore as a repository of mid-1980s-style discourse of postcolonial identity-formation and cultural critique. In the mid-1980s, many of the scholars and creative writers who are working *today* to supply the lacks and answer the needs identified in Dabydeen's *The Black Presence in English Literature* were still very, very young. And others were not yet born.

The Status of Black British Literature in 1990

By 1990, the broad category of literature that the April 2000 Howard University symposium addressed, *black British literature*, was still not officially on the literary maps. Alistair Niven of the British Council protested that "conventional definitions of Commonwealth literature leave out [black] British writing virtually in its entirety," thus allowing black British writers to go "under-recognized both internationally and at home,"[34] and Niven predicted that until "positions of influence in the formal and public education sectors are held by more black people with literary interests there will be little powerful advocacy for black British writing within them—or, indeed, for Caribbean, African or Asian literature either."[35]

That same year, Tim Brennan, the guest editor of a special issue of *The Literary Review* introducing "Writing from Black Britain," could truthfully ask:

> In a land as literary as Britain, why are its black writers invisible—at least as *British* writers? The world knows the rockers and the rastas—Aswad, Fine Young Cannibals, Nenah [*sic*] Cherry, Soul II Soul—and at least five major studies of the rise of reggae and its spin-offs in Britain can be found

today in any decent bookstore. Black British film . . . has its high-profile programs at London's Institute of Contemporary Arts, or gets picked up for foreign distribution at special festivals in New York, or even (in the case of Hanif Kureishi's *My Beautiful Laundrette*) the Hollywood distribution networks. But barring some illustrious exceptions, black authors have been greeted with suspicious stares and a few snarls.[36]

Brennan's special issue of *The Literary Review* is a good place to start for an early introduction to the scholarship that calls contemporary *black British writers* by that name. Here, Brennan asks, "Why should the literary field be more intractable . . . than music or film?" And he answers:

> . . . because British identity has for a long time been so tightly bound up with literature [and because] . . . studying English always meant consuming literature as a means of learning one's civilizational roots. The resistance to allowing "intruders" into the British canon is, then, motivated by much more than aesthetic taste. Individuals, if they are allowed to enter, must do so as proof of Britain's fabulous tolerance and sense of fair play rather than as the inevitable outcome of a Britain that is now a rainbow of colors, cultures, and talents. If one were to concede that there was such a thing as black *British* literature, an earlier version of civilization as that which othered "them" and defined "us" would crumble . . . .[37]

Brennan surveys the scholarly and creative projects of the 1980s dedicated to establishing the presence of blacks in Britain,[38] he attributes the poor showing of young black writers in Britain to censorship by Anti-Racism efforts of all but the most "positive images," and he sketches the inspiriting influence of black publishers "in combating official neglect and in setting new agendas at a time of great vulnerability for black British writing."[39] Brennan defines his selection of featured creative black British writing as "work [that] could not have arisen as 'British literature' in India, Africa, or the Caribbean" because its authors so clearly are "based in the UK."[40] Besides Brennan's introductory essay, there is only one other full-length essay in this special issue "introducing" black British writing: Ambalavaner Sivanandan's "The Liberation of the Black Intellectual," where (as in the writings of Frantz Fanon, Jacques Roumain, Aimé Césaire, Jean Genet, and Dunduzu Chisiza) the term *black* is used in a symbolic way to designate "the oppressed."[41] In theorizing the "oppression" of blacks and surveying the field of liberatory essayists listed earlier, Sivanandan endorses Brennan's endeavor to draw critical attention to something extraordinary happening in black Britain. The roster of then-relatively unknown creative writers featured in Brennan's introductory sampler of contemporary black British literature is, in hindsight, impressive: Grace Nichols, David Dabydeen, Obi Egbuna, John Agard, Farrukh Dhondy, Edgar White, Ben Okri, Jean Binta Breeze, Michael Smith, Linton Kwesi Johnson, Barbara Burford, Sonia Boyce, H. O. Nazareth, Buchi Emecheta, and Mustapha Matura. Throughout this special issue, the authors' axes are being finely ground. In Barbara Burford's short story "Dreaming the Sky Down," for example, the main character, Donna, answers Miss Howe's question "What country do you come from?" politely and laconically with "Battersea, Miss Howe," but she exclaims to herself when Miss Howe is out of earshot: "Not from outer space, Miss Howe! Not from some strange foreign place, Miss Howe! Battersea, Miss Howe!" Like Burford's Donna, the characters in Brennan's collection of poems and stories all want desperately to be recognized as the British citizens they feel they are. In short, even as late as 1990, the generation of black writers "introduced" by Brennan and who were living and working in the United Kingdom were not feeling quite so "centered" there, in the main place they had learned to call home, as Stuart Hall had presciently proclaimed of the yet younger set. But, of course, most of the writers that Brennan included in his issue of *The Literary Review* were not nearly so generally well known in 1990 as they are today. Furthermore, as Kadija George Sesay argues in her essay in this volume (chapter 6), the writers whom Brennan featured belong to a cluster of creative artists that is, after all, almost a generation older than the writers in whose works Sesay detects the benchmarks of a major literary "transformation."

Unsurprisingly, given the ethos of the literary marketplace in the mid-1990s, many important white critics were still assigning extraneous "places" to contemporary writers whose citizenship and addresses were British—and whom the British political and police establishments designated quite simply as "black." Malcolm Bradbury's ambitious *The Atlas of Literature*, first published in 1996, for example, does not address *black British writers* as such.[42] In Bradbury's survey, Derek Walcott, Caryl Phillips, and V. S. Naipaul are simply "of the Caribbean," as are Fred D'Aguiar and David Dabydeen;[43] Buchi Emecheta is apparently not even worth mentioning although, by 1996, she had been a British citizen for decades, was *even then* the subject of much scholarly discussion, and was producing best-sellers in Britain (and the world) at a fairly regular clip; Hanif Kureishi belongs to a "dislocated" London scene because he is half-British and half-Indian, just as Timothy Mo belongs to that same "dislocated" scene because he is half-Chinese; Salman Rushdie belongs to the Bombay crowd along with Anita Desai and Vikram Seth (even though Seth was in fact born in Calcutta and did not live there very long); and Kazuo Ishiguro (who wrote *The Remains of the Day*, whose mother is English, and who grew up in England and writes in English) is not mentioned anywhere in Bradbury's compendious book. It is instructive to compare Malcolm Bradbury's earlier *The Modern British Novel*,[44] where David Dabydeen, Ben Okri, and Caryl Phillips are mentioned as *bona fide* British novelists, but not distinguished as "black." Obviously, for Bradbury and his publishers, birthplace (because of Margaret Thatcher's British Nationality Act of 1981) counts (Dabydeen and Phillips were born in the British Caribbean; Okri in British Nigeria), but who the author's parents are (or were) and where they were born counts even more. Thus, although Kureishi and Mo are begrudgingly accorded a place in the British "metropolis" because they are British-born and part English, that "place" of belonging is *déclassé* and qualified as a "dislocated" place. Of many then-contemporary black female writers born in Britain—such as the poet Barbara Burford—no mention at all appears in the major surveys of contemporary British literature. In his popular *vade mecum*, Randall Stevenson includes Salman Rushdie, Kazuo Ishiguro, Ben Okri, and Timothy Mo in the constellation of important writers, but he calls them "migrants"[45] and adds to their number Angela Carter and Jeanette Winterson (who are white lesbians) because they, too, "come from areas belonging in one way or another to the margins rather than the mainstream of influence in British society."[46] White male gays like W. H. Auden, E. M. Forster, and A. E. Hausman, nevertheless, are everywhere considered mainstream writers.

The weird logic of such classifications and, thus, of the politics of belonging, becomes more comprehensible after one reads Ian Baucom's 1999 book *Out of Place: Englishness, Empire, and the Locations of Identity*. Baucom provides a rousing exposition of the legal history of citizenship in the British Isles and the British Empire; of public and literary responses to official revisions in the definitions of Englishness and Britishness, a history to which Maria Lima also refers in her essay in this volume (chapter 3). An important point Baucom makes is that the closely reasoned and passionate reactions of such black British writers as V. S. Naipaul and Salman Rushdie to the British Nationality Act of 1981 stirred up the younger generation of black Britons into an unprecedented intellectual and literary activism. Rushdie's essays "The New Empire within Britain" (1982) and "Outside the Whale" (1984), both reprinted in *Imaginary Homelands*, inspired awareness of an irresistible and proud "black" tradition of intelligence and determination—one that, as Peter Fryer put it, "those who at present rule the country . . . would be ill-advised to underestimate."[47]

Some of that literary activism began to ramify rather spectacularly after 1993. Between 1990 and 1997, the common point running through scholarly and critical writing about black writers in Britain was that they were struggling to be recognized by the public and the academy, both as creative writers *and* as citizens of England. For instance, Bernardine Evaristo, British and black, wrote in 1993 that "there has been an over-emphasis on plays about the Caribbean, America and Africa, as these seem to appeal to both funders and theatre directors alike, thus suppressing the Black British experience. The developmental work needed to escalate Black British women playwrights does not happen . . . .[T]here is still a long road ahead."[48]

At about the same time, Carole Boyce Davies reviewed black British women's postimperial writing (up to 1993), and her overview accentuated what she called the theme of "Unbelongingness" in the works of black women in Britain, especially in Joan Riley's 1985 novel *The Unbelonging* and Vernella Fuller's 1992 novel *Going Back Home*.[49] But 1993 may well have been a bit early even for attentive scholars to note that, while the words *belonging* and *longing* are everywhere to be seen and heard in the writing of black women in Britain, these words are more and more to be found in contexts that give them assertive inflections. The "centered" self of which Stuart Hall speaks is a version of the pragmatic position Grace Nichols takes in *Fat Black Woman's Poems*, where she says: "To tell the truth / I don't know really where I belaang" and nevertheless concludes: "Wherever I hang me knickers—that's my home."[50] Nowadays, black British writers are hanging their knickers, so to speak, in London, Birmingham, Manchester, Luton, Glasgow—and the list goes on.

Robert A. Lee's collection *Other Britain, Other British*, published in 1995, embodied another breakthrough. It featured important, new criticism on individual authors or small groupings of them: essays by Abdulrazak Gurnah (on V. S. Naipaul and Salman Rushdie), Stewart Brown (on Gurnah), Lyn Innes (on the treatment of women characters by Caryl Phillips, Ravinder Randhawa, Joan Riley, and Buchi Emecheta), Susheila Nasta (on Sam Selvon), Louis James (on George Lamming), Lee himself (on Mike Phillips, David Dabydeen, Hanif Kureishi, Pauline Melville, Timothy Mo, and Kazuo Ishiguro), and Rod Edmond (on New Zealand and Australian fiction).[51] The themes explored—here critically instead of creatively—were still, however, displacement, migration, befuddled national and cultural identity, and other downbeat effects of living and working in a postimperial Britain or a former British colony. Of particular note is the fact that all but three of the authors discussed in this publication were foreign-born—Kureishi, Mo, and Ishiguro being the sole exceptions. A different and more robust theme was sounded that same year by the poet SuAndi with her slim volume *There Will Be No Tears*,[52] but the book has not yet received the critical attention that it richly deserves.

1996 and After

Today, the literary landscape has changed considerably. From an academic perspective, several scholarly accomplishments marked the shift. A flurry of valuable scholarly texts were published in 1996 and 1997 (among them an updated *Reader's Guide to Westindian and Black British Literature*,[53] Clare Alexander's *The Art of Being Black*,[54] and Houston Baker et al.'s collection of critical essays titled *Black British Cultural Studies*, cited earlier). Perhaps even more significantly, two remarkably influential cultural events took place. One was the international "Re-inventing Britain" conference, held in London in March 1997.[55] The other was the "Tracing Paper" conference in October 1997 at the Museum of London.[56] Black British writers participated in both fora, recognizing and insisting—as Stuart Hall (among them) observed—that they *did indeed* belong in England and to British society. Trend-watchers were alerted to a new wave of black British authorship. London-born Diran Adebayo's Saga Prize–winning first novel, *Some Kind of Black*, and London-born Kadija George Sesay's second literary anthology, *Burning Words, Flaming Images*, came out in 1996; Essington-born Myra Syal's *Anita and Me* and London-born Bernardine Evaristo's first novel in verse, *Lara*, in 1997.[57] London-bred Judith Bryan's Saga Prize–winning first novel, *Bernard and the Cloth Monkey*; London-born Courttia Newland's acclaimed first novel, *The Scholar*, London-based Karen McCarthy's *Bittersweet* anthology of poems by black women, and Mancunian poet Lemn Sissay's anthology of new poems by young black Britons, *The Fire People*—all were published in the following year.[58] Cultural commentators began to remark that Andrea Levy had been publishing notable novels for some years,[59] that Jackie Kay was an outstanding poet with several volumes of poetry to her name and a new novel in print,[60] and that black British literary culture—however "complex and unstable"[61]—was a phenomenon that was coming increasingly into mainstream view.

By 2000, black Britons were writing emphatically about how the general culture must change to accommodate black British citizens and their lifestyles. The World Wide Web was teeming with the homepages of new black British writers, on-line literary magazines, serious book reviews, and reading lists of fiction and non-fiction by black British authors.[62] And the tone of the writing was new. The most recently published non-fiction, novels, and poetry fully manifested the centeredness that Stuart Hall had noted and described. Gary Younge, in a non-fictional narrative very much worth reading, told of becoming fully aware of and affirming his Englishness while traveling across the Southern United States.[63] Judith Bryan was using fiction as exorcism for the personal and cultural trauma of black Britons, as a way of *ringing out the old* and of "re-inventing" an authentic black British identity. Kadija George Sesay, as much a literary activist as a creative writer, was intent on defining writing that is black *and* British and differentiating it from the contemporary literatures of the Caribbean and Africa—the new black British emphasis being on *belonging* to a new society, on *owning* it. Courttia Newland's most recent novels *Society Within* and *Snakeskin* and Zadie Smith's *White Teeth* portrayed, with abundant verve, young people living adventurous, multicultural lives in London.[64] Patsy Antoine and Kadija Sesay each collaborated with Courttia Newland to publish anthologies of new black British writing[65] and launched on world tours to promote their authors.

Indeed, some current black British writers, like Susan Yearwood (who in this volume [chapter 8] analyzes Buchi Emecheta's fiction), are today engaged in the important critical work of reading and reviewing the enormous output coming from the newer generation,[66] a generation younger than Salman Rushdie, Hanif Kureishi, and Caryl Phillips. Others—including Dorothea Smartt, author of *Connecting Medium*, and Patience Agbabi, author of *Transformatrix*, both members of the Bittersweet Writers Tour[67]—are engaged in taking their popular brand of performance poetry to enthusiastic audiences around Britain and the world. One surefire way to find out what is going on in Britain's literary and artistic circles is to check the notices and reviews posted on the Internet. There, the daily activities of hundreds of black British poets, playwrights, novelists, reviewers, scholars, and critics are announced and commented on.[68]

There is truly a popular explosion of creative writing. While Courttia Newland is not yet thirty years old as we go to press, he has already written three highly praised novels, several filmscripts, four plays that have been performed in Edinburgh and London, numerous reviews, and the script for a television series about life in the London he knows. "What I am writing about," he says, "is a society within another one. It's got its own rules, a society with its own language."[69] Newland, on the same occasion, predicted that for every Newland writing today, there "will soon be 50 or 60" brand new writers: "That *is* gonna happen," he avowed. "And so, boy, if you're worried about that, I'd start worrying now!"

At Howard University, for the past eighteen years or so, we have been seriously and incrementally implementing an academic program that embraces the black British presence in all our British literature courses. But the point of the Howard University symposium on teaching black British writing was that there is a "new thing"—not just some new black writers, but an academic interest in retrieving the lost history of the presence of blacks in what is now called the United Kingdom—a presence that goes all the way to the Roman era B.C. The sensational young black British writers whose ideas and creative works we featured at Howard on April 15, 2000 (Judith Bryan, Susan Eastwood, Kadija George Sesay, Courttia Newland, Dorothea Smartt, and, of course, E. R. Braithwaite,[70] who is eternally youthful!) were all honored with a special reception that evening at the British Embassy in Washington, D.C., the premier U.S. city. Stuart Hall would have been pleased to see that they looked there, too, "as if they own[ed] the territory" because "they . . . are centered, in place" in the modern world. They have e-mail addresses, their own publishing firms, their own booking agents, their own touring companies. And their writing is self-affirming, confident, and growing in worldwide popularity. Who wouldn't be just a little "envious," as Stuart Hall teased. Black British writers are "the happenin' thing" in our world, and the other Britons know it.

In "The New Empire Within Britain" Salman Rushdie wrote: ". . . when Mahatma Gandhi, the father of an earlier freedom movement, came to England and was asked what he thought of English civilization, he replied: 'I think it would be a good idea.' "[71] We think so, too. And something like a sea change is occurring in that regard as well, for young writers like Zadie Smith, Diran Adebayo, Bernardine Evaristo, Andrea Levy, Meera Syal, and those poets and short-story writers represented in Patsy Antoine's *Afrobeat*, Karen McCarthy's *Bittersweet*, Lemn Sissay's *The Fire People*, Kadija George Sesay's *Burning Words, Flaming Images*, to name just a few, are centered, constructive, and civilizing. What they are saying is an affirmation of what C. L. R. James announced prophetically when he said (in 1958!), "It is in ageing, creaking, conservative Britain that there flourishes as solid, as cohesive and as powerful a national concentration of the new society as exists anywhere on the face of the globe."[72] James, of course, was speaking of black Britons.

For their contributions to the teaching of Black British writing, the essays of Judith Bryan, Kadija George Sesay, Tracey Waters, and Susan

Yearwood (first presented at the Howard symposium) are here offered as further scholarly evidence of the salutary participation of black Britons in the development not only of a revitalized "English civilization," but also of a vibrant new field of world literature.

Notes

1. Stuart Hall, "Minimal Selves," *Black British Cultural Studies*, ed. Houston A. Baker, Manthia Diawara, and Ruth Lindeborg (University of Chicago Press, 1996), 114–115.
2. Prepared by Fred Leventhal, president of NACBS, et al., the "NACBS Report on the State and Future of British Studies in North America" (published on the Internet at the NACBS Webpage) addresses the "widespread perception among members of the profession that British Studies does not occupy the same position of importance within the academy that it once had"(section A) and proposes a number of intellectual arguments that can be made to university administrators, funding agencies, and students to "promote and strengthen" the field: (1) "The history of Britain is arguably the most important 'national' history precisely because it has been the most intertwined with, and influential upon, other histories worldwide, in all their dimensions—political, economic, social and cultural." (2) "The huge diaspora of peoples from the British Isles has created . . . a worldwide community" that, in sharing a language among other things, has made "English the closest thing to a world language." (3) The story of the British Empire is "a story of complex relationships between the colonizing and the colonized, and of two-way flows of influence" and a rich site for the decentered study of colonial and postcolonial institutions and cultures. (4) "British history is perhaps the best single avenue of inquiry into the large processes of 'globalization' in all its many dimensions—political, economic, social and cultural" inasmuch as the British [claim to] have been the "creators of the first true 'world system' and the first world market, and . . . [were] the originators of industrialism." The NACBS points out that some of the latest, large-scale trends in academic offerings (cultural studies and critique, colonial and postcolonial studies, studies in globalization, literatures in English) are all, *ipse dixit*, facets of British studies.
3. The 1999 NACBS report (cited earlier) acknowledges a "decline" in British Studies as well as "a shrinking number of courses and [teaching] positions"; but insists that "Market trends are not our nemesis, but our opportunity. In future, rather than relying on a strong Anglophilia among students and their families, the study of Britain [and the literature of Britain] must stand or fall on its broader significances for the history and present situation of humanity" (section D).
4. Robert Hewison, in his address to the international "Re-inventing Britain" conference held in London, England, in March 1997, noted that the center/periphery model of British culture and empire has given way to a model more like a "net" of connections and "links" so that those English people

"whose identity is that of middle-England" are now only *part* of the fabric, not *the* national fabric, 2. http://www.britishcouncil.org/studies/reinventing_ britain/hewison.htm.

5. Texts of keynote speeches presented at the international "Re-inventing Britain" conference (March 1997, London, England) are available on-line. Some important ideas set forth there are excerpted here: In his "Introduction," Nick Wadham-Smith of the British Council addressed the question, "How does a new wave of cultural fusion in music, drama, dance and writing change the nature of national boundaries and the beliefs and traditions which now travel and combine so freely across them?" He added that the "Re-inventing Britain" conference was planned around the prospect of exploring "an alternative perspective that claims that culture is less about expressing a pre-given identity (whether the source is national culture or 'ethnic' culture) and more about the activity of negotiating, regulating and authorizing competing, often conflicting demands for collective self-representation." For Wadham-Smith's full text, see http://www.britishcouncil. org/studies/reinventing_britain/manisfesto.htm.

In his presentation titled "The Nub of the Argument," Stuart Hall connected the "absolute explosion of creative work in the arts, both serious and popular, especially from young practitioners from Asian, African, Afro-Caribbean and other so-called minority communities now living in Britain" with the suggestion that "marginality has become a productive space" since "Cultural diversity is not something that is coming in from the outside, it is also something that is going on, inside, in relation to Britishness itself. After Cultural diversity, Britishness cannot be what it was before. And that is why the conference is not called, 'Welcome Cultural Diversity' but 'Re-inventing Britain.' " http://www. britishcouncil.org/ studies/reinventing_ britain/ hall_2.htm.

Robert Hewison, ibid., argued that English people "whose identity is that of middle-England" are now only *part* of the fabric, not *the* national fabric.

6. Hall, "Minimal Selves," 114.

7. Maya Jaggi, "Englishmen Born and Bred . . . Almost: A New Generation of British-Born Black and Asian Writers is Emerging," *Mail & Guardian* Review Books Page (February 24, 1997).

8. "Tracing Paper: Black Writing in London, 1770–1997," which took place on Saturday, October 11, 1997, at the Museum of London, billed itself as the "first conference to trace black writing in London from its early origins through to today's writers and publishing industry" (Conference Flyer). The day-long program featured writers, publishers, publicists, and arts activists— including Moniza Alvi, Bernardine Evaristo, Andrea Levy, Pauline Melville, Q., Mike Phillips, Steve Martin, Jessica Huntley, Tony Fairweather, John Hampson, Angela Royal, and Onyekachi Wambu. Professor Lola Young of Middlesex University, United Kingdom, introduced the program; Mike Phillips presented the keynote speech, titled "The Dark Side of the Moon— Black English Writing in the 21st Century." Funded collaboratively by The Museum of London, The London Arts Board, and Spread the Word, "Tracing Paper" provided a forum for black British writers to meet with members of the publishing industry and to address "the tradition of exclusion" and the

"almost insuperable difficulties in representing the total experience of what it means to be British in the present day" (as Mike Phillips expressed the problem on that occasion). In short, the "Tracing Paper" conference was a professional, not an academic, one. *The Re-inventing Britain Project*, which began in May 1997, inaugurated a series of meetings on rethinking British national and cultural identity. Among those who spoke at the inaugural meeting in 1997 were Nick Wadham-Smith of the British Council, Homi Bhabha, Stuart Hall, and Robert Hewison (Prof. of Literary and Cultural Studies at the University of Lancaster). Their objective was primarily to promote a national dialogue on change in a civil society, not to discuss pedagogy relating to the works of black British writers.

9. Besides subventing travel expenses for individual black British writers to travel abroad to read from their works (e.g., novelist Courttia Newland's tour of the Czech Republic in 1999 and his and Judith Bryan's trips to the Howard symposium in 2000), the British Council helps support the publication of journals and anthologies featuring their work. It also subvents the expenses of such prestigious international events as the Annual Cambridge Seminar (ACS) on British Writing. In 2000, for its twenty-sixth annual gathering (on *The Contemporary British Writer*) the ACS hosted fifty-five Fellows from around the world, including Nigerian-born (black British) playwright Biyi Bandele and black British performance poet Patience Agbabi, "both fine representatives of the new boom of black writing in Britain today" (Terri Merz, "Letter from Cambridge," *Book World The Washington Post* [Sunday, September 3, 2000]: 10). On April 5–7, 2000 a major conference on the multicultural history of Britain titled "From Strangers to Citizens: Integration of immigrant communities in Great Britain, Ireland and the Colonies 1550–1750" took place at Dutch Church, Austin Friars, London. On April 27, 2000 a panel discussion on "Our Cosmopolitan Future" (sponsored jointly by The Arts Council of England and The British Council and held at the University of Warwick, Coventry, England) continued the discussion of themes explored in the *Re-inventing Britain* project. The conferences spinning out from the *Re-inventing Britain* project and supported by the British Council continue: the call for papers for the September 20–23, 2000 international, multidisciplinary conference titled "Writing Diasporas: Axial Writers, Plural Literacies, Transnational Imagination" requested abstracts along "six strands": Axial Writers; Transnational Cinema; On-line Diasporas; Marketing Ethnicity; Performance, Poetry and Song; and Plural Literacies and Policy. After 2000, even a partial listing of similar government-sponsored events grows too lengthy to print here.

10. Peter Fryer, *Staying Power: The History of Black People in Britain* (London and Boulder, Colorado: Pluto Press, 1984), 399, emphasis added.

11. Ian Baucom, *Out of Place: Englishness, Empire, and the Locations of Identity* (Princeton: Princeton University Press, 1999), 13.

12. Among the most influential critical responses to the 1981 British Nationality Act were Salman Rushdie's "The New Empire Within Britain" (first published in 1982) and "A General Election" (first published in 1988),

reprinted in his collection of essays and reviews *Imaginary Homelands* (New York and London: Penguin, 1991), 129–138, 159–165, respectively.

13. Paul Gilroy, *There Ain't No Black in the Union Jack* (London: Routledge, 1987).

14. Vincent Carretta, in his paper read at the NACBS meeting in Santa Barbara on April 1, 2000, presented an extensive list of scholarly achievements following Peter Fryer's *Staying Power: The History of Black People in Britain* (1984): among them, William Andrews's *To Tell a Free Story: The First Century of Afro-American Autobiography, 1760–1865* (1986), Angelo Costanzo's *Surprising Narrative: Olaudah Equiano and the Beginnings of Black Autobiography* (1987), Keith Sandiford's *Measuring the Moment: Strategies of Protest in Eighteenth-Century Afro-English Writing* (1988). A specialist himself in eighteenth-century black British writers, Carretta meticulously noted the "authoritative and deeply researched editions" of Phillis Wheatley, Sancho, Cugoano, and Equiano; the controversial works of Paul Gilroy, *The Black Atlantic: Modernity and Double Consciousness* (1993) and *Black Atlantic Writers of the Eighteenth Century* (1995).

15. Carretta, *Unchained Voices: An Anthology of Black Authors in the English-Speaking World of the Eighteenth Century* (Lexington: University of Kentucky Press, 1996).

16. *Black British Cultural Studies*, ed. Baker et al.

17. Dennis Walder, *Post-Colonial Literatures in English: History, Language, Theory* (Oxford: Blackwell, 1998).

18. Hall, "Minimal Selves," 116.

19. Ibid., 117.

20. Bill Ashcroft, Gareth Griffiths, and Helen Tiffin, *The Empire Strikes Back: Theory and Practice in Post-Colonial Literatures* (London and New York: Routledge, 1989), 196.

21. Mike Phillips and Trevor Phillips, *Windrush: The Irresistible Rise of Multi-Racial Britain* (London: HarperCollins, 1998).

22. The term *black literature* has roots in the Black Arts Movement in the United States. But its use within the British context has been inflected in another way. Stuart Hall explains, "the term 'black' was coined as a way of referencing the common experience of racism and marginalization in Britain and came to provide the organizing category of a new politics of resistance, among groups and communities with, in fact, very different histories, traditions, and ethnic identities. In this moment, politically speaking, 'The Black Experience,' as a singular and unifying framework based on the building up of identity across ethnic and cultural difference between the different communities, became 'hegemonic' over other ethnic/racial identities—though the latter did not, of course, disappear. Culturally, this analysis formulated itself in terms of a critique of the way blacks were positioned as the unspoken and invisible 'other' of predominantly white aesthetic and cultural discourses" (Baker et al., *Black British Cultural Studies*, ch. 7, 163–164).

23. Ivan Van Sertima, *African Presence in Early Europe* (London: Transaction Press, 1985).

24. David Dabydeen, *The Black Presence in English Literature* (Manchester: Manchester University Press, 1985). The same year Dabydeen also published *Hogarth's Blacks: Images of Blacks in Eighteenth-Century English Art* (Athens: University of Georgia Press, 1985).

25. Brian Street, "Reading the Novels of Empire: Race and Ideology in the Classic 'Tale of Adventure,' " (95–111) *The Black Presence in English Literature*, ed. Dabydeen, 96.

26. Ibid.

27. Ibid., 108.

28. See, e.g., Stuart Hall, James Donald, and P. Willis, *Culture and the State. Language, Literacy and Schooling* (Milton Keynes: Open University Press, 1982). For further references, please consult http://simsim.rug.ac.be/2000literacies/themes/algemenebiblio/gelbibl0b1.html. See also David Dabydeen's essay "On Not Being Milton: Nigger Talk in England Today," *Crisis and Creativity in the New Literatures in English*, Geoffrey Davis and Hena Maes-Jelinek, eds. (Amsterdam and Atlanta: Rodopi, 1990).

29. David Daniell, "Buchan and 'The Black General,' " *The Black Presence in English Literature*, ed. David Dabydeen, 135–153.

30. Abena Busia, "Manipulating Africa: The Buccaneer as 'Liberator' in Contemporary Fiction," *The Black Presence in English Literature*, ed. David Dabydeen, 168–185.

31. Ibid., 182.

32. Kenneth Parker, "The Revelation of Caliban: 'The black presence' in the classroom" (186–207) *The Black Presence in English Literature*, ed. Dabydeen, 205.

33. Ashcroft et al., ibid., 224–239.

34. Alistair Niven, "Black British Writing: The Struggle for Recognition," *Crisis and Creativity in the New Literatures in English*, Geoffrey Davis and Hena Maes-Jelinek, eds. (Amsterdam and Atlanta: Rodopi, 1990), 325–326.

35. Ibid., 331.

36. Tim Brennan, "Writing from Black Britain," *The Literary Review* 34, 1 (Fall 1990): 5.

37. Ibid., 6.

38. Brennan cursorily lists (7–9) many valuable publications issued after the race riots of 1981. The most important are given here with their full bibliographical information: Rozina Visram, *Ayahs, Lascars and Princes: Indians in Britain 1700–1947* (London and Dover, New Hampshire: Pluto Press, 1986); Dabydeen, *Hogarth's Blacks: Images of Blacks in Eighteenth-Century English Art* (1985); Prabhu Guptara, *Black British Literature: An Annotated Bibliography* (Sydney and Oxford: Dangaroo Press, 1986); David Dabydeen and Nana Wilson-Tagoe, *A Reader's Guide to Westindian and Black British Literature* (London: Hansib, 1988); Rhonda Cobham and Merle Collins, *Watchers and Seekers: Creative Writing by Black Women* (New York: P. Bedrick Books, 1987); Kwesi Owusu, *Storms of the Heart* (London: Camden Press, 1988); Rasheed Araeen's *The Essential Black Art* (1988); Kobena Mercer's *Black Film, Black Cinema* (London: Institute of Contemporary Arts,1988); Paul Gilroy's *There Ain't No Black in the Union*

Jack (1987); apposite articles published in the Institute for Race Relations' journal *Race and Class*, edited by Ambalavaner Sivanandan; and a spate of journals and magazines on the black arts, including *Third Text* (founded by Rasheed Araeen in 1987), *Bazaar, Black Arts in London, Emergency* (now defunct), *Voice*, and *Artrage*. Another manifestation of scholarly enterprise following the riots was the spate of publications on Black British English and its sociopolitical ramifications that appeared in linguistics journals and scholarly anthologies, for instance: David Sutcliffe, "British Black English and West Indian Creoles" in *Language in the British Isles*, ed. Peter Trudgill (Cambridge: Cambridge University Press, 1984), 219–237; Mark Sebba and Shirley Tate, "You Know What I Mean? Agreement Marking in British Black English," *Journal of Pragmatics* 10 (1986): 163–172; Viv Edward, "The Speech of British Black Women in Dudley, West Midlands," in *Women in Their Speech Communities: New Perspectives on Language and Sex*, eds. Jennifer Coates and Deborah Cameron ([©1988] London and New York: Longman, 1989), 33–50.

39. Brennan, "Writing from Black Britain," 8.
40. Ibid., 10.
41. A. Sivanandan, "The Liberation of the Black Intellectual," *The Literary Review* 34, 1 (Fall 1990): 12–25. See note 22 for Stuart Hall's comment on the use of the term *black* in Britain.
42. Malcolm Bradbury, *The Atlas of Literature* (London: Websters International Publishers/De Agostini Editions, 1996).
43. Ibid., 280–283.
44. Malcolm Bradbury, *The Modern British Novel* (London: Secker & Warburg, 1993).
45. Randall Stevenson, *A Reader's Guide to the Twentieth-Century Novel in Britain* (Lexington: University of Kentucky Press, 1993), 135.
46. Ibid., 140.
47. Fryer, *Staying Power*, 399.
48. Bernardine Evaristo, "Black Women in Theatre" and "The Theatre of Black Women: Britain's First Black Women's Theatre Company" [14–17] *Six Plays by Black and Asian Women Writers*, ed. Kadija George [Sesay] (London: Aurora Press, 1993), 15.
49. Carol Boyce Davies, "Black British Women Writing the Anti-Imperialist Critique," *Writing New Identities: Gender, Nation, and Immigration in Contemporary Europe*, ed. Gisela Brinker-Gabler and Sidonie Smith (Minneapolis: University of Minnesota Press, 1997).
50. Grace Nichols, *Fat Black Woman's Poems* (London: Virago, 1984), 10.
51. Robert A. Lee, *Other Britain, Other British: Contemporary Multicultural Fiction* (London and East Haven, Connecticut: Pluto Press, 1995).
52. SuAndi, *There Will be No Tears* (Manchester: Pankhurst Press, 1995). SuAndi advertises herself as a "sussed blackwoman celebrating life" (public relations postcard).
53. David Dabydeen, Nana Wilson-Tagoe, and Floraine Eastelow, eds., *A Reader's Guide to Westindian and Black British Literature* (London: Hansib, 1997). Kadija Sesay (in her essay in the present volume [chapter 6]) expresses disappointment that the editors did not update their profile of

"Black British literature" to reflect the radically new perspective of the youngest set of black British writers, those who began publishing after 1988.

54. Claire E. Alexander, *The Art of Being Black: The Creation of Black British Youth Identities* (Oxford: Oxford University Press, 1996).

55. See note 5.

56. See note 8.

57. Diran Adebayo, *Some Kind of Black* (London: Virago, 1996); Kadija George [Sesay], *Burning Words, Flaming Images: Poems and Short Stories by Writers of African Descent* (London: SAKS Publications, 1996); Bernardine Evaristo, *Lara* (London: Angela Royal Publishing, 1997); Meera Syal, *Anita and Me* (New York: New Press, 1997).

58. Judith Bryan, *Bernard and the Cloth Monkey* (London: Flamingo, 1998); Courttia Newland, *The Scholar* (London: Abacus, 1998); Lemn Sissay, *The Fire People* (Edinburgh: Payback Press, 1998); Karen McCarthy, *Bittersweet: Contemporary Black Women's Poetry* (London: The Women's Press, 1998).

59. Andrea Levy, *Every Light in the House Burnin'* (London: Headline Book Publishing, 1994), *Never Far From Nowhere* (London: Headline Book Publishing, 1996). Her novel *Fruit of the Lemon* (London: Headline Book Publishing, 1999) was anticipated enthusiastically.

60. Jackie Kay, *The Adoption Papers* (poetry; Highgreen, Tarset, Northumberland: Bloodaxe Books, 1991); *Other Lovers: Poems* (Highgreen: Bloodaxe Books, 1993); *Off Colour* (poetry; Newcastle upon Tyne: Bloodaxe Books, 1998); *Trumpet* (novel; London: Picador, 1998).

61. Alison Donnell, editor's "Introduction" to *Companion to Contemporary Black British Culture* (London: Routledge, 2002), xv. This book is an indispensable resource for readers and researchers in this field of study, providing detailed information about black Britons' achievements in fashion and design, film and cinema, intellectual life, music, organizations, performance arts, print-based media, television and broadcasting, visual and plastic arts, writing and publishing as well as extensive definitions and discussions of key terms and public figures.

62. Among the most useful are afronet.com (one of the largest collections of black poetry). Readers eager for a list of book titles may also wish to visit the GriotWorld site on the World Wide Web at http://www.griotworld. demon.co.uk/HTML/BOOKS/NL_bbbook.html (where they will find a ranking of the forty contemporary black British fiction and non-fiction books most esteemed by black British readers) and HOTSPOTWRITERS@ compuserve.com (the web address for Kadija George [Sesay]'s SAKS Publications and British news bulletins). The most comprehensive, worldwide listserv bulletin board for black literature news and information is Kalamu ya Salaam's at kalamu@aol.com (the CyberDrum listserv).

63. Gary Younge, *No Place Like Home: A Black Briton's Journey Through the American South* (London: Picador, 1999).

64. Courttia Newland, *Society Within* (London: Abacus, 1999) and *Snakeskin* (London: Abacus, 2002); Zadie Smith, *White Teeth* (London: Hamish Hamilton, 2000).

65. Patsy Antoine and Courttia Newland, eds., *Afrobeat: New Black British Fiction* (London: Pulp Faction, 1999); Courttia Newland and Kadija George Sesay, eds., *IC3: The Penguin Book of New Black Writing in Britain* (London: Hamish Hamilton/Penguin, 2000).
66. Among the most vibrant organs of this youngest generation are *Calabash*, ed. Andrea Enisuoh, published in London since 1990 (a monthly periodical of literary news and reviews of the latest books by young black British authors), *Sable* ed. Kadija Sesay, and *Wasafiri* ed. Susheila Nasta. Susan Yearwood, is a regular book reviewer for *Calabash* and a frequent contributor to book reviews on www.blackbritain.co.uk and www.darkerthanblue.co.uk.
67. Dorothea Smartt, *Connecting Medium* (Leeds: Peepal Tree Press, 2001); Patience Agbabi, *Transformatrix* (Edinburgh: Payback Press, 2000).
68. Among the most useful web addresses are these:

    Netnoir.com (one of the largest black sites on the Internet), http://www.arts.org.uk/directory/regions/longon/whats_new (a comprehensive calendar), www.blackbritain.co.uk (Black Britain Online), www.fixstudio.com/scribble (on-line poetry workshop), apples@snakes.demon.co.uk (Apples & Snakes, Battersea Arts Center, London), boxoffice@bl.uk (British Library box office), postmaster@renaiss.demon.co.uk (Melanie Abrahams, agent for numerous new writers, including Courttia Newland, Bernardine Evaristo, Biyi Bandele, Ferdinand Dennis, Kwame Dawes, Colin Channer, Judith Bryan, Jacob Ross, Jacob Sam-La Rose, Malika B, *Bittersweet* anthology authors, Roger Robinson, Dorothea Smartt), http://trace.ntu.ac.uk/poets (literature initiatives, arts based program, and a whole list of other literature, arts, writers, arts social workers), http://paublodemon.co.uk/company_background.htm (direct supplier of multicultural books), http://www.darkerthanblue.co.uk/darkhalf/9909/darkhalf_02.html (recommended books by black British writers, brief book reviews), baa@baas.demon.co.uk (Black Arts Alliance).

69. Courttia Newland, Star Interview, BBC Education, on-line, March 11, 2000.
70. Edward Ricardo Braithwaite (born 1920 in Guyana) is the author of the novel *To Sir with Love* (1958) about the experience of a young black teacher of white students in England after World War II. His novel was made into a popular Hollywood moving picture starring Sidney Poitier.
71. Rushdie, *Imaginary Homelands*, 138.
72. Brennan, "Writing from Black Britain," 9.

Works Cited

Adebayo, Diran. *My Once Upon a Time*. London: Abacus, 2000.
———. *Some Kind of Black*. London: Virago, 1996.
Alexander, Claire E. *The Art of Being Black: The Creation of Black British Youth Identities*. Oxford: Oxford University Press, 1996.
Antoine, Patsy and Courttia Newland, eds. *Afrobeat: New Black British Fiction*. London: Pulp Faction, 1999.
Araeen, Rasheed. "The Essential Black Art," Wolverhampton Art Gallery 1988.

Ashcroft, Bill, Gareth Griffiths, and Helen Tiffin. *The Empire Writes Back: Theory and Practice in Post-Colonial Literatures.* London and New York: Routledge, 1989.

Baker, Houston A., Manthia Diawara, and Ruth Lindeborg, eds. *Black British Cultural Studies.* Chicago and London: University of Chicago Press, 1996.

Baucom, Ian. *Out of Place: Englishness, Empire, and the Locations of Identity.* Princeton: Princeton University Press, 1999.

Bradbury, Malcolm. *The Atlas of Literature.* London: Websters/De Agostini Editions, 1996.

———. *The Modern British Novel.* London: Secker & Warburg, 1993.

Brennan, Tim. "Writing from Black Britain." *The Literary Review,* 34, 1 (Fall 1990): 5–11.

Bryan, Judith. *Bernard and the Cloth Monkey.* London: Flamingo, 1998.

Busia, Abena. "Manipulating Africa: The Buccaneer as 'Liberator' in Contemporary Fiction." In *The Black Presence in English Literature. Q.v.* Dabydeen, ed. 168–185.

Carretta, Vincent, ed. *Unchained Voices: An Anthology of Black Authors in the English-Speaking World of the 18th Century.* Lexington: University Press of Kentucky, 1996.

Cobham, Rhonda and Merle Collins, eds. *Watchers and Seekers: Creative Writing by Black Women.* New York: P. Bedrick Books, 1987.

Dabydeen, David. "On Not Being Milton: Nigger Talk in England Today." In *Crisis and Creativity in the New Literatures in English.* Geoffrey Davis and Hena Maes-Jelinek, eds. Amsterdam and Atlanta: Rodopi, 1990.

———. *The Black Presence in English Literature.* Manchester: Manchester University Press, 1985.

———. *Hogarth's Blacks: Images of Blacks in Eighteenth-Century English Art.* Athens: University of Georgia Press, 1985.

Dabydeen, David, Nana Wilson-Tagoe, and Floraine Eastelow. *A Reader's Guide to Westindian and Black British Literature.* London: Hansib, 1997.

Daniell, David. "Buchan and 'The Black General.'" In *The Black Presence in English Literature. Q.v.* Dabydeen, ed. 1135–1153.

Davies, Carol Boyce. "Black British Women Writing the Anti-Imperialist Critique." In *Writing New Identities: Gender, Nation, and Immigration in Contemporary Europe.* Gisela Brinker-Gabler and Sidonie Smith, eds. Minneapolis: University Press of Minnesota Press, 1997.

Donnell, Alison, ed. *Companion to Contemporary Black British Culture.* London: Routledge, 2002.

Edward, Viv. "The Speech of British Black Women in Dudley, West Midlands." In *Women in Their Speech Communities: New Perspectives on Language and Sex.* Jennifer Coates and Deborah Cameron, eds. London and New York: Longman, 1989, © 1988. 33–50.

Evaristo, Bernardine. "Black Women in Theatre" and "The Theatre of Black Women: Britain's First Black Women's Theatre Company." In *Q.v.* George, ed. 14–17.

———. *Lara.* London: Angela Royal Publishing, 1997.

Fryer, Peter. *Staying Power: The History of Black People in Britain*. London and Boulder, Colorado: Pluto Press, 1984.

George (Sesay), Kadija, ed. *Burning Words, Flaming Images: Poems and Short Stories by Writers of African Descent*. London: SAKS Publications, 1996.

——, ed. *Six Plays by Black and Asian Women Writers*. London: Aurora Metro Press, 1993.

Gilroy, Paul. *There Ain't No Black in the Union Jack*. London: Routledge, 1987.

Guptara, Prabhu. *Black British Literature: An Annotated Bibliography*. Sydney and Oxford: Dangaroo Press, 1986.

Hall, Stuart. "Minimal Selves" in Houston A. Baker, Jr. et al., 114–119.

Hall, Stuart, James Donald, and P. Willis, eds. *Culture and the State: Language, Literacy and Schooling*. Milton Keynes: Open University Press, 1982.

Jaggi, Maya. "Englishmen Born and Bred . . . Almost: A New Generation of British-Born Black and Asian Writers is Emerging." Internet (Cyberspace Arts On-line), *Mail & Guardian* Review Books Page (February 24, 1997).

Johnson, Catherine, ed. *Playing Sidney Poitier and Other Stories*. London: SAKS Media Publications, 1999.

Kay, Jackie. *Off Colour*. Newcastle upon Tyne: Bloodaxe Books, 1998.

——. *Trumpet* (novel) London: Picador, 1998.

——. *Other Lovers: Poems*. Highgreen: Bloodaxe Books, 1993.

——. *The Adoption Papers*. Highgreen, Tarset, Northumberland: Bloodaxe Books, 1991.

Lee, A. Robert. *Other Britain, Other British: Contemporary Multicultural Fiction*. London and East Haven, Connecticut: Pluto Press, 1995.

Levy, Andrea. *Fruit of the Lemon*. London: Headline Book Publishing, 1999.

——. *Never Far From Nowhere*. London: Headline Book Publishing, 1996.

——. *Every Light in the House Burnin'*. London: Headline Review, 1994.

Leventhal, Fred et al. "NACBS Report on the State and Future of British Studies in North America." North American Conference on British Studies Webpage, Spring 2000.

Mercer, Kobena. *Black Film, Black Cinema*. London: Institute of Contemporary Arts, 1987.

Merz, Terri. "Letter from Cambridge." *Book World, The Washington Post* (Sunday, September 3, 2000): 10.

Newland, Courttia. *Snakeskin*. London: Abacus, 2002.

——. *Society Within*. London: Abacus, 2000.

——. *The Scholar*. London: Abacus, 1998.

Newland, Courttia and Kadija George Sesay, eds. *IC3: The Penguin Book of New Black Writing in Britain*. London: Hamish Hamilton/Penguin, 2000.

Nichols, Grace. *Fat Black Woman's Poems*. London: Virago, 1984.

Niven, Alistair. "Black British Writing: The Struggle for Recognition." In *Crisis and Creativity in the New Literatures in English*. Geoffrey Davis and Hena Maes-Jelinek, eds. Amsterdam and Atlanta: Rodopi, 1990.

Owusu, Kwesi. *Storms of the Heart*. London: Camden Press, 1988.

Parker, Kenneth. "The Revelation of Caliban: 'The Black Presence' in the Classroom." In *The Black Presence in English Literature. Q.v.* Dabydeen, ed. 186–207.

Phillips, Mike and Trevor Phillips. *Windrush: The Irresistible Rise of Multi-Racial Britain*. London: HarperCollins, 1998.

Rushdie, Salman. *Imaginary Homelands: Essays and Criticism 1981–1991*. New York and London: Penguin, 1991.

Sebba, Mark and Shirley Tate. "You Know What I Mean? Agreement Marking in British Black English." *Journal of Pragmatics*, 10 (1986): 163–172.

Sissay, Lemn, ed. *The Fire People*. Edinburgh: Payback Press, 1998.

Sivanandan, A. "The Liberation of the Black Intellectual." *The Literary Review* 34, 1 (Fall 1990): 12–25.

Smith, Zadie. *White Teeth*. New York: Random House, 2000.

Stevenson, Randall. *A Reader's Guide to the Twentieth-Century Novel in Britain*. Lexington: University of Kentucky Press, 1993.

Street, Brian. "Reading the Novels of Empire: Race and Ideology in the Classic 'Tale of Adventure.' " In *The Black Presence in English Literature*. Q.v. Dabydeen, ed. 95–111.

Sutcliffe, David. "British Black English and West Indian Creoles." In *Language in the British Isles*. Peter Trudgill, ed. Cambridge: Cambridge University Press, 1984. 219–237.

Syal, Meera. *Anita and Me*. New York: New Press, 1997.

Van Sertima, Ivan. *African Presence in Early Europe*. London: Transaction Press, 1985.

Visram, Rozina. *Ayahs, Lascars and Princes: Indians in Britain 1700–1947*. London and Dover, NH: Pluto Press, 1986.

Walder, Dennis. *Post-Colonial Literatures in English: History, Language, Theory*. Oxford: Blackwell, 1998.

Younge, Gary. *No Place Like Home: A Black Briton's Journey Through the American South*. London: Picador, 1999.

CHAPTER 3

THE POLITICS OF TEACHING
BLACK *AND* BRITISH

Maria Helena Lima

Put the GREAT back into Britain
and my GREAT GREAT GREAT grandparents'
ghostly hands
touch my face
and ghost faces claim my restless
roving eyes
to whisper

And you
would you, then,
be part of the GREAT British nation, too,
when Britain regains its GREAT?
    —Merle Collins, "When Britain Had Its Great" in *Rotten Pomerack*

The imperial English may have carried British passports—as did the Scots, Welsh, and some of the Irish—but they really didn't need to think too hard about whether being "English" was the same as being "British": the terms were virtually interchangeable. Nowadays, nothing will so infuriate a Scot as to confuse the terms English and British, for England's Celtic neighbours are increasingly for striking out on their own.
    —Jeremy Paxman, *The English: A Portrait of a People*

From the moment when I first wondered about teaching "black" and "British" together, to the time I sat down to write the first incarnation of this article (prompted by a rereading of Michael Eldridge's "The Rise and Fall of Black Britain") and now, the meanings of both words—*black* and *British*—have been shifting. Indeed, in these last decades, they have seemingly realigned themselves in yet another configuration. Although readers may assume that this essay is a direct response to Eldridge's somewhat negative position, I would like you to consider it, instead, my own attempt at continuing to historicize what it is I have been trying to do in teaching black British literature.

While I have been including black British writers in "African Diaspora," "Women's Studies," "Contemporary British Literature," "Women's Literature," and the other courses I have developed over the years, the Spring 2004 semester is the first time at the State University of New York at Geneseo that the course has a *permanent* place in curriculum, with a number and a title all of its own: English 318, "Black British Literature and Culture." If what I have been telling my students is right—that it is literature only when it gets *regularly* taught in English Departments—I would be curious to find out how many similar courses exist in the United States, in Britain, and elsewhere in the former Commonwealth nations. If, indeed, "the primary duty of any literature department is to illuminate the spirit animating a people, to show how it meets new challenges, and to investigate possible areas of development and involvement," as F. R. Leavis claims, now seems to be the moment not only to recognize the complicity of literature (and the other arts) in the constitution of the national imaginary, but also to endorse it.[1] My guess is that Eldridge's critique of what he calls "the reification of *black British* as a term affixed to magazine articles, book titles, art exhibits, conference panels, college courses, and a certain practice (or certain practitioners) of cultural analysis" is still premature.[2] Of course, from my point of view as a teacher and an activist, the issue becomes not only whether such courses exist in any significant numbers, but instead *how* they have been structured and taught—and for what purposes.

For example, the first time I incorporated black British texts was in a Women's Studies class I taught years ago as a graduate student at the University of Maryland at College Park. At that point I was not yet interested in delineating the *legitimate*, as distinct from the merely formal and legal, enfranchisement in the British *nation*.[3] The editors of the anthology I used, *Charting the Journey: Writings by Black and Third World Women* (1988), explain in the preface that their "book is about an idea, [an] idea of "Blackness" [with a capital *B*] in contemporary Britain." This anthology was indirectly a product of the cumulative experience of the Black Power and Black Consciousness movements in the United States, of their influence on other peoples in the Diaspora to "Think Black, Talk Black, Create Black, Buy Black, Vote Black and Live Black," in an attempt (according to Paul Gilroy) to forge "a countercultural identity."[4] The editors recognize that "Blackness"—both as an idea and a process—is inevitably self-contradictory in its conceptualization because it transcends color. The term, then, encompassed African,

South Asian, and Caribbean U.K.-passport–carrying citizens, as well as political exiles from other parts of the world, including South America. Although the material substance of this "idea" was the arrival in the British Isles of people from the former British colonies (the first section of the anthology is entitled "Alien Nation: Strangers at Home"), *Charting the Journey* was also, if not primarily, a reaction to the conservatism of the Thatcher years and its effects on black women's politics and lives.[5] We can hear the longing and nostalgia for a past of real activism in the editors' voice:

> *Once* there was a plethora of local Black women's groups up and down the country; groups which had mushroomed in a heyday of Black political activity attempting to force a change in the status quo of our lives. As women and as feminists . . . we campaigned in solidarity with each other and with those of us still "at home" struggling for National Liberation— the Irish and Palestinians, Eritreans and Namibians, Chileans and the people of El Salvador. *Once* we fought local authorities over injustices meted out to us . . . . *Once* we formed our own political agendas and argued in our own terms about how best to go forward; *once* we had networks, national conferences, and our campaigning took many forms, depending on the situation we found ourselves in and our assessment of what needed to be done.[6]

The signifier *Black*, at that historical conjuncture (the mid-1980s), was synonymous with political activism and change. Already, the word meant something different in the U.K. context: it was more an idea to be achieved through politics than either a race or a textual horizon. It implied the "business of transforming transplanted ways of being, seeing, and living . . . into a 'Black British' way of being."[7] *Charting the Journey*, the editors claimed, was to document that process. Although the myth of British culture as insular and racially specific had crumbled under the manifest evidence of a multicultural reality, many attempts were made at preserving that national imaginary. During the 1983 election campaign, for example, with the aid of the advertising firm Saatchi and Saatchi, the Conservative Party produced a now notorious poster featuring a black man, dressed in a suit and carrying a briefcase. The caption read: "Labour says he's black. Tories say he's British." "Implicit in the new Thatcherite concept of nationhood," as Caryl Phillips writes, was the idea that one could not be both British *and* black:

> Black equals bad. British equals good. We will take you as British as long as you look like you belong—no afros, no dashikis, no beads, no shoulder bags, only a suit, tie and briefcase, thank you very much. For the first

time in British history, two types of black person were now being officially recognized: the "good" and the "bad." The nation had certainly moved on from the "Powellite" model in which *all* blacks were to be excluded from the national narrative and encouraged to go "back to where they came from."[8]

With Powell, however, racism was out in the open, and Black Power became, according to A. Sivanandan, "the other side of the Powellite coin." Bringing together over fifty African, West Indian, Indian, and Pakistani organizations, the Black People's Alliance came about *because* of Powell's speech.[9] Thatcher's new idea of British nationality, "with its dependency on economic virility and on codes of behavior," was to be, as Phillips notes, "culturally and not racially constructed."[10] Not quite hidden, however, was the true agenda of the Conservative Party: assimilate or you will never belong. Although the 1980s saw the first non-white citizens being elected to Parliament and even becoming captains of national sports teams, creating, in Phillips's evaluation of the decade, "a space for the black community in Britain to begin to come of age," what Thatcher truly achieved by including her version of black people in her concept of nation was a new generation who did not know who they were. If "divide and rule" had worked for empire building, Phillips concludes in his analysis of the Thatcher years, why not try it in the domestic arena.[11]

The 1990s seem to have started from an altogether different premise, one that positioned blackness within and against what Stuart Hall calls "the burden of representation," his term for a primarily discursive reality.[12] For Hall, the central concern is the quest for a "new language" that articulates the experience of black people in Britain as a distinctly British or English experience. It was as a response to this moment that the first version of my "Black British Writers" course was created. Because *black* and *British* were not words normally seen together in the Geneseo universe in 1998 (they are now), I started the semester exploring the questions raised on the syllabus: Who is English in that nation's imaginary? Who is not? Does Englishness mean white only, as Catherine Hall has so persuasively demonstrated by retelling some of that country's history in relation to its colonies.[13] To explore that history, I also used Linda Colley's *Britons: Forging the Nation 1707–1837*. Colley contends that it was not so much consensus or homogeneity at home, but a strong sense of dissimilarity from those outside, which proved to be the essential cement of England's national identity. The British came to define themselves as a single people, Colley argues, "not because of any political or cultural consensus at home, but rather in reaction to the Other beyond their shores."[14]

The focus of our course was on what happens when the Other beyond Britain's shores comes to settle in the mother country. I told my students that, unfortunately, we did not have time to explore fully the black presence in British cultural history.[15] That black presence in Britain dates to as far back as the invading Roman army. Steve Martin, the historian who runs the "London Black Heritage Walking Tours," claims that "you can throw a dart at any area of London and find a black contribution to its history." While the most commonly given date for the arrival of black people in Britain is 1555, when five Africans were carried there by British traders to learn English and facilitate trade with Africa, there is a poem about a black woman by William Dunbar, a Scot, in the early sixteenth century, and toward the end of that same century the inclusion of young black servants in the portraits of aristocrats had become a common practice. While we were *not* going to subscribe to the fiction that there were no black people in England before 1945, the class was going to focus on the immigrants who came in at the end of World War II. Originally invited to the mother country by the Labour government in its attempt to solve the immediate labor crisis following the War, and commonly known as the "Windrush generation," these islanders moved to Britain expecting to improve their standard of living.[16]

According to Harry Goulbourne, until the British Nationality Act of 1948, there was a common set of assumptions regarding nationality throughout the British Empire. The basic understanding was that all who came under the Crown's power were British subjects. The British Nationality and Aliens Act (1914), for example, sought to define British citizenship for an empire that was, obviously, scattered, multiracial and multinational. Rushed through Parliament during the first week of August as England was about to enter the Great War, the 1914 Act sought to consolidate "the law" relating to British nationality as it had developed piecemeal over the centuries. As Goulbourne explains, the 1914 Act defined those who were henceforth to be considered British citizens, the means whereby an alien could be naturalized, and also how she or he could lose the status of being British. In sharp contrast to postimperial British nationality law, the 1914 Act seems to have been concerned with who could be *included*, rather than who should be *excluded* from being a part of the Pax Britannica.[17] The Conservative Party's main contribution (in more recent times) to the search for a new definition of postimperial British nationality has been to give it an ethnic dimension. Nowhere has this contribution been more clearly demonstrated than in the 1962 Commonwealth Immigration Act, the 1971 Immigration Act, and the 1981 Nationality Act. The 1962 Act marked the abrupt end of free entry of people from non-white Commonwealth countries into Britain. And the term "new Commonwealth" was to become more familiar as a code term for non-white people. It is also worth noting that this new political label has tended to encourage the thinking that the countries of the "new Commonwealth" have only recently established connections with Britain, which is, of course, far from the truth. Some of these "new" Commonwealth societies (such as several of the Caribbean countries) were established by Britain herself in the early part of the sixteenth century, and part of India was under British control (through the East India Company) long before the formal establishment of the British Raj in 1857. The change in the relationship, however, provided part of the justification for a voucher system that was then introduced. Intending migrants, as Goulbourne notes, had to prove that they had a job to come to. Only dependents, such as a wife and minor children, could join the head of the family.[18] The majority of the Conservative Party felt that there were three things that had to be done: integrate those "immigrants" already here, "send the bad hats home," and restrict further immigration "until we have digested what we have here already" (the Conservative Party, 1961). But the question of integration was not agreed upon by all. Norman A. Pannell, a Liverpool Member of Parliament, argued that quite apart from the housing question, immigrants posed a danger to health and morals because of their contribution to the births of unwanted children.[19]

Already a classic in its representation of this period is the first novel on our syllabus, Samuel Selvon's *The Lonely Londoners* (1956). The other texts we read also attempt to tell the immigrant story of great expectations and shattered illusions. More recent novels even address the riots of 1981 and 1985 directly.

A parallel development, I have told my students, can be observed in the arts other than literature. In the early 1960s, for example, with the creation of the Commonwealth Institute of London, there was fostered an interest in the arts of "others," but no real change in the perceived national culture was attempted. (The Arts Council of Great Britain is linked to that much later development.) The recognition of black film-making in Britain and the notion of a black British cinema are also phenomena of the 1980s. During that decade, the politics of race and ethnicity, of diversity and difference, emerged as signifiers of the ways in which Britain had to confront its colonial and imperialist history. It is precisely that history that the filmmaker Maya Jaggi and other black Britons have been revisiting, claiming it a "right of citizenship to see [themselves] reflected in what the nation preserves and values."[20] There was indeed almost an urgency in adding "blackness" to the national imaginary, for many Britons still wanted to associate Englishness with whiteness and all that is "proper," a reflex deriving from the myth of cultural superiority that England exported to the colonies to justify its imperial presence there. Immigrants raised on images of Britain as the epitome of civilization searched, often in vain, for the solid reality of that ideal English metropolis, a world that had grown up in their imaginations on dubious, artificial, and often literary foundations. When immigrants from the colonies began to arrive in England after World War II, they soon realized that the non-fictional English people were a far cry from what they had been led to expect. In "Nation and New Identities," Patricia Waugh sums this up best:

> What did Englishness continue to mean in this context? . . . English reserve was in any case a legacy of that national identity promoted by an imperial civil service, with its view of the foreigner as exotically other and in need of safe containment, a threat both outside but also potentially within the national psyche as a lurking evolutionary throwback. But it was a convenient myth to rehabilitate for the eighties . . . .[21]

Most of the texts we read actually explore the newcomers' shock at the reality of England when compared to the myth imperialist Britain had previously exported to the colonies. In Hanif Kureishi's *The Buddha of Suburbia* (1990), for example, a novel that depicts what it meant to grow up in the 1960s and early 1970s in London, Karim's father's first encounter with the English people conveys the impact of such a realization in the following passage: "[Haroon] had never seen the English in poverty . . . when Dad tried to discuss Byron in local pubs no one warned him that not every Englishman could read."[22] The immigrants were also surprised and saddened to discover that they were not readily accepted as English citizens, even though they had been told their whole lives they were English. They confronted, instead, skinhead violence that—although later "explained" as a response to unemployment, poor housing, and deplorable working conditions—always came as a surprise to the black British. In an interview, Hanif Kureishi contextualizes the drugs, sex, and punk rock scene in *The Buddha of Suburbia* as the only possible escape that the youth of his generation found from the violence surrounding them (he was born in 1954).[23]

Samuel Selvon's *Moses Ascending* (1975) is another black British novel on our syllabus that portrays an entirely different Englishness from the veneer of refinement and intellectualism the colonizers disseminated throughout the far-flung empire for emulation by the colonial natives. In the novel, although Moses has been trying to move up in the world by becoming a landlord, he knows he will never be treated like the average Englishman because he is not white. Still, *Moses Ascending* indirectly poses the same question that E. M. Forster asks in *Howards End* (1910): who will inherit England? Although on the surface Selvon seems to be saying that only the white man can inherit England (especially since, at the end of the novel, readers will find Moses confined to the basement of what used to be his own house), other futures are possible, for Moses is left planning ways to rise again in society.

When we started discussing Selvon's *Moses Ascending*, however, one of the first comments I heard from a student was about the novel's style: "but this is old style realism!" How have I justified conventional realism to English majors used to the complexity they have learned to value in Modernist and Post-Modernist texts? Well, I have kept trying. I explained, first of all, that English fiction after 1945 was already beginning to return to its eighteenth-century roots: the realism of Daniel Defoe and Henry Fielding was to be self-consciously revived. That postwar realism, I explained, was indeed radical. Realism is radical because any purposeful attempt to change the world depends on a conviction that it can be realistically represented. The later fiction of James Joyce and Virginia Woolf does not convey a belief that the world could or would ever be changed. Realism, I argued, is a way of *looking hard* at *the world*; any nation needs to look hard at itself, and report on what it sees, if it is ever to grow and change.

When I was thinking of giving up the attempt to "sell realism" to my students, a colleague gave me *Questions of Third Cinema* to read (Jim Pines and Paul Willeman, eds.), a collection that includes Clyde Taylor's article "Black Cinema in a Post-Aesthetic Era," where I have found some pedagogical answers. For, as Taylor notes, "the question of aesthetics is always a non-dialogue between those who subscribe to the conditioned world order and those who stand to gain from a reconstructed forum."[24] A rationale for some of the interpretive practices in my "Black British Writers" class has been what Taylor characterizes as a "post-aesthetic" process. Since, according to Taylor, black art is one of the "crucial site[s] out of which the human is being rewritten," how do we as literature teachers convey such a dynamic idea? Best, probably, by reconceptualizing the use of "aesthetics" in our classrooms. If we ask our students to think of the function of aesthetics in human life—how its concepts correlate with our present social order—they will understand, in Sylvia Wynter's formulation, the correlation between aesthetics and the nonlinear structuring dynamics of our present global order. For Wynter, the aesthetic imperative is to secure the social cohesion of the specific human order of which it is a function. It aims to produce a unitary system of meanings, a "paradigm of value and authority," against which every "newcomer" must be measured—and is usually found "lacking."[25]

In these texts my students and I have also been able to trace the critique of the English reluctance to talk about race. While Stuart Hall characterizes "race in Britain as the modality in which class is lived" and Michael Eldridge attempts to turn that around to say that "class is the modality in which race is lived" and that "both sides of the equation are *divided* by ethnicity,"[26] we came out with a much more inclusive (even if somewhat idealized) imagined community in our reading of *Bhaji on the Beach*. For the purpose for art now seems to be the creation of such new imagined communities in England. We saw Gurinda Chadha's and Meera Syal's film *Bhaji on the Beach* (1994) as, in a way, a precursor of the types of film that will characterize yet another realignment of the ethnic identities comprising the British. We focused our discussion on contemporary black filmmaking in Britain as being not only about the contestation of Englishness but also, perhaps more importantly, about exploring the diversity and intrinsic complexity that constitute a British Asian, African, or African-Caribbean (English) identity in Britain. My students read a version of "No Pure Spaces in *Bhaji on the Beach*," a article I delivered at the NYCEA Fall 1999 Conference, "Bridges and Borders in Literature and Film," where I argue that Chadha and Syal want their audience to reevaluate what it means to be Indian in England at that point in history, particularly in light of the ways in which their original culture has been used to exclude them from full citizenship. Reading the film against a background of court decisions on domestic violence, I emphasize how that context is indeed crucial to understanding the filmmakers' agenda. Bravely using comedy to treat the issue of violence against women, Chadha shows her audience the complexity of Asian women's lives in England: the conflict between modern ways and tradition, the price some women refuse to pay for the so-called comforts of home, and the tensions that arise in recognizing the state as both oppressor and protector. In campaigns against domestic violence, for example, Asian women have made demands for their right to leave oppressive family environments and for the state to criminalize domestic violence, dismantling the notion of the family as a sacred and private space. At the same time, British Asian women have also needed to demand that the state recognize the right to family unity in immigration cases where racist laws and policies separate and even criminalize some members of minority families. To keep silent about domestic violence for the sake of preserving the mythical notion of a united Asian com- munity means to support and collude in their own oppression as women. There are many women like the fictional Ginder in Chadha's film, who have fled violent homes and are living in battered women's shelters. What I see *Bhaji on the Beach* accomplishing without loud-speakers and big demonstrations is the reconceptualization of commu-nity for Asian women living in Britain today. For very few women at the end of the movie will have any sympathy left for Ginder's mother-in-law, to whom we are introduced in one of the film's initial scenes, at the breakfast table, reminding her family that Ginder is too dark and maybe that's the reason why "since she stepped into [her] house, she's been nothing but trouble" and now wants a divorce: "she's brought the English Court into my house!" she tells her son, and that cannot be the last thing happening to her before she dies.

By suggesting how mainstream British society itself is riven by con-flict, movies like *Bhaji on the Beach* help interrogate the idea of national identity, thus invigorating the project of forging alternative social iden-tities and practices. The filmmakers' depiction of the seaside resort of Blackpool exposes the extent to which there has never been an uncon-tested set of values—Queen, Church, and Commons notwithstanding. What is left of whiteness in the movie, for example, is fittingly perfor-mative: an old English actor who wanders the streets of Blackpool in search of ladies in distress with whom to recall his and England's past glories. Rather than depending on the dominant values of the existing society, Chadha's cinematography attempts to forge a new consensus. After acknowledging the necessary fictions of identity the British have attempted to preserve, her audience is ready to move on to create the society of the future.

Gurinder Chadha's last film, *Bend It like Beckham* (2002), takes the national allegory a step further. According to Chadha, what has changed since the release of *Bhaji on the Beach* is "the British audience's appetite for films about Britain."[27] She claims "people don't see the film in terms of race and culture clash," managing instead to "identify with characters regardless of their background." Chadha captures the national passion in a film but bends it a little, for her protagonist is a teenage girl named Jess (Parminder Nagra), who must choose between following the tradi-tions of her Sikh family or pursuing her dream of becoming a soccer star. That the team's coach, an Irishman named Joe (Jonathan Rhys-Myers), chooses Jess over Jules (Keira Knightley), her best friend (who happens to be white) and also a great player, adds to the idyllic imagined community Chadha achieves with her last creation. For Jess's cousin can come out as a gay man and not be ostracized by the entire community, and Jess is allowed to leave for California to play for the college team that recruits her. Rather than criticizing Chadha's script for taking "every easy way out" and never recognizing "the possibility of real pain," as the reviewer for *The Observer* does, I prefer to consider the "liberal ecumenicism" of the final scenes where "everyone comes to appreciate everyone else's religion and taste" as a *telos*, a goal to be achieved as England slowly enters the European Union (EU).[28]

What becomes interesting for me to continue to observe in this strategic realignment is the role of "blackness" in cementing British identity—or should I say *English* identity here, since nothing much of *Great* Britain is left. Many British intellectuals have been wondering what it means to be English after the end of empire and the pressures for the English to plunge into Europe. Indeed, if Linda Colley is right, now that it is part of the EU, the United Kingdom can no longer comfortably define itself against the European powers at all. Whether it likes it or not, Britain is fast becoming "part of an increasingly federal Europe," as Colley notes, "though the agonies that British politicians and voters of all partisan persuasions so plainly experience in coming to terms with Brussels and its dictates show just how rooted the perception of Continental Europe as the Other still is." In these circumstances, Colley argues, the reemergence of Irish, Welsh, Scottish, and indeed English nationalisms, which have been so marked in recent decades, can be seen not just as the natural outcome of cultural diversity, but as a response to a broader loss of *national*, in the sense of *British*, identity. While I agree with Colley that the *Other* in the shape of militant Catholicism or a hostile Continental European power or an exotic overseas empire is no longer available to make Britons feel that—by contrast—they have an identity in common, I cannot understand why the predictable result needs to be a revival of internal divisions.[29]

According to Stuart Hall, "Black British culture is today confident beyond its own measure in its own identity—secure in a difference which it does not expect, or want to go away. . . . We are fully confident in our own difference, no longer caught in the trap of aspiration which was sprung on so many of us who are older, as part of the colonial legacy described in Fanon's famous phrase as Black skins, white mask. Black identity today is autonomous and not tradable."[30] Not all the writers in our Fall 2003 syllabus for "Black British Women Writers" share this confidence, however. Apart from a handful of headliners such as Zadie Smith and now Monica Ali, a vast majority still faces the challenges of writing against cultural imperatives and conventions, of being published, reviewed, and—ultimately—fully understood. What really was more surprising to me during my sabbatical in London in spring 2002 was not to be able to find "Black British Literature" courses at the university level. At the University of London, for example, Benjamin Zephaniah can be read before or after Toni Morrison in a course called "Black Writing," a practice that in my view does justice to neither author. While Mike Phillips gets "half a dozen invitations a year from foreign universities to lecture on [his] fiction" and acknowledges that, "in his experience, the most knowledgeable and well-read academics in the field are likely to be attached to universities in Germany, France, Italy or the U.S.," the majority of critics in Britain continue to categorize black British literature as "minority writing," "postcolonial," and/or "marginal."[31]

Until black British writers earn their place in the national imaginary and in literature departments, it will be a long time before the "nation/state as a paradigm for the consideration of art," as Bronwyn Williams foresees, will be "supplanted by new, more fluid, transnational and transcultural forces."[32] While, as Williams urges, critics and teachers should continue to attempt *not to* "essentialize the Black British subject or experience," we will also have to continue "to unpack how both 'Black-ness' and 'Britishness' are culturally constructed for themselves and for the dominant culture."

For these reasons, I cannot find much use for Paul Gilroy's latest argument in *Against Race: Imagining Political Culture Beyond the Color Line*. Yes, we are officially through with "the century of the color line," and it would be beautiful if the world's peoples did not have the grid of race against which to perceive ourselves, but we do. It will take more than a discursive attempt, an exercise in wishful thinking, to enact an alternative reality. Gilroy's "nano-political struggles of the biotech" (17) do not seem to address race either systemically or at the level of the imaginary. Race-thinking does not stop (or start) at the individual gene/body. It has *never* been about science—the volumes that Gilroy draws from have been there all along. So what is the point of the exercise, when now—for the first time—young black Britons seem to have found a voice? Despite the contradictions of this moment, when in economic terms, as Hall notes, young black people still "continue to be at the receiving end of systematic structures of deprivation and victimization because of their race" and at the same time "find themselves at the center of the host culture as its object of desire,"[33] I wonder whether Gilroy's "strategic universalism" and "planetary humanism" can really do the job of equipping "black European mentalities for the perils of the twenty-first century."[34]

Will "planetary humanism" help us understand why better levels of education for almost all ethnic groups living in Britain today have *not* translated into equality in the world of work? If not systemic racism, how do we explain that the "political, legal and business establishment remains largely white."[35] Because now there are more than four million "non-white" Britons—more than the population of the Republic of Ireland as Sunder Katwala points out—"with as many differences within and between different ethnic groups as can be found by comparing the 'ethnic minorities' to the general population," it becomes harder, but not impossible, to conceive of "blackness" as an idea, an organizing force around which *all* disenfranchised peoples can organize.

Daniel Defoe, as Jeremy Paxman writes, had a much more accurate idea of the ethnic origins of the English three centuries ago. When he heard English people disdaining foreigners as having corrupted blood, Defoe described "the most scoundrel race that ever lived," the English: the English are a mongrel race, and, according to Paxman, it has taken the development of communities living in England that are visibly different to demonstrate the point.[36] Lord Parekh's Report on the Future of Multi-Ethnic Britain stresses that British history was racially exclusive and that Britain "as an imagined community . . . urgently needs to re-imagine itself."[37] That history produced a contrived, class-based, Anglo-centric narrative grounded in Protestantism, patriotism, and a sense of imperial mission almost ordained because of her democratic traditions. The qualities of honesty, courage, and endurance are at the core of the English national character, and the process of absorption into Englishness until recently implied pride in the British Empire. Ironically, it is the former empire that once more will allow for a British identity in common. As my first epigraph indicates[38] (and of course it is my reading of Merle Collins's poem), an EU identity will be achieved based on the presence of the descendants of the former colonial subjects, but not as black culture for consumption only, which seems to be Eldridge's main fear.

Caryl Phillips offers the synthesizing new world vision of the Caribbean as the perfect model for the age in which we live—"an age in which migrations across boundaries are an increasingly familiar part of our individual lives as national borders collapse and are redrawn." We should be able to "explain our new hybrid selves," he claims, "without recourse to the simplistic discourse of race."[39] For Phillips, Britain should define itself as a nation with a "synthesis of Indian takeaways, baked beans, soccer, Jamaican patties, St. Patrick's Day, pub on Saturday, Notting Hill Carnival, church on Sunday, mosque on Friday and fish and chips." Whereas George Orwell claimed that "it needs some very great disaster, such as prolonged subjugation by a foreign enemy, to *destroy* a national culture," Phillips argues that "the truth is that it needs some very great fortune such as continual waves of immigration to *create* a national culture."[40] He concludes:

> As a nation Britain is now reluctantly postcolonial, but stubbornly pre-European. While it was the pioneer generation of Caribbean migrants who helped to introduce Britain to the notion of postcoloniality, it is their children's and grandchildren's generation who will help Britain cross the Rubicon of the English Channel and enter the European age of the twenty-first century.[41]

I tend to agree. Teaching black British literature over the years has enabled me to identify ways in which texts produced on the margins of a dominant discourse have earned the authority not only to subvert but also to transform its central notions. From where I stand the future looks bright for black Britons.

Notes

1. F. R. Leavis, *The Great Tradition* (New York: New York University Press, 1973), 9–18.
2. Michael Eldridge, "The Rise and Fall of Black Britain," *Transition* 74 (1998), 39.
3. Enoch Powell, e.g., argued that a person of either West Indian or Asian background born in England could not become English. See one version of that very complex history in Harry Goulbourne, *Ethnicity and Nationalism in Post-Imperial Britain* (Cambridge and New York: Cambridge University Press, 1991), 4–5, for this point.
4. Paul Gilroy, *There Ain't No Black in the Union Jack* (London: Hutchinson, 1987), 176–177.
5. Forty years after the landing of *SS Empire Windrush*, Margaret Thatcher boasted that "the story of how Europeans explored and colonized and—yes, without apology—civilized much of the world is an extraordinary tale of talent, skill and courage" (qtd. in Goulbourne, Ethnicity and Nationalism 167).
6. Shabnam Grewal et al., eds., *Charting the Journey: Writings by Black and Third World Women* (London: Sheba Feminist Publishers, 1988), 2–3, emphases added.
7. Ibid., 1.
8. Caryl Phillips, *A New World Order: Essays* (New York, Vintage International, 2002), 247–248.

9. Kwesi Owusu, "The Struggle for a Radical Black Political Culture: An Interview with A. Sivanandan," *Black British Culture & Society*, ed. Kwesi Owusu (London and New York: Routledge, 2000), 421.

10. Phillips, *A New World Order*, 279.

11. Ibid.

12. Stuart Hall, "New Ethnicities," *Black British Cultural Studies: A Reader*, ed. Houston A. Baker, Jr., Manthia Diawara, and Ruth H. Lindeborg, (Chicago and London: University of Chicago Press, 1996), 165.

13. Catherine Hall, "Gender Politics and Imperial Politics: Rethinking the Histories of Empire," *Engendering History: Caribbean Women in Historical Perspective*, Verene Shepard et al., eds. (New York: St. Martin's Press, 1995), 48–59.

14. Linda Colley, *Britons: Forging the Nation 1707–1837* (New Haven and London: Yale University Press, 1992), 17.

15. I have since that first class taught Bernardine Evaristo's *The Emperor's Babe* (London: Hamish Hamilton, 2001), a novel in verse that documents African presence in Londinium, Britannia, when the city was a remote northern outpost of the Roman Empire. In her presentation at Geneseo (Fall 2002), Evaristo emphasized the importance of rewriting British history, for not many people realize that Septimius Severus, ruler of the Roman Empire from A.D. 193–211, was African. The novel's epigraph by Oscar Wilde, "The one duty we owe to history is to rewrite it," illuminates the narrative's daring irreverence, shifting from Latin to twenty-first-century teen slang and never losing its punch.

16. In response to this call, in June 1948, a ship carrying about four hundred and fifty people from the Caribbean docked at Tilbury. For more on the literary representation of the Windrush Generation, read Susheila Nasta, "Setting up Home in a City of Words: Sam Selvon's Novels," *Other Britain, Other British: Contemporary Multicultural Fiction*, A. Robert Lee, ed. (London: Pluto Press, 1995).

17. Goulbourne, *Ethnicity and Nationalism*, 91.

18. Ibid., 115.

19. Ibid., 116.

20. Maya Jaggi, "Casting Off the Shackles of History," Guardian Weekly (November 18–24, 1999).

21. Patricia Waugh, *Harvest of the Sixties: English Literature and Its Background* (Oxford and New York: Oxford University Press, 1995), 160–161.

22. Hanif Kureishi, *The Buddha of Suburbia* (New York: Penguin Book, 1991), 24.

23. The interview ("Fresh Air," January 17, 1996) was to promote his then-new novel, *The Black Album* (1995), which, according to Kureishi, depicts Islamic Fundamentalism in the 1990s ("the fatwah business," as Kureishi's protagonist, Shahid, calls it) as offering a similar kind of relief for the young from the disillusionment of rejection that in the 1970s was treated with drugs and punk rock. Islamic Fundamentalism is also at the center of Selvon's *Moses Ascending* (1975) and Zadie Smith's *White Teeth* (2000).

24. Clyde Taylor, "Black Cinema in a Post-Aesthetic Era," *Questions of Third Cinema*, ed. Jim Pines and Paul Willeman (London: British Film Institute, 1989), 90.
25. Sylvia Wynter, "Rethinking 'Aesthetics': Notes towards a Deciphering Practice," *Ex-Iles: Essays on Caribbean Cinema*, ed. Mbye B. Cham (Trenton, New Jersey: Africa World Press, 1992), 241, 244, 245, 249.
26. Eldridge, "The Rise," 38, emphasis added.
27. Gurinder Chadha, "Call that a Melting Pot?" The Guardian (April 11, 2002): See http:/film.guardian.co.uk/Print/0,3858,4391544,00.html.
28. Philip French, "Bend It Like Beckham," *The Observer* (April 14, 2002): See http://film.guardian.co.uk/News_Story/Critic_Review/Observer_review/0,4267,683987,00.
29. Colley, *Britons*, 7.
30. Stuart Hall, "Frontlines and Backyards: The Terms of Change," *Black British Culture and Society*, ed. Owusu (London and New York: Routledge, 2000), 127.
31. Mike Phillips, "From Slaves to Straw Men," *The Guardian* (August 30, 2003). See http://books.guardian.co.uk/print/0,3858,4743025–110738,00.html.
32. Bronwyn T. Williams, "'A State of Perpetual Wandering': Diaspora and Black British Writers." See http://social.chass.ncsu.edu/jouvert/v3i3/willia.html.
33. Stuart Hall, "Frontlines," 128.
34. Paul Gilroy, *Against Race: Imagining Political Culture Beyond the Color Line* (Cambridge, Massachusetts: The Belknap Press of Harvard University Press, 2000), 12.
35. "The Truth of Multicultural Britain," *The Observer* (November 25, 2001). See http://www.observer.co.uk/Print/0,3858,43066676,00.html.
36. Jeremy Paxman, *The English: A Portrait of a People* (Woodstock and New York: The Overlook Press, 2000), 59.
37. Runnymede Trust, *The Future of Multi-Ethnic Britain: Report of the Commission on Multi-Ethnic Britain* (London: Profile Books, 2000), 15.
38. Ashaki Charles, a student in the 2000 version of my "Black British Writers" class, suggested that I use Merle Collins's poem as an epigraph, after hearing my trial run of this article, and still after I reminded her that "Put the 'Great' back into Great Britain again" was a popular Tory Party campaign slogan. Even if Thatcher's Britain was invested in images of Britain as a colonial power, one could signify on the idea of greatness, and that is what I was persuaded Merle Collins could be doing in the poem. Margot Backus and Kevin Meehan have offered invaluable feedback on earlier versions of this essay, for which I remain grateful.
39. Phillips, *A New World Order*, 132.
40. Ibid., 281.
41. Ibid., 282.

CHAPTER 4

THE EVOLUTION OF BLACK LONDON

Judith Bryan

The works of writers such as Olaudah Equiano and Ignatius Sancho give us detailed accounts of the lives of people in England from the eighteenth century, contradicting the often-held belief that black people only began to arrive *en masse* in Britain from the 1950s. Britain is a nation of hybridity, since many other "classic" British writers were not born in Britain either, but in the colonies, whether as colonizers or the colonized. A by-product of Britain's cultural history and identity is that it has produced a vigorous and dynamic literature. "As soon as one defines oneself as 'British,' " says novelist Caryl Phillips, "one is participating in a centuries-old tradition of cultural exchange, of ethnic and linguistic plurality."[1] This essay will show how Britain's black writers give us access to information about and knowledge of a section of the British population that historians have neglected and, consequently, have omitted from British history.

* * *

Artifacts prove that people of African descent have been present in London from Roman times. By the 1500s, in addition to being Britain's capital city, London had established itself as a premier port, its wealth and success built largely on the profits of empire building and the slave trade. Contemporary writings from the seventeenth century—such as the diaries of Samuel Pepys—indicate an increasingly visible black presence in the capital. By the turn of the eighteenth century, the black population in London alone numbered somewhere between 5,000 and 10,000. In portraits, newspapers, and pro-slavery tracts, black people were portrayed either as decorative accessories or as valuable, though troublesome, chattel. It is only in recent decades that black Britons have had an opportunity to reevaluate our contribution to the making of a nation and to place our contribution in its proper context. And, even so, significant gaps in the story remain.

I should like to focus here on four of Britain's earliest black writers: Ignatius Sancho, Olaudah Equiano, Robert Wedderburn, and Mary Seacole. By sketching their biographies and examining the social context in which their work was written, I hope to show that black history and Britain's history are inextricably linked. Black Londoners have played pivotal roles in these histories. And today's black British writers are not unaware of the fact.

Slavery in England was abolished in 1807, but it was not until 1834 that the practice was outlawed throughout the territories. Because of London's association with the slave trade, the majority of black people living in the capital up to that time were domestic slaves, runaways and ex-slaves. Domestic slaves generally lived with their "owners," often moving with them from place to place so that the black population was constantly shifting. Some, like Ignatius Sancho, were enabled to better themselves through the philanthropic interventions of wealthy patrons. Others were subject to the every whim of the slave owner. In addition to physical violence, there was the constant threat of being sold on, or returned to plantation slavery. In *Longest Journey*, her history of black Lewisham, Joan Anim-Addo offers the case of Jonathan Strong, who, in 1765, survived a brutal beating by his master.[2] He made his way to the house of the brother of the noted abolitionist, Granville Sharp. Anim-Addo says: "The Sharps took him to hospital where they paid for treatment. Two years later, having recovered from the near fatal beating, Jonathan was discovered after his master hired two professional slave hunters. Arrangements were made for his sale to another captain whose ship was bound for the West Indies."[3]

Free blacks tended to be those who had been released by their "owners" or had purchased their own freedom. Their numbers were significantly increased in 1783, as a result of America's victory in its War of Independence. Thousands of black men fought for the British. Some were free but most were slaves who had enlisted in return for their freedom. Hundreds were evacuated to London at the end of the war. In *Black Londoners, 1880–1990*, Susan Okokon tells us that "While some were able to continue their trades, such as cookshop owners and shoemakers, the vast majority joined the London poor as beggars and street musicians, being deprived of even Army back pay and compensation for war injuries, and denied work due to prejudice."[4]

Their predicament was aggravated by the fact that earlier, in 1731, the Lord Mayor of London had banned black people from taking up apprenticeships. Nor did these sufferers have recourse to government relief through The Poor Law. That law provided for the minimal maintenance of those poor people born in the parish. Since most black people had been born in Africa, the West Indies, or America, they did not qualify.

By the 1780s, philanthropists and abolitionists were beginning to speak out against the plight of London's black poor. Repatriation was seen as the best solution. With financial assistance from the Royal Navy, it was decided to establish a colony of free blacks in Sierra Leone, on the west coast of Africa. The plan was fraught with problems from the start, not least of which was the fact that Sierra Leone was an important slaving area and transport point. Olaudah Equiano, an ex-slave who became a noted writer, was appointed by the admiralty as Commissary for Stores to the Expedition. Around seven hundred black Londoners signed up for the passage. However, as his friend Ottobah Cugoano, another ex-slave living in London, wrote that same year, "Many more of the Black People still in this country would have, with great gladness, embraced the opportunity, longing to reach their native land; but as the old saying is, a burnt child dreads the fire."[5] In the event, the expedition proved disastrous, and many of the three hundred or so that eventually sailed were indeed recaptured as slaves.

In 1791, a second attempt was made to establish the Sierra Leone colony. This time, over a thousand free blacks who had settled in Nova Scotia were successfully resettled in what is now Freetown. The process did nothing to reduce the population of black Londoners, as had been the original aim. In fact, it directly increased the numbers. In *West Africans in Britain, 1900–1960*, Hakim Adi writes that a school was established in Clapham, south London, "to educate Africans who could then be placed in situations, 'as would afford the best means of promoting the great ends of the settlement,' which included the spreading of Christianity throughout West Africa as well as the suppression of the slave trade. Thus began the tradition of educating teachers, priests, and prospective West African rulers in Britain."[6]

By the 1850s, this tradition had developed to the extent that William Wells Brown, a fugitive American slave who visited London, later wrote, "In an hour's walk through the Strand, Regent-street or Picadilly, one may meet half a dozen coloured men, who are inmates of the various colleges in the metropolis. These are all signs of progress in the cause of the sons of Africa."[7]

But what of the intimate lives of black Londoners? How did they feel about their predicament, and what personal experience informed their political activity? Prior to the 1780s we have no first-hand information with which to address these questions. The first black Londoners to illuminate us are Ignatius Sancho and Olaudah Equiano. Their writings, published in 1782 and 1789 respectively, represent the beginnings of black British literature. They both confirm and contradict the picture of black London seen so far.

Even before 1807, our presence in Britain was not dictated solely by the whims of slavery, but was also a result of the will of black people themselves. London was a place where adventures began or ended, where travelers stopped to recover and consolidate before the next foray into the outreaches of the Empire. Equiano's writings show that black people were attracted to the capital in this same spirit. In his autobiography, *The Interesting Narrative of the Life of Olaudah Equiano or Gustavus Vassa*, he writes that, as a free man in 1767, he hired himself to "a hairdresser, in Coventry-court, Haymarket" and thence to a "Dr. Charles Irving, in Pall Mall"—during which time he also studied arithmetic and the French horn. However, by May 1768 his funds were severely depleted, and he "thought it best to try the sea again in quest of more money, as I had been bred to it, and had hitherto found the profession of it successful."

London became for Equiano a staging post. Captured from West Africa at the age of about eleven (so he recalled), he became the property of an English naval captain. On a visit to London, when Equiano was around the age of fourteen, his master dispatched him to work as a servant for two sisters named the Misses Guerin. As well as sending him to school, he reported, "They often used to teach me to read, and took great pains to instruct me in the principles of religion and the knowledge of God." But his master's ship was being prepared for sea again, and Equiano had no choice but to leave with it. Thus began a life during which he traveled all over the world, under many masters and many captains, even eventually joining an expedition to the Arctic in 1773. Although enslaved—and having no legal right to money or property— Equiano became something of an entrepreneur, earning enough money through the buying and selling of goods that in 1766 he was able to buy his freedom. It was as a free man that he returned to live in London, between bouts at sea.

In the last twenty years of his life, he became an active campaigner against slavery—writing letters to the press, participating in public debates, and assisting the victims of kidnapping and resale. His brief involvement with the Sierra Leone expedition ended with his dismissal, due to disagreements with the organizers. His memoirs were published in London two years later, and he used the book's success and his income from it to travel throughout Britain, speaking out against the continuing slave trade. The *Interesting Narrative* quickly became famous, translated into three languages and going to eight editions within his lifetime. When he died, in 1797, the abolitionist Granville Sharp was at his bedside. Equiano was survived by his wife, a white Englishwoman, and one of their two daughters.

Ignatius Sancho's beginnings were very different, in that he was born on a slaveship and therefore had no experience of life as a free African. However, the personal transformation he effected was no less extraordinary. As a young boy, he was the property of three sisters living in Greenwich, south London. When he expressed a desire to become literate, they threatened to sell him into plantation slavery. He ran away to the Duke and Duchess of Montague, who employed him as a butler in their home in neighboring Blackheath. It was in the library of Montague House that Sancho taught himself to read and write. As Amin-Addo says, "That he envisaged such a possibility for himself and created the opportunity was a remarkable act of resistance to the narrowly prescribed routes mapped out for African slaves."[8]

Sancho married a white Englishwoman, Anne, with whom he had six children. After retiring from a life of service in the homes of the wealthy, he and Anne ran a grocer's shop in London's fashionable Charles Street, Westminster. His friends were well-known novelists, actors, and artists, with whom he regularly corresponded. Writing to a friend in 1778, he refers to the poems of Phillis Wheatley, saying, "The perusal affected me more than I can express;—and indeed I felt a double or mixt sensation—for while my heart was torn for the sufferings—which, for aught I know, some of my nearest kin may have undergone—my bosom, at the same time, glowed with gratitude—and praise toward the . . . learned Author."[9] A book of his missives, *The Letters of Ignatius Sancho*, was published posthumously, in 1782. He also wrote poetry, two plays, and a book on musical theory, and he was a respected critic of the arts. From the most inauspicious of beginnings, Sancho reinvented himself as a middle-class man of letters, a successful London merchant, and well-known citizen of that town.

Because Sancho's letters and Equiano's autobiography survive, we may discover that, even at a time when newspapers advertised slaves and shackles, some dared to assert their right to lead full and complex lives, to educate themselves, to travel, to set up in business, to marry, and to raise families. None of this was achieved without trial, nor without an awareness of the prevailing condition of other black people. Equiano wrote, "Did I consider myself a European, I might say my sufferings were great: but when I compare my lot with that of most of my countrymen, I regard myself as a particular favourite of heaven, and acknowledge the mercies of Providence in every occurrence of my life."

Slavery formed the context of every black Londoner's life. Yet the political concerns of black Londoners did not stop there. Many were also involved in some of the significant stirrings of popular discontent that marked the second half of the Industrial Revolution. In 1820, for example, William Davidson, the son of a slave woman, was hanged for his part in a plot by a group of radical working-class men to assassinate the cabinet. Another political activist was the mild-mannered tailor William Cuffay. The son of a free black immigrant to Chatham, England, Cuffay became a leading member of another working-class movement, the Chartists'—a vigorous and popular campaign for the right of universal (male) suffrage. In 1848, he was the acknowledged leader of London Chartism. He developed plans for a major uprising in the capital that same year. Cuffay's involvement in the conspiracy led to his arrest and sentence: transportation and twenty-one years banishment to Tasmania (Australia). It is important to recognize the degree of black participation in labor and civil rights movements taking place in Britain proper during the nineteenth century.

Our third writer, however, is Robert Wedderburn, a contemporary of Davidson. Like him, he was the son of an enslaved Jamaican woman and a Scottish plantation owner. Like Cuffay, Wedderburn was a tailor, and, like Equiano, he spent many years at sea, serving in the British Navy and as a privateer. There, however, ends the likeness to his peers. Wedderburn's character stands in stark contrast to Sancho's gentility and to Equiano's self-controlled determination. Born in 1761 in Jamaica, by around 1780 Wedderburn had settled in London. Influenced by Thomas Paine's *Rights of Man*, he established himself as a Unitarian preacher. But this was no ordinary man of God. In their anthology *Black Writers in Britain, 1760–1890*, Edwards and Dabydeen describe Wedderburn thus: he "lived on the fringes of criminality and troubled the authorities with his fiery and popular preaching that it was the Christian duty of his flock to do all in their power to bring down the establishment."[10] In 1820, he was jailed for blasphemy and in 1831 served a sentence of two years hard labor, "not simply for running a brothel but for brawling in the street outside it."[11] As part of the working- class Society of Spencean Philanthropists, Wedderburn argued publicly for the right of slaves to kill their masters.

An insight into the motivations of this extraordinary man can be found in his three published works: *Truth Self-Supported* (1800), *The Axe Laid to the Root* (1817), and *The Horrors of Slavery* (1824). This last details his early years, including the fact that, at the age of eleven, he witnessed his seventy-year-old grandmother "flogged . . . to that degree, that she would have died but for the interference of a neighbor."[12] It is largely through personal accounts such as this that we discover some of the harsher realities of black women's lives during this period. General evidence suggests that they were employed in a variety of domestic occupations, working as seamstresses, laundry maids, and children's nurses. Edwards and Dabydeen provide glimpses of other sorts of lives, of "a black actress . . . playing Shakespeare's Juliet in the 1770s," and they add: "Many were forced into prostitution . . . such as Black Harriet, whose clients were said to include 20 members of the House of Lords."[13] In 1831, the transcript of an oral narrative, *The History of Mary Prince*, was published in London. This item represents the first British account of a black woman's life, although most of her years as a slave were spent abroad. *The History* details a life of brutality, sexual harassment, and overwork, making sad and shocking reading. Twenty-six years later, Mary Seacole published *The Wonderful Adventures of Mary Seacole in Many Lands*. Hers is a very different story, both in content and presentation. It gives us a picture of an indomitable woman who, unlike Mary Prince, retains a strong sense of herself as mistress of her own fate. The primary differences between the two women are slavery and education.

Seacole's mother, a free woman and noted doctoress, ran a boarding house in Kingston, Jamaica. It was popular with army and naval officers and their families, many of whom came seeking medical advice or to convalesce from illness. It was here that Seacole learned "the prognosis and treatment of tropical diseases, general ailments and wounds." In 1854, shortly after the outbreak of war in Sebastopol, she arrived in Belgravia, London, and offered her services to the officials in charge of recruiting nurses to the field hospitals of the Crimea.

In their introduction to the 1984 edition of Seacole's memoirs, Alexander and Dewjee state, "It is doubtful whether there were any white women who could equal her expertise and training, since at that time in Great Britain few females of any class had the opportunity of acquiring such extensive practical experience or of seeking higher education."[14]

Although she carried references from civilian and military doctors, Seacole was repeatedly rebuffed by the authorities. Undaunted, she made her own way to the Crimea. For two years she provided food and home comforts at her establishment, the British Hotel, as well as venturing onto the battlefield to give medical treatment to the wounded. In recognition of her heroic work, she was awarded no less than four medals of honor. Like Sancho and Equiano, she made a number of influential friends, including Alexandra Princess of Wales. She died in London in 1881, leaving a substantial estate, "equivalent to tens of thousands of pounds in today's money."[15]

Seacole's legacy would be a triumphant note on which to end. However, within thirty years of her death, and despite being fêted in public and the media during her lifetime, knowledge of her impact on history had all but disappeared. It has taken determined efforts on the part of Britain's latter-day black Londoners to rescue her reputation from obscurity, along with that of earlier black writers. It is interesting that Robert Wedderburn, who, in relation to the Establishment, was the most pugnacious and least palatable of the four, remains the least well known.

There are, of course, many more writers who have influenced and been influenced by London. However, it would be a mistake to locate the experience of black people solely in the capital. Wales, for example, has one of the oldest black populations in Britain. Edinburgh boasted a significant population of black students throughout the eighteenth and nineteenth centuries. By investigating and reimagining the historical experience of black Britons, today's black British writers have a peerless opportunity to participate in that "centuries-old tradition of cultural exchange"[16]—something that Caryl Phillips himself is doing. As Susan Okokon states in *Black Londoners*, "With greater curiosity and more research, we may come to realise that most of these personalities carry within their stories access to yet more hidden histories."[17] The scholarly recovery of writings by black people in Britain only points out what many black Britons have long known: that black people have made crucial contributions to the long and interesting evolution of London.

Notes

1. Caryl Phillips, *Extravagant Strangers* (New York: Vintage, 1999), xv–xvi.
2. Joan Anim-Addo, *Longest Journey: A History of Black Lewisham* (London: Deptford Forum Publishing, 1995).
3. Ibid., 45.
4. Susan Okokon, *Black Londoners, 1880–1990* (Stroud, Gloucestershire: Sutton Publishing, 1998), 31.
5. Paul Edwards and David Dabydeen, *Black Writers in Britain, 1760–1890* (Edinburgh: Edinburgh University Press, 1991), 51.
6. Hakim Adi, *West Africans in Britain, 1900–1960* (London: Lawrence & Wishart, 1998), 7.

7. Ibid., 8.
8. Anim-Addo, *Longest Journey*, 48.
9. Edwards and Dabydeen, *Black Writers in Britain*, 28.
10. Ibid., 139.
11. Ibid., 138.
12. See *Horrors of Slavery*, qtd. in Edwards and Dabydeen, *Black Writers in Britain*, 145.
13. From the "Introduction" to Seacole in Edwards and Dabydeen, *Black Writers in Britain*, 165.
14. Ziggi Alexander and Audrey Dewjee, eds., *The Wonderful Adventures of Mary Seacole in Many Lands* (Bristol: Falling Water Press, 1984), 17.
15. Ibid., 37.
16. Phillips, *Entravagant Strangers*, xvi.
17. Okokon, *Black Londoners*, 12.

Works Cited

Adi, Hakim. *West Africans in Britain, 1900–1960*. London: Lawrence & Wishart, 1998.

Alexander, Ziggi and Audrey Dewjee, eds. *The Wonderful Adventures of Mary Seacole in Many Lands*. Bristol: Falling Water Press, 1984.

Anim-Addo, Joan. *Longest Journey: A History of Black Lewisham*. London: Deptford Forum Publishing, 1995.

Cugoano, Ottobah. *Thoughts and sentiments on the evil and wicked traffic of the slavery and commerce of the human species, humbly submitted to the Inhabitants of Great-Britain* (1787). Paul Edwards, ed. London: Dawson Colonial History Series, 1968. Extract rpt. in Edwards and Dabydeen.

Edwards, Paul and David Dabydeen, *Black Writers in Britain, 1760–1890*. Edinburgh: Edinburgh University Press, 1991.

Equiano, Olaudah. *The Interesting Narrative of the Life of Olaudah Equiano or Gustavus Vassa* (1789). Paul Edwards, ed. Heinemann African Writers Series, 1969.

Okokon, Susan. *Black Londoners, 1880–1990*. Stroud, Gloucestershire: Sutton Publishers, 1998.

Phillips, Caryl. *Extravagant Strangers*. New York: Vintage, 1999.

Prince, Mary. *The History of Mary Prince*. London: 1831. Extract rpt. in Edwards and Dabydeen.

Sancho, Ignatius. *The letters of Ignatius Sancho*. London: 1782. Paul Edwards, ed. London: Dawson's Colonial History Series, 1968.

Seacole, Mary. *The Horrors of Slavery*. London: 1824. Extract rpt. in Edwards and Dabydeen.

———. *The Axe Laid to the Root*. London: 1817.

———. *The Wonderful Adventures of Mary Seacole in Many Lands*. London: 1857. Wedderburn, Robert. *Truth Self-Supported*. London: 1800.

CHAPTER 5

IDENTITY AND BELONGING IN CONTEMPORARY BLACK BRITISH WRITING

Chris Weedon

Our culture shapes and determines our identity. To convey our sense of self, as Black women, we must first generate a positive understanding of the long cultural tradition, which has fashioned our way of life here in Britain. . . . The unique feature of our culture is that its roots and base is Africa. To acknowledge its origins is also to identify the unchanging seam, which is common to all Black cultures in the diaspora. Our African origin is the cornerstone of our lifestyle and our perception of the world, the internal dynamic, which has enabled us continuously to resist new assaults on our way of life.[1]

[B]eing "black" in Britain is about a state of "becoming" (racialized); a process of consciousness, when colour becomes the defining factor about who you are. Located through your "otherness" a "conscious coalition" emerges: a self-consciously constructed space where identity is not inscribed by a natural identification but a political kinship. Now living submerged in whiteness, physical difference becomes a defining issue, a signifier, a mark of whether or not you belong. Thus to be black in Britain is to share a common structural location; a racial location.[2]

Contemporary African-American resistance struggle must be rooted in a process of decolonization that continually opposes re-inscribing notions of "authentic" black identity. This critique should not be made synonymous with a dismissal of the struggle of oppressed and exploited peoples to make ourselves subjects. Nor should it deny that in certain circumstances this experience affords us a privileged critical location from which to speak, this is not a reinscription of modernist master narratives of authority which privilege some voices by denying voice to others. Part of our struggle for radical black subjectivity is the quest to find ways to construct self and identity that are oppositional and liberatory.[3]

Recent decades have seen the publication of a rich and exciting body of writing by black British writers. In this writing the long history of slavery and colonialism and the more immediate history of postwar migration and life in contemporary Britain are main points of reference. This chapter takes up the themes of identity and belonging in examples of this writing, focusing on the novel, and examining four different approaches to these questions in separate sections. The first involves texts that testify to the black experience of migration from ex-colonies to a racist "Mother County." The second highlights the importance of history to identity and the role of imaginative rewritings of marginalized or forgotten histories. The third looks at how black people negotiate life in contemporary Britain, and the fourth examines a related theme: how racism affects identity and belonging. The chapter does not attempt to offer an overview of black British writing nor of my chosen themes. Rather, it selects examples that highlight some of the issues at stake in texts that address the issues of identity and belonging.

Theorizing Identity

Identity is an important issue in contemporary Britain where there are ongoing struggles to redefine both "Britishness" and the nature of a desirable, culturally diverse society.[4] The factors that have influenced these debates include migration, devolution, globalization, the end of Empire, Britain's long-term decline as a world power, the development of a widespread moral and cultural pluralism, and an increasing degree of integration with Europe. For black people in Britain, another crucial factor is racism, which has both shaped their relationship to Britishness and produced various forms of resistance.

Writing, together with other forms of black cultural production such as film and performance, is an important site for the articulation of old and new forms of black identity and for exploring the place of black people in Britain.[5] In his essay on new Caribbean cinema, "Cultural Identity and Diaspora,"[6] Stuart Hall argues that recent diasporic black cultural production is "putting the issue of cultural identity in question." "Who," Hall asks, "is this emergent, new subject of the cinema? From where does he/she speak?"[7] Similar questions could be asked of recent black British writing. Hall suggests that creative practices—cinema, or in this case writing—are important, not as reflections of an already existing black identity, but in the *production* of identities. He argues:

> There are at least two different ways of thinking about "cultural identity."
> The first position defines "cultural identity" in terms of one, shared culture,

a sort of collective one true self, hiding inside the many other, more superficial or artificially imposed "selves," which people with a shared history and ancestry hold in common. Within the terms of this definition, our cultural identities reflect the common historical experiences and shared cultural codes, which provide us, as "one people," with stable, unchanging and continuous frames of reference and meaning, beneath the shifting divisions and vicissitudes of our cultural history.[8]

From this perspective, the discovery of a true black identity involves decolonizing the self and recovering an identity no longer distorted by the colonial experience and by racism. It is a project that lies at the heart of Afrocentric discourses that look to discover a true identity rooted in African heritage, an example of which can be found in the first epigraph from *The Heart of the Race*[9] Hall offers an alternative approach to the question of black identity:

There is, however, a second related but different view of cultural identity. This second position recognizes that, as well as the many points of similarity, there are also critical points of deep and significant difference, which constitute "what we really are," or rather—since history has intervened—"what we have become." . . . Cultural identity, in this second sense, is a matter of "becoming" as well as of "being." It belongs to the future as much as to the past. It is not something which already exists, transcending place, time, history and culture. Cultural identities come from somewhere, have histories. But like everything, which is historical, they undergo constant transformation. Far from being eternally fixed in some essentialized past, they are subject to the continuous "play" of history, culture and power. Far from being grounded in a mere "recovery" of the past, which is waiting to be found, and which, when found, will secure our sense of ourselves into eternity, identities are the names we give to the different ways we are positioned by, and position ourselves within the narratives of the past.[10]

It is this second understanding of identity as a process, constituted at least in part in and through cultural production, that primarily concerns me in this chapter. The first understanding of identity as a shared collective true self that one must uncover, usually by looking to African or diasporic black societies, is, however, also important, featuring in several of the texts that I am discussing.

Testimonies of a Generation

While Britain has had a small black and mixed-heritage population for centuries, the second half of the twentieth century saw major black migration to the United Kingdom. In June 1948 the *Empire Windrush* arrived at Tilbury Docks on the Essex coast with 500 passengers from the Caribbean who had come to take up jobs in Britain. This ship was the first of many ships to transport African-Caribbean migrants to Britain over the next two decades, and all together they would bring more than 500,000 settlers.[11] Although many West Indian migrants initially saw themselves as coming to work, not to settle, most of them would stay permanently. The history of this major migration, which helped to change the face of Britain, remains largely unknown to Britain's white population. The process of documenting the migrants' stories, and making this hidden history widely available, has only just begun. A major step in this direction was the four-part series made by Mike Phillips for BBC Two on the history of black people in Britain since World War II.[12] Using oral history and archive footage, the programs covered the decades between 1940 and 1998. These were years, fraught with racial unrest, that saw the reemergence of the extreme Right in Britain, protests against immigration, violence toward black and South Asian people, riots, organized black resistance, and the beginnings of acceptance as black Britons achieved wider positive visibility in music, sports, and the media.

The experience of African-Caribbean migration to Britain is part of the little known history of post–World War II Britain. It not only shaped first-generation migrants but also the lives and identities of their children. It was one important basis for the subsequent development of a multiethnic and culturally diverse Britain. It is a history that features strongly in the work of black writers and filmmakers. The experience is depicted, for instance, in the works of two writers, Caryl Phillips and Joan Riley, both of whom immigrated as young children accompanying their parents and attended schools and universities in the United Kingdom. Their novels offer testimonies to aspects of postwar Britain that most white people would rather forget. I turn first to Caryl Phillip's debut novel, *The Final Passage* (1985).

Dedicated to his parents, who belonged to the *Windrush* generation of migrants, *The Final Passage* describes life on an unnamed Caribbean Island and migration to Britain around 1960. The narrative is focused on Leila, the nineteen-year-old, mixed-race daughter of a black mother and a white father whom she has never known. Unhappily married to a man who has been living with another woman and who feels overly constrained by his marriage to a mixed-race woman with a higher social status, Leila persuades her husband (Michael) to move with her to Britain. Her mother, who is barely forty years old, has already departed for England to obtain medical treatment—just one week before the birth of Leila's first child. Leila hopes that she and Michael can make a new start in London, but finds that her mother's letters home have revealed nothing of her London experience of racism and social exclusion. Leila's mother dies soon after Leila arrives and is buried in a pauper's grave. Leila and Michael find themselves living in degrading conditions in London and are unable to make a success of their marriage. Michael leaves Leila, once more pregnant, for a white woman. Ill and emotionally disturbed, Leila resolves to return to the Caribbean.

One of the most striking features of the text is the contrast that it offers between life in the Caribbean and in London. This recurrent theme in black writing is evoked by images of color versus greyness and warmth of human relations versus cold indifference. For example, the text contrasts the port from which the couple leave with their port of arrival in Britain:

> At 6.30 the harbour had been a blaze of colour and confusion. Bright yellows and brilliant reds, sweet smells and juices, a lazy deep sea nudging up against the land, and looking down upon it all the mountains ached under the weight of their dense green vegetation.[13]

Two weeks later:

> On the fifteenth day the wind died and Leila saw land; the high and irregular cliffs of England through the cold grey mist of the English Channel. She clasped together the collar of her light cotton dress and shivered. Overhead a thin fleet of clouds cast a bleak shadow across the deck, and the sluggish water swelled gently, then slackened.[14]
> . . .
> Leila looked at England, but everything seemed bleak. She quickly realized she would have to learn a new word; overcast. There were no green mountains, there were no colourful women with baskets on their heads selling peanuts or bananas or mangoes, there were no trees, no white houses on the hills, no hills, no wooden houses by the shoreline, and the sea was not blue and there was no beach, and there were no clouds, just one big cloud, and they had arrived.[15]

Leila is depicted as having an ambiguous relation to her home country. As she boards the SS *Winston Churchill*, she reflects: "This small proud island, overburdened with vegetation and complacency, this had been her home. She looked, feeling sorry for those satisfied enough to stay. Then she stiffened, ashamed of what she had just thought. Then she relaxed."[16]

For her husband, Michael, as for his grandfather before him, migration is an economic question: "Me, I want a car and a big house and a bit of power under my belt, like any man does want. This country breed too many people who just cut cane in season and happy to be rum-jumbie out of it."[17] As a young teenager Michael had been warned by his grandfather, who had traveled and worked in Central America, about the effects of racism on black subjectivity and identity: "You must hate enough, and you must be angry enough to get just what you want but no more! No more! For, if you do, you just going to end up hating yourself."[18] When Leila suggests to Michael that they go to England, he sees it as an opportunity to earn a better living. Walking through Baytown, the island's capital, he tries not to look at "the defeated faces that lined these streets, men in grease-stained felt hats and women in deceptively gay bandannas, their eyes glazed, arms folded, standing, leaning, resting up against the zinc fencing of their front yards, their children playing, racing scraps of wood in liquid sewage."[19] He visits Alphonse Walthers, who has just returned from Britain and is now living in poverty. Walthers tells him how, when working in England, he had knocked over some acid which burnt his skin: "They give me £100 and tell me to go home, but I stay another five years just doing nothing, boy, begging in truth. But now I back home and you can see how I living."[20] He warns Michael about the dangers of living in England: "England don't be no joke for a coloured man."[21] Yet letters home from emigrants tell a different story: "They say every coloured man in England have a good job that can pay at least $100 a week."[22] The letters do not mention the racism and hostility of the white British or the poor living conditions. Thus, on arrival in England, Leila experiences shock at what she finds and wonders "what else her mother had left unsaid."[23] She soon discovers this, to her cost.

The novel offers a historically accurate picture of the experience of new migrants. Looking for accommodation in London, Leila is met by signs in the windows that say: "No Coloureds," "No Vacancies," and "No Children." Those householders without signs make lame excuses that make her feel grateful for the honesty of the "No Coloureds" signs. Eventually Leila rents a house from an agency in Marble Arch, but it turns out to be a dirty, damp slum, and Michael blames her for this. Seeing London through Leila's eyes, the reader learns the realities of racialized, class distinctions. Whereas in the Caribbean black people constitute all social strata, in London they are restricted to particular areas of the city and particular jobs. Leila notes that they do not drive big cars or wear suits or carry briefcases. They look sad and cold.

She notices graffiti: "If you want a nigger neighbour vote Labour."[24] Edwin, Leila's mother's landlord, who attempts to help the couple, warns Michael about the various types of racism that he will encounter and its effects on black subjectivity:

> Well, all you need to remember is that they treat us worse than their dogs. The women expect you to do tricks with your biceps and sing calypso, or to drop down on one knee and pretend you're Paul Robeson or somebody . . . . Well, you better know. He's a cunt and he [Michael's new employer Jeffries] is going to call you names, man, and you going to behave like a kettle, for without knowing it you going to boil. It's how the white man in this country kills off the coloured man. He makes you heat up and blow yourself away.[25]

When Leila arrives in Britain, she already has a deep-seated fear of white people, instilled by her mother while Leila was a child. The novel recounts how one time during her childhood, when she was lying beside some white people on the beach, her mother hit her:

> Don't never let me catch you lying with white people again or as God is my witness I'll take a stick to you and beat you till the life leaves your body. . . . You think you can trust them. You can't. And if you think the white woman was sleeping you were wrong. White women never sleep with both their eyes closed if a coloured woman is around, and they never see a coloured man without something moving inside of them. Still, you going to live to find that out.[26]

Despite this, Leila allows herself to be befriended by Mary, a fifty-year-old white neighbor; but even this relationship is poisoned for Leila when Michael takes up with a white woman, confirming in Leila's mind both her mother's warnings and her best friend Millie's words to her before Leila left the Caribbean: "I hear the white women do anything to get their hands on a piece of coloured man."[27] Millie already knows something that Leila will only learn through painful experience: "home is where you feel a welcome."[28] Leila's rejection of Mary is, however, not depicted as an easy process:

> Mary posed to Leila the hardest part of her new life to consider, for now more than ever before she was white, and Michael's woman was white (the hair blond). Even without knowing it Mary might hurt her in some way, for she had come too close to Leila, and Leila cursed herself for being foolish enough to allow this to happen. Mary's voice alone, not even her presence, would always worry her, and what now followed

would be in Leila's mind as strained and as artificial as their first meetings were honest and spontaneous. Leila thought again of the uniformed woman at the train station, then Mary again, all in quick succession, trying to root her among cruel and stupid people, but Mary would not stay still. The moments of help and the laughter they had shared came flooding back.[29]

Leila's sense of self in the novel is shown to be undermined by racism, together with unresolved problems that she has brought with her from the Caribbean. For her, return to her home as a single parent with two children comes to be the only option she can contemplate.

Life for women who stayed on in Britain is the theme of Joan Riley's novel *Waiting in the Twilight* (1987). It takes up and develops the themes of identity and self-respect for first-generation migrants to the United Kingdom. The narrative tells the story of a Jamaican woman, Adella Johnson, a successful seamstress in Kingston, who follows her husband to London, where racism and ill-health reduce her to being a crippled office cleaner living on low wages in a council flat (government subsidized housing). Even working for the council, with its positive action policies, she finds herself subject to daily racist encounters:

"Johnson!"
The insolence ran through her and she gripped the mop tighter with her feeling hand, forcing back anger that still bubbled up after so many years. "Thou shalt rise up before the hoary head," she muttered under her breath, "No wonda yu treat yu old people dem so bad."
"Yes, mam . . ." she said aloud, turning to see a young white girl, not more than seventeen years old. Her feet had left a fresh trail of mud, and Adella's mouth thinned. This one had been working less than six months and already she had learnt how to treat the cleaning staff. Adella wanted to ask if this was how she was at home; bit back the words. Of course, this was how they all behaved: everybody knew what white people were like.[30]

The narrative offers the reader Adella's perspective on her life in Britain and flashbacks to Jamaica, which help to explain how she has become what she is. The depiction of Adella's Jamaican experience marks the cultural differences between the two societies and sets the scene for her subsequent life in Britain, where class, gender, poverty, disablement, and lack of family support magnify the effects of racism. Gender relations in Jamaica, where she was seduced by a married man and forced to live as his mistress in return for support for herself and their children, are depicted as patriarchal. Women are shown to have little power outside the structures of the family, but the extended family offers an important material and emotional support network that is absent in Britain. On moving to Britain, the novel suggests, African-Caribbean women become exposed to much harsher forms of patriarchal oppression within the isolation of the nuclear family, and black men are more likely to be emotionally and physically violent and less responsible because of their own experience of racism in the wider society. Moreover, cultural difference, the difference between the family, religion, and codes of respectability in Jamaica and Britain make it impossible for Adella to explain, even to her children, why she cannot return to live in Jamaica.

Looking to History

If testimonies to recent black experience form an important theme within contemporary black British writing, fictional evocations of earlier black history are also crucial to reclaiming a sense of history and tradition that allows for positive identities in the present. They are also important for historicizing the interrelation of black and British histories and challenging narratives of British history that see it as exclusively white. This matters profoundly, since having a history and set of traditions with which one can identify and within which one can position oneself, other than as victim, gives the individual a position of dignity from which to speak.

Perhaps the most prolific body of historical fiction has so far been produced by Caryl Phillips. Here, I examine just one example: his novel *Cambridge* (1991)—which combines a sophisticated, multi-perspectival retelling of black history with an interesting exploration of the formation of black subjectivity and identity. It depicts examples of black–white relationships from 200 years ago, pointing to the long history of these relations. *Cambridge* tells the story of the visit by Emily Cartwright, an absentee planter's daughter, to her father's estate in the Caribbean. It describes her voyage from England to the island (the same unnamed island that features in *The Final Passage*) and her stay on the plantation. The novel offers details of the workings of the plantation from a white perspective, drawing on period sources and incorporating nineteenth-century white racist ideas about African and Creole slaves. Set in the years between the abolition of the slave trade and the abolition of slavery in the West Indies, the novel raises questions about the nature and legitimacy of slavery from the perspective of the period in which it is set, and it juxtaposes the planter's daughter's narrative with that of an educated African slave, Cambridge, who had been freed by his master in Britain and re-enslaved by the trickery of the captain of the ship taking him back to Africa as a missionary.

The novel offers a sophisticated account of the way the plantation system functions and shapes the subjectivities and identities of both its black and white subjects. On Emily Cartwright's arrival, she finds that the manager who had been treating the slaves humanely by standards of the period (Mr. Wilson), has been forcibly replaced by Mr. Brown, a cruel man. Brown is hostile to Emily until an incident transpires between Emily and the black slave woman with whom Brown is sleeping. Emily's threat to have him replaced radically changes his behavior and he becomes overly friendly, showing her the island, seducing and ultimately impregnating her. After Brown is killed by Cambridge, Emily and her black maid Stella retreat to a cottage in the hills where Emily has a stillborn baby. The novel ends with Emily reflecting on her return to Britain but not welcoming her future prospects.

The text's multi-perspectival form involves the juxtaposition of competing versions of events. It comprises a prologue set in England, Emily's narrative, Cambridge's narrative, the local press version of the killing, and an epilogue in which Emily gives birth. Initially, in traveling to the Caribbean, Emily has abolitionist aims: "Perhaps my adventuring will encourage Father to accept the increasingly common, though abstract, English belief in the iniquity of slavery."[31] Yet her views of black people are shown to be formed by the racist discourses of the day, which blur her vision, and, as she lives on the plantation and associates with the harsh manager, the views expressed in her journal change: "For the negroes this is indeed a happy hedonistic life, with ample food, much singing and dancing, regular visits to the physicians, hospitals a-plenty, good housing, healthy labour, and an abundance of friendship."[32] On arrival she is assigned the personal services of Stella, one of the house slaves, of whom she writes that she "carried herself with comical self-assurance, quite as if she were white."[33] The idea that black people can have dignity and self-assurance is foreign to her, and she is surprised, when she goes into Baytown, to see free blacks and house slaves, wearing shoes. She writes, "the dress, manner and gait of these relatively civilized town slaves marks them off as a wholly different breed from their brutish country cousins."[34] Although contradictory, her experience of black people does not enable her to transcend the racist ideology of the day. While she comes increasingly to value Stella, she finds ways of interpreting her behavior that serve as proof of those inferior racialized characteristics commonly ascribed to black people:

> Stella's loyalty is, I am led to understand, typical of her people. It would appear that Mr. Wilberforce and his like have been volleying well wide of

the mark, for the greatest fear of the black is not having a master whom they know they can turn to in times of strife.[35]

Emily's perceptions are shown to be shaped by contemporary racist attitudes that extend across classes and professions. Thus, reiterating racial science of the period, she comments, "A milkier hue signified some form of white blood, and it should be clear to even the most egalitarian observer that the more white blood flowing in a person's veins, the less barbarous will be his social tendencies."[36] These beliefs are bolstered by the racist attitudes of the island's white professionals, for example, Dr. MacDonald, the local doctor, who assures her that

> Constant association with an inferior race will weaken the moral fibre of a white man and debase the quality of his life. A mere glance should be sufficient to convince an observer that the West Indian negro has all the characteristics of his race. That he steals, lies, is witless, incompetent, irresponsible, habitually lazy, and wantonly loose in his sexual behaviour, is apparent to even the most generous of those who would take *Sambo's* part.[37]

Such is the power of racist discourse that even Emily's personal encounters with Cambridge do not lead her to ask why he is as he is. She recounts how Cambridge is ordered to keep guard outside her door to protect her from Christiania, Cambridge's wife and the black woman with whom Brown is sleeping:

> My dark sentry looked at me, and I noted that I appeared to have disturbed him in the most unlikely act of studying the Bible. I asked if this was his common form of recreation, to which he replied in highly fanciful English, that indeed it was. You might imagine my surprise when he then broached the conversational lead and enquired after my family origins, and my opinions pertaining to slavery. I properly declined to share these with him, instead counter-quizzing with enquiries as to the origins of his knowledge.[38]

When he smiles broadly in reply, she shuts the door on him. For Emily, a black slave who addresses her as an equal is unthinkable.

Based on period sources, the novel also offers insight into Cambridge's sense of self-worth and identity through *his* narrative, which he composes in prison as he awaits execution. It tells his life story from his capture as a fifteen-year-old in Africa up to the killing of Brown. It informs the reader about the slave trade and attitudes toward slavery and blacks in Britain. It details the capture of slaves and the middle passage. In the course of his life—on the slave ship, as a house servant in London, and as a missionary—he is renamed three times. As a servant he receives an education in reading, writing, arithmetic, and religion, and he marries a white woman, Anna. After the captain's death he is sent on a fund-raising missionary trip around England, during which he preaches the evils of slavery. Anna and their child die in childbirth, and he sets out as a missionary to Africa with his legacy from the captain. He is robbed and re-enslaved on his journey to Africa and transported to a plantation in the Caribbean.

On the plantation, he is renamed a fourth time. Remaining a devout Christian, he refuses to see himself as slave and lives in the hope that justice will be done and that he will once again be freed from slavery. When Brown takes over the plantation, Cambridge refuses to become a driver and thus makes a vicious enemy. To punish him, Brown starts sleeping with Cambridge's (second) wife and flogs him for no reason. Despite this, Cambridge, who continues to inhabit the subject position of free Englishman, equal and often superior to the plantation whites, believes he can reason with Brown, but Brown dies in the struggle that ensues from their meeting, and Cambridge is charged with his murder.

The novel suggests that neither blacks nor whites inevitably have to conform to the dominant racist discourses of the day. Resistances and different identities and modes of behavior are possible, but they, too, emerge from historically specific social relations. The ship's captain, who pays for Cambridge's education, frees him from slavery and bequests him 400 guineas; Cambridge's white wife and his white teacher all point to other modes of relation between whites and blacks. In setting Cambridge's complex identity—shaped by a Christian, English liberalism—against the narrowness of both white British racism in England and black and white identities on the plantation, the novel challenges the hegemonic racial discourses in play both historically and at the time of its publication. It endows Cambridge with dignity and a positive identity that, even while subscribing to the Christian colonial discourse of the need to convert Africans, offers him a way of resisting his definition and victimization as a slave.

Negotiating Contemporary Britain

As early as 1975, Sam Selvon, one of the *Windrush* generation of Caribbean writers,[39] published *Moses Ascending*. That book—his third London novel and a sequel to Selvon's classic, *The Lonely Londoners* (1956)—is set in the early 1970s, the era of Black Power.[40] Like Selvon's earlier novels, *Moses Ascending* is written in what Mervyn Morris describes as "a literary version of Trinidad speech," which uses "creole not in dialogue only but also as the language of narration."[41] It features Moses, the central character from *The Lonely Londoners*, and tells of how he buys a decrepit house with a five-year lease, due for demolition by the council (local governmental authority) on expiration, and becomes a landlord. In a reversal of the usual roles, Moses employs a white "man Friday," Bob, to look after the tenants and retires to the penthouse flat to write his memoirs.

A key theme of the text is the difference in sense of identity between the *Windrush* generation of migrants—with their respect for authority and disappointed belief in Britain as the "Mother Country"—and the younger London black people. The Moses of this text is depicted as an apolitical man who is in search of a quiet life. Yet, inadvertently, in his role as a landlord and in his quest for material for his book, he finds himself involved both with members of the Black Power movement, who organize from his basement, and with Pakistanis, who trade in illegal South Asian immigrants, using his house as a staging post. On two occasions in the narrative, he comes to experience police brutality at first hand, and the combined effect of both experiences forces him to reflect on police behavior and to abandon his "philosophy of neutrality" that marks him off from younger and more radical black people.[42]

Selvon's novel is important for the insights it provides into black British lives and identities in the 1970s, the years when ideas from the Black Power movement began to make an impact in Britain. Foremost in shaping both experience and identities is the black community's relationship with the police. Moses's first violent encounter with the police is at a Black Power demonstration in Trafalgar Square that he comes upon by chance. When a fight breaks out, the police descend on the crowd, and Selvon gives a vivid evocation of the experience of arrest:

> A set of Blacks was being towed, propelled, and dragged across Trafalgar Square. The place like it was full up of police as if the whole metropolitan force was lurking in the side streets waiting for signal. Blue lights flashing, radio-telephones going, sirens blowing, Alsatians baring their teeth for the kill, and Black Maria [a police van] waiting with the doors fling wide open in welcome.[43]

Commenting on the experience, Moses betrays important aspects of the effects of racism on black subjectivity, combining references to black history with images from Hollywood cinema.

I do not know about you, but it is a shuddering thought for a Black man to be locked up by the police. Once you are in, it is foregone conclusion that they will throw away the key. There was no protests from any of the passengers saying that they was innocent and shouldn't be here, nobody struggling to get out like me, nobody saying anything at all. Like we was all in the hold of a slave ship. I remember them stories I used to read, how the innocent star boy get condemned to the galleys. Next thing you see him in chains, with beard on his face, wrestling with one of them big oars like what stevedores have in Barbados when they loading the ships. Any minute now the timekeeper was going to crack a whip in the Black Maria. I wonder if I play dead if they would jettison me in the Thames. And I could make my escape.[44]

On the second occasion, Moses is present when the police break up a peaceful Black Power meeting and people leave the hall in panic. He tries to understand what is going on and is forced to realize that the police are far from neutral:

I try to rationalize the situation. Okay. So it must have had some wanted criminals in the hall, in spite of the respectable aspects of the meeting. Right? So the police make a raid and bust up the gathering. Right? That was it, simple and plain. Right? I catch a bus 52 in Ladbroke Grove and went to Notting Hill Gate and catch a 88 and went home, but I still couldn't convince myself that it was a simple as all that. I was beginning to get vex now; my dignity was affronted as I imagined myself pelting down the road terror-stricken when I didn't do nothing at all, not even spit on the pavement or smoke in a non-smoking compartment. Was all of we in the hall criminals that we had to jump up and flee for our very lives? There we was, sitting down, and I was just writing down the words of the Party anthem, when we was so rudely interrupted. My blood begin to boil. I had half a mind to get back there and ask the Inspector himself what was the meaning of this outrage? "How dare you intrude on this peaceful gathering," I would say, "and strike terror into the hearts of these innocent people." And I would ask him for his name, number and rank, and report him to the Chief of Scotland Yard.[45]

These experiences begin to transform Moses's subjectivity, as he is forced to see society in the way younger black people do—that is, as fundamentally racist. This puts into question his preferred identity as a respectable, nonpolitical, retired landlord. Reflecting on his life in Britain, he has to conclude that his experience of the "Mother Country" has been far from positive:

I don't know if I can describe it properly, not being a man of words, but I had a kind of sad feeling that all Black people was doomed to suffer, and that we would never make any headway in Brit'n. As if it always have a snag, no matter how hard we struggle or try to stay out of trouble. After spending the best yeas of my life in the Mother Country it was dismal conclusion to come to, making you feel that one and one make zero. It wasn't so much depression as sheer terror really, to see you life falling to pieces like that.[46]

Many of the themes and issues that are central to *Moses Ascending* resurface almost twenty years later in the debut novel *Some Kind of Black* (1996) by Diran Adebayo, the British-born son of Nigerian migrants. Set in 1993, the story tells of a few months in the life of Dele, a young British Nigerian man who has been brought up in London in a traditional Nigerian family and is currently in his final year of study at Oxford. The narrative evokes his life, in London and Oxford, before and after a police beating that injures him and nearly kills his sister, who has sickle cell anemia. The incident leads him to become involved in a campaign for justice for his sister. The text offers a panoramic picture of student life in Oxford, politics among blacks in London, police brutality, and the lives of disaffected young urban blacks. The issues raised include forms of white racism (from the primitivism of the upper-class Oxford students to the brutality of the London police), social deprivation, class, religion, generational differences, relationships between black men and white women, different forms of black politics (including Black Nationalism), and drug culture.

The narrative moves between Oxford University, an elite, supposedly liberal institution, and black life in London. Oxford is shown to have its own forms of racism, which have profoundly alienating effects on black subjectivity and identity. Among the white elites, black students are feted in primitivist terms as exotic or primitive others:

Dele wasn't necessarily talented or beautiful either, but up here there just wasn't a big enough supply of brothers to go round. Well, there were the bloods who laboured at the British Leyland plant and lived on the big estates down Cowley way, on the east side, but they didn't count in the student scale of things. Up here, Dele was what you'd call a Mr. Mention. A player. X amount of invites to events and launches littered his college pigeon-hole. After three years of sharing his sense and flexing across the city, Dele was now the undisputed number one Negro.[47]

The effects of the Oxford experience on the identities of black students—the sons of African elites and a small number of British-born blacks—are shown to be varied. Dele describes Colin:

> Of Bajan natural parentage but adopted by a liberal English couple. Hitherto lumbered with a nondescript mid-Afro, Colin had gone AWOL and returned only today sporting long, braided extensions. He was shaking his funky locks around and twirling a canapé by the food table. But still, with his Home Counties burr, his cords and his brogues, Colin was coming like an English gentleman of the old school.[48]

Commenting on the students who attend a short-lived black student discussion group held during his second year at Oxford, Dele reflects:

> It was funny, though. There was a certain wanky air of self-satisfaction bubbling under the surface at these Black Chats. Folk felt that whatever the problems had been out there, *they* had overcome them, they must be the *crème de la crème*. As the evening wore on and tongues got loose, some would invoke hoary myths of the integrity of strong African cultures and contrast that with the Caribs' lack of coherent identity to explain their minuscule representation there. But when he checked it, Dele could barely find a person in the room, himself included, who was truly sorted. Most of them were unreconciled either to their families or to their role here, if any. Their heads were mash-up, frankly.[49]

Dele eventually abandons mixing with other black students for a "less right-on crowd," where he functions as "court entertainer."[50] Yet some Oxford student rituals may go too far, even for him, for example, a rag week slave auction at an elite Oxford party. (Rag week is the week once a year when university students organize events to raise money for charities.)

Home life for Dele is depicted as in stark contrast with his student life. The son of a strict Nigerian Seventh Day Adventist family, his father is a repressive figure who believes in authority and is "a One Nation Heathite Tory Man and proud of it."[51] Like other London Africans, Dele's father is hostile to African-Caribbean black people, whom he sees as bad influences on his children. He recalls how "When he first arrived in England, he was staggered to find all these Jamaicans called Winston, named after Britain's wartime premier, when over in Nigeria Winston Churchill had been castigated as a reactionary, who could not bear to dismantle the Empire."[52] He is profoundly disappointed in his children and denies Dele the closeness that he craves. He tries to counteract what he sees as the evil influences of life in Britain by wielding iron discipline over his family. Thus, for example, on one occasion he finds Dele in London, when he should be studying in Oxford, and he takes extreme and violent measures, beating his son severely. Like many first-generation migrants, he wants his son to be a Nigerian not a hybrid British black. On the occasion of the beating, after Dele's mother has tended to his injuries, he tells his son: "But for your mother, I would throw you and your complexes out of the house, until you understand that you are an African, not some Follow-Follow boy! It were better that you spent some time in Africa and then you would know."[53] Dele's mother is depicted as supportive of her children, but oppressed by her traditional husband and rejected as a role model by her daughter, Dapo. It is Dapo's hospitalization and coma, the result of police brutality, that motivates a large part of the subsequent narrative, bringing Dele into contact with various black groups and organizations and eventually reuniting him with his father.

The picture of black London life in the novel focuses on black organizations and drug culture. The text emphasizes the differences between London Nigerians and African-Caribbeans. At an African-Caribbean party there is none of the networking and constant pressure to succeed, which British-born people of Nigerian descent are shown to find so stressful:

If it was a Nigerian do now, he might have to pop outside for a smoke; the sounds would be down and the chat would be thick and fast: who was doing business in Germany or in America on a Master's course, and whose family had been spotted in the papers bringing shame on the homeland. He would be introduced to eligible Nigerian-Nigerian girls, now at Buckingham University or Holborn Law Tutors in a meaningful way. And Dele would turn to Dapo or any other renegade UK Africans in the house and bemoan the fact that there weren't enough of them around to have a party all their own.[54]

The novel gives a largely critical picture of both Far Left politics and black activism, including a visit by a Black Nationalist from the United States. While some activists are depicted as having good intentions, others display corrupt practices, sectarianism, and self-interest. Some are also involved in drugs. The picture of young black people's relationship with the police is bleak. The police are depicted as racist, violent, and vindictive. As with Selvon's work, the language of the text, which draws on black modes and style of speech, is important as a marker of difference and specificity, serving to ground the narrative in the realism of everyday life.

Identity and Belonging

The impossibility of achieving a sense of belonging in a racist, white society is the central theme of much black British writing. Here, three examples illustrate the point: Joan Riley's first novel, *The Unbelonging* (1985), and two texts by two women of mixed heritage, Lucinda Roy's *Lady Moses* (1998) and Charlotte Williams's autobiographical text *Sugar and Slate* (2002). *The Unbelonging* evokes the effects of leaving Jamaica as a child and growing up black in Britain in an uncaring family and in children's homes. It depicts social relations through the eyes of its central character and has the rhetorical power of texts that appear to offer us direct access to authentic subjective experience. The novel presents an extremely bleak picture of paternal sexual abuse and white racism. Eleven-year-old Hyacinth leaves Jamaica to join a father she does not know. The narrative traces her life in Britain until her return to Jamaica as a grown woman. It is written exclusively from Hyacinth's perspective and shows how her experiences in Britain deny her the possibility of achieving a positive sense of identity—other than one rooted in an imaginary Jamaica, derived from childhood memories.

Beaten and threatened with sexual abuse by her father, Hyacinth's experience of home life in Britain instills in her a deep fear of black men and a sense of guilt and shame. In the white environments of school and the children's home, she comes to hate her blackness and to see herself as fundamentally different from other African-Caribbean people. Her university experience reintroduces her to black people, but threatens her sense of herself. This danger is anchored in the repression of her experience with her father and in her childishly innocent and romantic image of Jamaica, which turns out to have nothing in common with the reality of the country to which Hyacinth returns at the end of the novel. Her contacts with other black students and with Black Nationalist thought offer her a framework from within which to make sense of her oppression. However, her experience of sexual abuse, which she is desperate to hide, and her fear of black male sexuality make it impossible for her to identify with Black Nationalism.

The Unbelonging is written with powerful and unrelenting realism, as the following passage illustrates:

"Hyacinth!"
The sharpness in the voice brought her back to present reality and the fear she had been trying to suppress mingled with remembered horror. "Yes sir?" she asked faintly. "I think Joyce did give you too much freedom," he said angrily. "I not going to stand for none of this dumb insolence, you hear." "Yes sir," she croaked hoarsely, desperately, swallowing hard. "I hear you wet the bed again," he said now, the eyes fixed unblinkingly on her. "Y . . . yes sir," she managed to get out in a frightened whisper, eyes falling, unable to stay averted. "And you know what

that means, don't you?" She nodded, swallowing hard to try to force the blockage from her throat. He wanted to frighten her and she could see that he was puzzled by the lack of tears. She knew she would suffer for it from the way his hand tightened on the wooden arms of the chair. She could feel the shaking that she could no longer control, the sting of salt tears in a fresh wave behind her eyes. "You know what to do, don't you?" he asked now. And the hands released the arm of the chair as the tears she had been fighting back started to flow. He was getting to his feet, and sick fear made her legs weak as she saw the lump in his trousers. The confirmation she had tried so hard not to see. Her tongue was large in her mouth, swallowing jerky and painful, and the tears flooded faster as the lump of his anger increased.[55]

The narrative juxtaposes two competing languages—Jamaican and English—which signify the colorful, escapist world of Hyacinth's dreams of her childhood in Jamaica, a world rich in metaphor and natural imagery, and the cold, prosaic reality of Hyacinth's life in England. Her dreams, however, are always liable to turn to nightmares as aspects of her real life impinge on them. Unable to take up a fully constituted subject position in either one of these languages, Hyacinth retains a fragmented and unfixed sense of identity throughout the novel. Even on her return to Jamaica as an adult, where she had hoped to rediscover a unified sense of self, she finds none. The Jamaica of her dreams is replaced by a reality of poverty, slum life, and disease. She does not belong there either. Her position has become marginal to both British and Jamaican cultures.

Mixed-Heritage Identity

If racism in Britain makes questions of identity and belonging difficult ones for many black writers, being of "mixed race" or of "mixed heritage" is perhaps even more problematic. In recent years, people of mixed heritage in the United Kingdom have begun challenging the categorizations, used in the collection of official statistics, that make them identify as either black or white; texts are now being published that explore the implications of this resistance for identity. A powerful example of such writing is Lucinda Roy's first novel, *Lady Moses* (1998), which tells the life story of a thirty-six-year-old, mixed-race woman, Jacinta Louise Buttercup Moses, born and brought up in Battersea in the late 1950s, 1960s, and 1970s. Jacinta is the daughter of a white English actress, Louise Buttercup, and a West African father, Simon Moses, who works in a brillo pad factory and writes stories about Africa, which only receive acclaim long after his death. Simon dies when Jacinta is five, leaving her with no black role model, and the story focuses on mother–daughter relationships placed within the wider immediate community with its poverty, social deprivation, and everyday racism. Jacinta lives with her mother and their lodgers in her parents' house, suffering from her mother's inability to come to terms with her husband's death. Although poor, Jacinta is educated at the local Catholic convent school, studies English at university, and marries a white American, Manny. She emigrates to the United States and gives birth to a daughter who is missing an arm. Her marriage founders when her husband rejects the child. Manny is killed in a car accident while they are living in West Africa, where they have gone to enable Jacinta to find her roots.

The story focuses on questions of identity and belonging in a racist Britain, where life is shaped by poverty and social class and where Jacinta finds herself marked out as different, as "the coloured child." Part One is set in London, where she spends her childhood:

> My father had a sense of humour. He had to. It was only a few years since Hitler had been defeated, and he was a black man married to a white woman—the first black man some English people had ever seen close up. He used to lick his lips when passers by stared for too long, and then they'd take off with all their fears confirmed. Luckily my mother despised humanity, so she didn't give a damn what anyone thought.[56]

To protect herself from racist abuse, Jacinta rejects what people around her say she is and identifies with the heroine in her father's stories of Africa. When her mother shouts at the five-year-old Jacinta on their way back from the hospital where her father is dying, Jacinta recalls

> women's white faces staring at the little coloured girl who was a fool not a genius, after all. I didn't know what to do. I wasn't a coloured child. I was the Jacinta-in-the-Story. I bit my lip and tried hard not to cry, but it spilled out of me anyway, and I hated the sound of me crying like a baby.[57]

Jacinta is racially abused by her mother's tenants who call her "wog" and "half-caste." She makes friends with the only black girl in the area, Alison Bean, whose family is African-Caribbean and asks her if she ever wishes she were white. Alison's answer does not help Jacinta resolve her identity crisis, since Alison's identity is rooted in being black like the rest of her large family, whereas Jacinta has only her white mother:

> "If I was white, then I wouldn't be like the others, Jassie. Me brothers 'n sisters would all look at me funny. When I went back to my granny, she'd say, 'Who are you, Missy?' I'd be the oddman out."

"Yes," I said, understanding for the first time that our homes were places where our skins belonged.[58]

This leads to Jacinta's search for a home, which eventually takes her, via the United States, back to her father's people in Africa:

I had left the country I grew up in. I was following my dreams, but there was still a gap inside me. I had never been to Africa. I didn't know who my father was. I had to find him in the contours of his own continent. I needed to find him in a place where blackness was a given cause for celebration. The African Americans in this country fascinated me because they took this land as their own. Black Britons didn't do that in the same way. We were always aliens; in the corners of our eyes was the fear of repatriation. I wanted to find a home like the Africa of Simon's stories— a place where no one would question my right to put down roots.[59]

In Africa she meets members of her father's family, but learns that there, too, she is different. She comes to recognize her white as well as her black ancestry:

I hadn't thought enough about my mother's race and my own. I was mixed race; Louise Buttercup was white, my father was African. Yet I wasn't simply the bringing together of two opposites. I was me. Distinct. A race apart. . . . I wanted to know other people like myself. It would be a luxury to talk with someone who understood what blackness meant from a white perspective and what whiteness meant inside the dark.[60]

Similar themes are to be found in the life story of black Welsh writer and sociologist, Charlotte Williams. *Sugar and Slate* provides an incisive study of the effects on subjectivity and identity of growing up mixed-race—"coloured"—in an all-white, small town on the North Wales coast. The question of color is central to Charlotte Williams's life from an early age. She spends her early childhood in Lagos, where she is seen as white. On returning to primary school in Wales, she is defined as "coloured":

There was no such thing as "black" where I grew up; Landudno wasn't that kind of place. We were "the coloured family" in polite English. . . . I grew up coloured, half-caste, and it took me a long time to realize that to be half-caste wasn't to be half of anything. It took me even longer to realize that to be mixed was not to be mixed up, or was it? How would I have known? You have to have knowledge of a wider experience to make sense of your own and that just wasn't available.[61]

Williams and her sisters are subject to a constant low-level racism that marks them out as different and refuses to allow them to belong:

> Are you from Africa? I bet it's hot in your country. Are you feeling the cold? Do you eat this sort of food where you come from? Are you that colour all over? Can you speak English? You people are so good at dancing. Is that your father? He's a proper gentleman isn't he? What part of Africa is he from? Can't tell when you're dirty can we? You don't need to wash so often I suppose? That's some suntan you've got there. Have they all got small ears like you? Let me feel your hair. People like you don't blush do they? I mean, there's no point.

Williams comments: "You mean I spent all those years with my cheeks burning and nobody knew any different?"[62]

Growing up in this environment with no other black or mixed families has profound effects on her identity. She reflects:

> Small town thinking has its own way of managing difference. It both embraces it and rejects it. In its ambivalence you become at one and the same time highly invisible and punishingly visible. "We never really noticed you were coloured," they would say in condescending tones, or "You're not really black, you're just brown," and we would all be relieved of the onerous impoliteness of being black. We would trade bits of ourselves for their white acceptance, denying ourselves to provide reassurance against the intrusion of difference. But it was the background assumptions embodied in the questions that caught me so unawares. The everyday assumptions of inferiority that eventually ground me down until I didn't know who or what I was.[63]

Later, when Williams travels to Guyana to discover her father's homeland, she realizes that, like Hyacinth in *The Unbelonging*, she has internalized white stereotypes and judgments of black people. In Guyana, where she hopes to find a place where she can belong, she is once more marked as different. Her attempt to form a friendship with a local black woman brings home to her that "[w]e were different although I didn't want us to be. I knew that my great-great grandmother had the experience of slavery like hers, and I thought of the generations of Negro women who were my ancestry. Somewhere we were joined at the root."[64] Eventually she comes to realize that she has been chasing an illusion in her search for identity and belonging: "until I changed my perception of what it was to be Welsh or what it was to be Guyanese, or both, I would never feel that satisfaction of belonging."[65]

Charlotte Williams's conjecture at the end of *Sugar and Slate* offers one answer to the questions of identity and belonging posed by many British-born or educated black and mixed-heritage people: "We may look to Africa or the Caribbean for or inspirational cues, we may inherit fragments of a traditional culture from our parents, but these we reformulate and reinvent and locate in our home places."[66] Claiming Britain as a home space is a first step. The problem for British society remains one of transforming those home places into nonracist spaces that allow both a sense of belonging and the development of positive forms of identity and belonging. As black British writing consistently demonstrates, such transformations are essential to developing a society that is truly diverse and in which difference is valued and celebrated, not merely tolerated. Recent black British writing is making a positive contribution to this process by rendering visible the issues at stake, by suggesting new ways of articulating Britishness, and by offering a range of narratives of the interrelation between British and black histories.

Notes

1. Beverley Bryan, Stella Dadzie, and Suzanne Scafe, *The Heart of the Race* (London: Virago, 1985), 183.
2. Heidi Safia Mirza, ed., *Black British Feminism: A Reader* (London and New York: Routledge, 1997), 3.
3. bell hooks, *Yearning: Race, Gender and Cultural Politics* (London: Turnaround, 1991), 29.
4. See Bhikhu Parekh, *Report of the Commission on The Future of Multi-Ethnic Britain* (London: Profile Books, 2000) and Chris Weedon, *Identity & Culture: Narratives of Difference & Belonging* (Maidenhead: Open University Press, 2004).
5. For more on recent black British culture, see Kwesi Owusu, *Black British Culture & Society: A Text Reader* (London and New York: Routledge, 2000). For more on black art, see the journal *Third Text*. For photography, see various publications by the London-based Association of Black Photographers. For recent work in film and television, see Karen Ross, *Black and White Media* (Cambridge: Polity, 1996).
6. Stuart Hall, "Cultural Identity and Diaspora," *Identity: Community, Culture, Difference*, ed. Jonathan Rutherford (London: Lawrence & Wishart, 1990), 222–237.
7. Hall, "Cultural Identity and Diaspora," 222.
8. Ibid., 51.
9. Bryan et al., *The Heart of the Race*, 183.
10. Hall, "Cultural Identity and Diaspora," 52.
11. For a history of black people in Britain, see Peter Fryer, *Staying Power* (London: Pluto, 1984).

12. *Windrush*, Four-Part documentary, BBC Two, 1998, produced by Mike Phillips and accompanied by *Windrush: A Guide to the Season* (London: BBC Publications, 1998).
13. Phillips, *The Final Passage*, 9.
14. Ibid., 137.
15. Ibid., 142.
16. Ibid., 20.
17. Ibid., 103.
18. Ibid., 41.
19. Ibid., 98.
20. Ibid., 101.
21. Ibid., 105.
22. Ibid., 104.
23. Ibid., 151.
24. Ibid., 122.
25. Ibid., 168.
26. Ibid., 129.
27. Ibid., 114.
28. Ibid., 115.
29. Ibid., 198.
30. Joan Riley, *Waiting in the Twilight* (London: The Women's Press, 1987), 2.
31. Caryl Phillips, *Cambridge* (London: Faber, 1991), 7–8.
32. Ibid., 67.
33. Ibid., 77.
34. Ibid., 104.
35. Ibid., 37.
36. Ibid., 25.
37. Ibid., 52.
38. Ibid., 92–93.
39. These writers included C. L. R. James, George Lamming, Wilson Harris, and V. S. Naipaul. Sam Selvon (1923–1994) was of mixed Indian and Scottish descent and came to London from Trinidad in 1950. He had served as a member of the Royal Navy Reserve during World War II, then worked as a journalist in Trinidad. In London he was employed as a civil servant while establishing himself as a writer.
40. *The Lonely Londoners* depicted the experience of migrants from the Caribbean who settled in Britain shortly after World War II, at a time when more than 25,000 migrants from the Caribbean were coming to settle in the United Kingdom each year. That novel was followed in 1965 by *The Housing Lark* and in 1975 by *Moses Ascending*.
41. Sam Selvon, *Moses Ascending* (Oxford: Heinemann 1975, rpt. 1984). xi.
42. Ibid., 97.
43. Ibid., 36.
44. Ibid., 36–37.
45. Ibid., 95–96.
46. Ibid., 35.
47. Diran Adebayo, *Some Kind of Black* (London: Virago, 1996), 19.

48. Ibid., 19.
49. Ibid., 21.
50. Ibid., 22–23.
51. Ibid., 44.
52. Ibid., 45.
53. Ibid., 5.
54. Ibid., 13.
55. Joan Riley, *The Unbelonging* (London: The Women's Press, 1985), 14.
56. Lucinda Roy, *Lady Moses* (London: Virago, 1998), 8.
57. Ibid., 22.
58. Ibid., 95.
59. Ibid., 216.
60. Ibid., 300.
61. Charlotte Williams, *Sugar and Slate* (Aberystwyth: Planet, 2002), 48–49.
62. Ibid., 48–49.
63. Ibid., 49–50.
64. Ibid., 133.
65. Ibid., 184.
66. Ibid., 191.

Works Cited

Adebayo, Diran. *Some Kind of Black*. London: Virago, 1996.
Bryan, Beverley, Stella Dadzie, and Suzanne Scafe. *The Heart of the Race*. London: Virago, 1985.
Fryer, Peter. *Staying Power*. London: Pluto, 1984.
Hall, Stuart. "Cultural Identity and Diaspora." In *Identity: Community, Culture, Difference*: Jonathan Rutherford, ed. London: Lawrence & Wishart, 1990. 222–237.
hooks, bell. *Yearning: Race, Gender and Cultural Politics*. London: Turnaround, 1991.
Mirza, Heidi Safia, ed. *Black British Feminism: A Reader*. London and New York: Routledge, 1997.
Parekh, Bhikhu. *Report of the Commission on the Future of Multi-Ethnic Britain*. London: Profile Books, 2000.
Phillips, Caryl. *The Final Passage*. First published in 1985. London: Faber & Faber, 1999.
———. *Cambridge*. London: Bloomsbury Publishing and Faber & Faber, 1991.
Riley, Joan. *Waiting in the Twilight*. London: The Women's Press, 1987.
———. *The Unbelonging*. London: The Women's Press, 1985.
Roy, Lucinda. *Lady Moses*. London: Virago, 1998.
Selvon, Sam. *The Lonely Londoners*. First published in 1956. Harlow: Longman, 1998.
———. *Moses Ascending*. 1975. Oxford: Heinemann, 1984.
Weedon, Chris. *Identity & Culture: Narratives of Difference & Belonging*. Maidenhead: Open University Press, 2004.
Williams, Charlotte. *Sugar and Slate*. Aberystwyth: Planet, 2002.

CHAPTER 6

TRANSFORMATIONS WITHIN THE BLACK BRITISH NOVEL

Kadija George Sesay

In the early 1990s, interest rekindled in black British literature. Nevertheless, many critics tended to regard this new black writing as merely a strand growing out of the already existing genre. But the emergence of 1990s black British writers, not only coincided with Britain's moving into a new century, it came at a crucial time, when the notion of what constitutes British culture was undergoing unprecedented changes. As I suggest here, this newest literary effusion surely has historical roots but it represents, just as clearly, several radical transformations of that venerable tradition.

Broad critical principles have been evolving ever since discussions in the 1960s and 1970s on "ethnic minorities"—from the notion, in those early discussions, that black writing and other ethnic forms of expression were the sole and unique possession of their specific ethnic communities—to the theorizing in the 1980s of a "multicultural" Britain, to the official acknowledgment in the 1990s of a "cultural diversity" that goes beyond ethnicity and race, but which, nevertheless, "involves far greater complexity."[1] In short, this evolving discourse has come to have a transformative effect on contemporary British culture. Proponents of "cultural diversity" hold that society is made up of an array of constituencies and cultural voices, all of them valid: these include ethnically based artists in general, as well women's arts and the arts for elderly people, young people, disabled people, and so on, as outlined in the Arts Council of England's Consultative Green Paper, *The Landscape of Fact, Towards a Policy for Cultural Diversity for the English Funding System.*[2] The theoretical argument for "Re-inventing Britain" is contained in the manifesto proposed by Homi Bhabha in 1997.[3] Bhabha there identifies a "third space," where very different British identities are being formed and re-formed in the collaborations and fusions occurring in the spaces in between cultures. For a younger generation of Britons, that "third space" continually becomes real and apparent.

This re-invention finds its basis in the nation's most recent literature, which includes the works of the "new breed" of young writers interpreting Britain from the perspective of the black British experience. R. Victoria Arana has referred to these writers (and similarly motivated artists) as the "neo-millennial avant-garde."[4] The common distinguishing mark of these writers is that, for the most part, they were born in Britain and are descendants of the wave of migrants from Africa and the Caribbean who began to arrive en masse starting from the late 1940s and throughout the 1950s and 1960s. David Dabydeen's initial definition of black British literature in *A Reader's Guide to Black British Literature*—that is, that literature which has been "created and published in Britain, largely for a British audience by Black writers, those born in Britain or who have spent a major portion of their lives in Britain"[5]—remained unchanged in the revised edition of the *Reader's Guide*, giving the misleading impression that black British literature remained static during those intervening ten years. The *Reader's Guide* definition fails to take into account the new black British writers who have been published since 1988 and the different dynamics that they contribute to black British literature.

A predominant number of black British writers do fall into the category of "those who have spent a major portion of their lives in Britain"—that is, both migrants and those whom Kwame Dawes has referred to as "the middle wave."[6] But the *language, themes,* and *imagery* of the newest black British novelists are notably different—and in a constant state of flux. Indeed, in *The Landscape of Fact*, the authors clearly conclude, ". . . the emergence of a larger younger generation calls for advance planning, and arguably a rather different approach. Art forms described by some as 'Second Generation' have developed their own distinctive character, and a sizeable coming generation will want to have the opportunity of experiencing them in arts centres, theatres and other venues."[7] Novelist Andrea Levy explains it thus: "As black British writers, we are kind of making it up as we go along, we don't have any sense of something else. *We've only got this culture to go on*" (my emphasis).[8] Therefore, neither do their works have to be identified as being "largely for a British audience"—with that phrase's suggestion of alterities— since the members of this group already see themselves as British.

As well as reiterating the changing terminology for blacks in Britain (from *ethnic minorities in Britain* to *multicultural Britain* and then, again, to *the cultural diversity of Britain*), Usha Prajar C. B. E., Chair of the Cultural Diversity Advisory and Monitoring Committee, acknowledges the significant practical and physical changes that have accompanied each stage in Britain's recent cultural development: "Unpacked, [this terminology] traces the shift from margins to mainstream, from communities to society—and this significant shift, this transformation, has taken place in the last twenty years."[9]

The new and distinctive character of the most recent black British literature can be aptly demonstrated by looking at the works of four new novelists of the 1990s: Bernardine Evaristo, Andrea Levy, Diran Adebayo, and Courttia Newland. Here we see marked changes in regard to (a) the theme of identity, (b) imagery, and (c) language, three areas in which these differences from earlier writings by blacks in Britain are quite apparent.

Identity

Lara, Evaristo's versified novel, depicts the growing face of a multicultural Britain as it traces the two dissimilar cultures of Lara, a Nigerian/ Irish girl growing up in the 1960s and 1970s. Half way through the text, at a pivotal point in the narrative, comes the moment in which Lara and her best friend, Susie, try to work out where Lara is from. The scene encompasses the various dilemmas of identity. It reveals how, although a distinct part of her heritage is African, Lara knows little, if anything at all, about the continent and relates much more directly to the country in which she has been raised, England.

> "Where you from, La?" Susie suddenly asked
> one lunch break on the playing fields. "Woolwich."
> "No, silly, where are you from, y' know originally?"
> "If you really must know I was born in Eltham actually."[10]

Lara also shows how Lara, herself, comes to realize that she may be an "other," not so much through the hurtful racist taunts she suffers, but because, in the country she calls home, she sees no depiction of her image in her everyday surroundings.

> *Home. I searched but could not find myself,*
> not on the screen, billboards, books, magazines,
> and first and last not in the mirror . . .
> . . .
> where in the silence of the sky I longed for an image,
> a story, to speak me, describe me, birth me whole.
> Living in my skin, I was, but which one?[11] (my italics)

Although she travels to Africa and Brazil to trace her family roots, Lara eventually returns to her real home: Britain, which she calls "my island."[12]

In *Every Light in The House Burnin'* (1995) and *Never Far From Nowhere* (1996), Andrea Levy also tells the stories of growing up black in Britain and dealing with the issue of acceptance within British society. In Levy's narratives, as in Evaristo's *Lara*, food plays a dominant role in revealing identity. In her first novel, *Every Light in The House Burnin'*, Levy's protagonist, Angela, prefers school dinners to those that her mother makes:

> I loved school dinners. I looked forward to them every day. My friends didn't. They all screwed up their faces and said, "Ehh!" a lot and that their mums cooked better things. Nicer. But my mum didn't. She couldn't cook steak and kidney pie with a rich crusty pastry that melted in your mouth . . . .
>
> And the puddings. Like no puddings we ever got at home . . . .
>
> But *my* mum cooked different things. She boiled rice in coconut with beans. She spiced chicken and meat until it was hot. She fried bananas. Everything she made tasted different.[13]

Her mother's cooking is depicted as embarrassingly odd, especially along with Angela's dissimulating declaration to her friend's mother that in Angela's house they eat "normal food" like other British people, "Most of the time."[14]

Both *Lara* and *Every Light in the House Burnin'* explore the values and politics of hair and the ways these are different for the girls growing up in England, as compared with their mothers. Levy spends an entire chapter in the only black hairdresser's place in town, where her protagonist cannot follow the conversation in the accent the women use. Levy's Angela considers that having her hair straightened gives her normal hair. In Evaristo's novel, Lara fakes normal hair by wearing her Irish mother's buttoned-up yellow cardigan on her head like a scarf, pretending that the swinging arms are flowing blond locks.

For Angela, acceptance as British means never being excited about being from Jamaica or going to Jamaica. Her unemotional response, when asked, is to answer that she's "from here."[15] In comparison, as Chris Weedon notes in her essay in this volume (chapter 5), there are more than a few novelists who would consider themselves black British and were publishing between the 1960s and the 1980s for whom these particular notions of identity and acceptance do not arise.

Works by the generation writing between the 1960s and the 1980s give the impression of being about *trying to be accepted* or about *not being accepted,* their characters feeling as though they have their two feet in two different continents despite the length of time they have lived in Britain, whereas for Levy's and Evaristo's protagonists, these notions are reversed. They see themselves, growing up, as being part of British society and are only made aware as they get older that they may constitute another blend. This difference in outlook reflects Bhabha's notion that mainstream British society may need to be coerced into accepting *access* between cultures; he has exhorted black British citizens to look for any reacceptance within this hybrid of British culture, rather than outside of it.

Language

In *Some Kind of Black* (1996), Diran Adebayo adeptly employs various styles of language in an attempt to exemplify the hybridity that exists *within* blacks in Britain. The protagonist, Dele, is an Oxford graduate of Nigerian parentage, and we watch how he straddles three different cultures—African, British, and Caribbean—in an effort to satisfy those around him, whilst putting his own identity into a "third space" sort of quandary.

Initially, the mix of languages used in the book feels uncomfortable, what with Standard English, Jamaican patois, and "street talk" (a mixture of American and English street slang)—all generally occurring within a few pages of each other. This mix is especially evident at the beginning of the book, where the abrupt changes in linguistic styles create the momentary effect of a disjointed story. For example, in chapter 1, "Nothing Can Contain," we read (on one page): ". . . so now Dele, mainly belled [*belled* = telephoned] Concrete [= his friend's name] when he was blitzing London [*blitzing* = "tearing up" or "painting the town red"] on weekends. His spar [*spar* = friend] definitely had access to the most parties . . ."; on the next page, we find a different mix: "His dad just picked him up by the scruff of the neck, didn't look at his mate or the colleagues and frog-marched him to the tube station."[16] But as the story progresses, the language does seem to blend more naturally. At the same time, its complexity affects the varying pace of the story, being much faster on the street.

Adebayo and Newland are both masterful employers of linguistic code. Yet, even though their stories take place just miles away from each other in the same city, with their books published just eighteen months apart and their age gap less than ten years, the difference in their two sorts of street language is still very striking. Courttia Newland's *The Scholar,* set on a West London housing estate, is paced at the same speed that the kids talk—and that is *fast!* By the time a third of the book is absorbed, the characters' style of talking is embedded even in an uninitiated reader's mind; the reader has learned the slang by immersion in it. Unlike Adebayo's protagonists, Newland's have never moved out from their tight community and know only one language, the one they have picked up from the street. They even talk the same way to their teachers at school and college and to their parents. In contrast, in Adebayo's *Some Kind of Black*, the pace of language slows down when Dele is speaking to his Nigerian parents, a mark of his regard for their notions of respect, which they demand that he uphold. Shaun's mother in *The Scholar*, younger than Dele's and from the Caribbean, not Nigeria, relates to language differently. In fact, adults in Newland's book try to identify as much as they can with the youth; and, quite often, they attempt to use the same slang. For example, Shaun's mother replies to Cory's, "Ruff innit?" with "Not as 'ruff' as looking at mash up ham sandwich."[17]

Compare these characters to Ferdinand Dennis's characters in *The Last Blues Dance*—all of them migrants from the Caribbean—who talk as if they still live in the same lifestyle they once had in the Caribbean, much slower and more easygoing than the rest of London, taking it all in stride.[18] Dennis, who was born in Kingston, Jamaica, and emigrated to England when he was eight years old, captures these Caribbean rhythms in his prose. Boswell Anderson's Sunset Café restaurant, for example, has been going downhill for the past twenty years, yet Anderson behaves as if he hardly notices its rundown condition, quite happy to have a busy lunchtime—and watching Caribbean folklife in England drift by.

In *The Language of the Black Experience*, David Sutcliffe compares language to a prism: "It refracts the light of experience through many different systems of expression and embodies it in many different oral traditions . . . Jamaican Creole and English."[19] This and other studies of the same type refer little or not at all to the input of West African Creole and African English. In the various languages of today's black Britons—particularly since a growing number of the new writers, like Adebayo, are of African parentage and have their experiences and speech patterns informed by their parents' African languages as well—subtle things are communicated by linguistic code shifting. Like those who reflect Caribbean speech patterns, especially those of Caribbean/Jamaican English along with other regional English speech patterns, African English writers use a tri-composite language in their work, that is, Jamaican English, African English, and Standard English.

It bears pointing out that, while West African Creole is quite commonly heard in England, people from the Caribbean have not found it necessary to express themselves in West African Creole or African English; these languages are rarely, if ever, found in their writing. Nevertheless, second- and third-generation black Britons are native speakers of a great spectrum of regional dialects, including "London English" (or Cockney), generally unfamiliar to migrants, who arrived in England speaking, first and foremost, "the Queen's English," which they had been taught in colonial schools. Indeed, Cockney is prevalent in many of the works of black British writers today, as it is one of the languages they ordinarily speak. Whereas second-generation black Britons may speak the "London Jamaican" and/or the Caribbean Creole of the island of one or both of their parents, they frequently also speak that new idiom that Mark Sebba has described as "Afro-Caribbean London English."[20] In short, the English language is *itself* being made over various ways in that "third space" that Bhabha has identified.

Imagery

The use of imagery is also helpful in distinguishing the differences between black immigrant (British) literature and the writing of blacks born in Britain. Migrant writers employ luxuriant imagery and focus on the colors and objects from their home countries or islands—using tropical foods and flora, in particular, in their tropes. In contrast, those born in England usually use only images and food references directly connected to England. In *their* stories, even plot tensions arise out of the divergent images the characters use in their everyday speech.

In *The Last Blues Dance*, Ferdinand Dennis describes Victoria's kisses as "sweeter than a Julie mango and twice as watery."[21] For many black British writers born in England, a comparison would more likely be made between a mango and another fruit. The British-born, having scant or no experience of the distinctive characteristics among mango varieties, do not think to evoke them for poetic effect. In Evaristo's *Lara*, mangoes are seen simply as black food. For *Lara*'s characters living in Britain, even for one with a strong consciousness of being black, simply knowing "the difference between yam and cassava" is an achievement to boast of.[22]

For those black British writers and readers who have never been to Jamaica or anywhere in the Caribbean, Dennis's atmospheric images are impossible to recreate from their own life experience: they cannot draw upon a nonexistent memory. Dennis's exotic images, like the simile in the following quotation, are not pertinent to everyday life in England: "He had always thought that the setting sun should have been red because that was how he remembered the sunsets in the Jamaica of his youth, a flaming red sun, '*red like a hibiscus or poinsettia*' " (my italics). The most recent crop of black British writers looks elsewhere—and closer to home—for poetic inspiration.

Although outside the "old" British mainstream, the works of Bernardine Evaristo, Andrea Levy, Diran Adebayo, and Courttia Newland represent very clearly the collaboration and fusion that is occurring in the spaces between cultures. Their roots are in Britain, as they have, or are certain of, no other topos. Their issues center more around acceptance (the other side of the "displacement" coin) than around alienation—displacement being the old theme, prevalent in the writings of the earlier, postcolonial era writers. Adebayo explains the newest trend as the consequence of black British writers trying to find their comfort zones amongst the different social systems: African, Caribbean, and British. For Newland, "this re-invented Britain" is defined through "a different point of view, different values, different food" from those of black British writers born outside Britain. "I'm writing about what I know, and I've been here all my life . . . . I see myself as different. I don't see myself as Caribbean, I've only been there once."[23]

For a growing number of *new* black British writers, the definition of "the black British writer" cannot be clear-cut. A singular definition would need to demonstrate the difference between the earlier generations and the latest one, made up of writers who have probably never been to Africa or the Caribbean, much less spent any significant part of their lives there, who cannot write about those places from a stance of reminiscence or remembrance, but write about Britain from a distinctive viewpoint all the same.

It has been suggested that these differences are only generational: but young migrant writers from Africa like Gbenga Agbenugba, the author of *Another Lonely Londoner* (1991) have created characters that (like his Akin, a young Nigerian coming to England) relate more readily to Moses in Samuel Selvon's *The Lonely Londoners* (1956) and *his* outsider experience of Britain (to which Selvon alludes in his novel's title) than they do to Shaun's and Cory's experiences in Courttia Newland's *The Scholar* or even to Dele's experiences in Diran Adebayo's *Some Kind of Black*. Agbenugba, who spent his youth in Nigeria, gives his young protagonist more of a postcolonial mind-set than a black British one. Newland, in contrast, did not travel outside of London until his twenties; the life experiences of his main characters are, therefore, shaped only by their immediate surroundings. In *The Scholar*, even having young African males playing football in the same park creates an "us and them" situation. Whereas Newland uses the street talk common amongst black British youth and nowhere acknowledges African English as a part of his characters' experiences, Agbenugba writes using African English and Standard English and only uses Cockney to a limited degree in street talk dialogue. Indeed, Adebayo's language usage is more like Newland's than Agbenugba's. Agbenugba narrates in African English, with some pidgin included, while Adebayo only uses African English for his parents' speech and does not himself narrate in it. These differences are marked and consistent between Agbenugba and Adebayo—and this despite their being in the same age group and both of Nigerian descent.

Conclusion

In essence, the new generation of black writers in Britain cannot write about some faraway home from a position of remembrance; they write about Britain from their own British viewpoints and put their own British spins on the world as seen from their very own perspectives. What characterized an earlier black British literature, the migrants' otherness, emanated from their coming to England and searching for a particular kind of perceived Britishness that did not necessarily exist. Black writers born in England have none of these illusions. They are developing within the British landscapes and social groups that they have been born into, writing about their own impressions of Britain from a new British perspective. In an interview with Courttia Newland in 1998, he explained it thus to me: "There is a culture over here that is a mixture of all three [British, Caribbean, and African]—but angled our way."

Notes

1. Quoted from the Arts Council of England's Consultative Green Paper titled *The Landscape of Fact, Towards a Policy for Cultural Diversity for the English Funding System* (London: Arts Council of England, February 1997), 15.
2. Ibid.
3. Homi Bhabha, *Re-inventing Britain: Identity, Transnationals and The Arts* (London: The British Council/British Studies: November 1997), 9.
4. R. Victoria Arana, "Black American Bodies in the Neo-Millennial Avant-Garde Black British Poetry," *Literature and Psychology: A Journal of Psychoanalytic and Cultural Criticism* 48, 4 (2002): 47–80.
5. David Dabydeen, *A Reader's Guide to Black British Literature* (orig. 1988; rev. ed. London: Hansib, 1997).

6. In his oral presentation to "Tracing Paper: Black Writing in London, 1770–1997," a conference that took place on October 11, 1997 at the Museum of London.
7. *The Landscape of Fact*, 21.
8. Andrea Levy, unpublished interview, 1998.
9. *The Landscape of Fact*, 21. This Green Paper was the first part of a process whose aim was to develop a national policy toward cultural diversity. In July 1994, the Arts Council agreed to the establishment of a Cultural Diversity Advisory and Monitoring Committee whose responsibilities would include the development of a policy for "Black and Asian arts."
10. Bernardine Evaristo, *Lara* (London: Angela Royal Publishing, 1997), 65.
11. Ibid., 69.
12. Ibid., 140.
13. Andrea Levy, *Every Light in the House Burnin'* (London: Headline Book Publishing, 1994), 44, 45.
14. Ibid., 46.
15. Ibid., 58.
16. Diran Adebayo, *Some Kind of Black* (London: Abacus, 1996), 2, 3.
17. Courttia Newland, *The Scholar* (London: Abacus, 1997), 11.
18. Ferdinand Dennis, *The Last Blues Dance* (London: Harper Collins, 1996).
19. David Sutcliff and Ansel Wong, *The Language of Black Experience* (Oxford: Blackwell, 1986), 3.
20. Mark Sebba, "How Do You Spell Patwa?" *Critical Quarterly* 38, 4 (1996): 50–63.
21. Dennis, *The Last Blues Dance*, 53.
22. Evaristo, *Lara*, 76.
23. Courttia Newland, unpublished interview, 1998.

Chapter 7

Contemporary Black
British Poetry

Lauri Ramey

HOME
Cleo is home when I wander
to far places
in this strange country
that longs for me to be far away
to where home is
a bright smile of welcome
in a buzzing throng of people
who never call me stranger
and never ask
where do you come from
but who would feed Cleo
if I left England

—SuAndi[1]

Nowhere does the poem "Home" identify itself as having been written by
a black British poet. It is free verse, nonmetrical, shows no signs of being
intended for performance, and does not rhyme. There is no indication of
the speaker's race. It is not written in vernacular or patois, and it contains
no direct references to cultural touchstones associated with blackness. Its
diction and vocabulary do not reveal themselves as specifically British.
How can such an ostensibly "generic" poem lead us into our investi-
gation of contemporary black British poetry? It can—and, in defying
certain pat expectations, it provides an excellent point of entry.

To begin with, SuAndi's "Home" depicts a speaker who wanders (l.1)
and is uncomfortable in the land where she lives, a "strange country"
(l.3). The country is personified (l.4) and longs for the speaker "to be far

away/to where home is," implying that in the mind of *this* "home" the speaker belongs elsewhere (l.5). The mind (or spirit) of the "strange country" (ll.4–5) metamorphoses into the imagination of the speaker (ll.6–7)—where, in the space to which the speaker has now mentally traveled, no one calls her stranger. This dreamlike reception contrasts with those (at "home") who ask her where she comes from (l.10). We are clearly operating with a double consciousness of home—a place where one resides but is a stranger and a place where one authentically belongs and feels appreciated. One puts on a face for those at "home" that does not need maintaining among the "buzzing throng" (l.7), the bright smiling others who are like oneself. In the closing two lines, we return to the frame of the cat who waits in the intimate space of the speaker's *actual* home. England is now identified as the real and particular location of that home, the (unproblematic) home also of the speaker's cat, Cleo. Naming bestows reality, connection, and specificity so that, together, cat and country add up to home in the realest sense, providing the all-important touchstones of connection. The poem closes with a rhetorical question and an "if" clause, leaving some lack of resolution to the poem's closure and adding a dimension of liminality. But it is implied that the speaker's true home is with the cat in England, the place where she has put down roots, in spite of places and people, real or imagined, to which she is connected elsewhere as an extended family of heart or history. SuAndi's poem is packed with signifiers as familiar to black Britons as their own cats.

The central themes of SuAndi's poem are identity, belonging, travel, alienation, isolation, separation, displacement, fragmentation, connection, and the strength to carry on ("who would feed Cleo" l.11). If the speaker is an "other," we must also infer the existence of "selves" who are insiders, unified and accepted. If we read "Home" as a black British poem, what do we gain, and if we do not, what do we lose? Hopefully, the answer is self-evident in that the emotional center of the poem, in fact, relies on our being able to read subtle themes into this poem of isolation, hostility, and difference within an explicitly English context. At the same time, the poem, by erasing race signifiers, cleverly checks a racially prejudiced response and challenges racism.

These are traits used in many and diverse ways in the poetry of contemporary black Britons. Some black British poets might be seen in roles that reflect African diasporic connections: some are "urban griots"; others, "trickster figures" (the writers' group that named itself Cave Canem—literally "beware the [angry] dog"—tropes richly along those lines).[2] The black British poets who view their roles as "urban griots" (Roi Kwabena, Breis, Fatimah Kelleher, Merle Collins, Adisa, Vanessa Richards, Malika B) narrate contemporary Britain as a citified and diverse diasporic village, partly defined by its external connections. The poets using trickster identities (SuAndi, Roger Robinson, Benjamin Zephaniah, Lemn Sissay, Anthony Joseph, Linton Kwesi Johnson, Patience Agbabi, Lorraine Griffiths) hold up British culture to a mirror, providing knowing reflection and pinpoint critique. In adopting these two tags, I do not mean to be prescriptive or pigeonholing, essentialist or totalizing; certainly, individual poems by many of these poets might place them in the other "camp." The phrases, in having emerged from their authors' critical self-examinations, do help us to situate certain exciting younger poets in relation to two nonexclusive and broad concepts of the poet's role, especially when the poets profess connections to practices of the African diaspora. My intent is to present poets as individuals while also suggesting new ways of conceiving of black British poetry and encouraging others to develop perspectives that enable further illuminations.

The questions that have recently begun to arise—Is there a canon of black British writing? What relationship does this brand of writing bear to British literature as it has commonly been studied? What might the special features *be* that identify black British writing?—are enormously pertinent to current critical and cultural debates. Numerous stereotypes surround black British poetry, the worst being that there is not very much of it and that its stylistic range is strictly circumscribed. It is easy to see how that impression could be conveyed, judging from the contents of anthologies, reading lists of English literature classes, and the limited availability of poetry books on both sides of the Atlantic.

In the introduction to his challenging and diverse anthology of contemporary black British poets *The Fire People*, Lemn Sissay refers to the "obvious names of Black poetry in Britain," by which he means Benjamin Zephaniah, John Agard, and Grace Nichols.[4] They may indeed be the closest thing to canonical black British poets (particularly the latter two, with Zephaniah often serving as more of a figurehead for certain kinds of critique and rebellion), but they remain far from canonical in terms of British poetry writ large, as we shall see. I would like to argue that black British poetry will not become canonical until it is widely recognized as a legitimate and valuable body of poetry—filled with range, dissension, variety, diversity, and a sophisticated cultural contribution: a poetry that carries special insight into the urgent global issues of race and nation, the individual and society. Until that time, we are dealing with tokenism, which results in conservative choices where respect and engagement with this poetry can be qualified, modulated, and controlled. Whether they see themselves as "angry dogs" or urban griots or in another role, contemporary black British poets tackle that sort of literary ghettoization, which masquerades as multicultural enlightenment.

In the British classroom, one sometimes comes across one of Nichols's "Fat Black Woman" poems, which are often described as "accessible" and "recognizable" in their expatriate-in-Britain mind-set of dislocation, struggle to assimilate, and cultural naivete. Take, for instance, such lines as "Shopping in London winter / is a real drag for the fat black woman": if read in isolation without realizing that they are working within a specified literary and cultural context, they might reinforce some of the stereotypical views of black British life and poetry as a mimetic and unmediated expression of a uniformly unsuccessful experience.[5] For the female immigrant who comes from a warmer climate, England is too cold, in terms of weather as well as the lifestyle and character of the English people (whose pink-cheeked heartiness and stiff-upper-lip reserve, one must remember, are commonly taken as British virtues and signifiers of Anglo-Saxon strength and resiliency). But the poem expresses no particular desire to grow accustomed to either literal or metaphorical coldness: just the opposite. In general, Nichols's personae tend not to exhibit much desire to adapt to an England that may *have to be* home, but that never feels warm and attractive. With a closer look and more experience of black British poetry as forming a canon of its own, Nichols's poems can be seen to perform the uncanny dance of subtly portraying the speaker's inability to fit in as a strength, rather than a failing, in a reversal of old-style British values. Her characters may complain, but they tend to be highly self-accepting and uninterested in changing to fit in—even flamboyantly resistant. The tropical "elsewhere" always sounds more enticing than the urban English "here." Clothing may not fit properly, implying that her fat black body and physical image are alien and negative in this place, but the speaker uses the word *fat* as a way of taking linguistic ownership of an identity that is self-defined. She neutralizes the power of external judgment to name and quantify her. The "fat black woman" uses the space of poetry, which has cultural esteem in Britain, to announce her jubilant acceptance of her fat black female body. The implicit criticism is not of herself, but of *British culture* for not "clothing" her—that is, for not protecting her from the elements, natural and manmade, and enabling her to feel that she belongs in it. Still, she does not need British culture to offer paternalistic membership in any national, psychological, social, or cultural club because she has an identity of her own. In a decisive act of self-assertion and reclamation of her body and identity, the speaker "curses in Swahili/Yoruba/and nation language under her breath," a whole linguistic black mix. Again, if read naively or taught in a decontextualized manner, such a gesture could be taken as reinforcing her linguistic otherness or impropriety in the centrist world of English-language dominance. But the speaker's strength is shown in a return to the originary language of orality—a self-liberating ironic juxtaposition as represented in the (here decolonized) form of a written poem in English that is, at the same time, a vibrant expression of communal African diasporic identity.

Frequently, the new black British poems are not wholly what at first they appear to be, but instead reflect the sly double voicing often associated with African American poetry and the archetypal personae of Carnival. Nichols's fat black woman, in keeping with a great deal of other black British poetry, actually resides in a liminal space—between slippery and rooted, combatively edgy and cheerfully assertive. Taught in schools as isolated examples of "poetry by those who have come from other cultures" (as I have often heard and seen such poems described), the complex poetry of Nichols and others might be mistaken as quaint ethnic alternatives to the female confessionalism of Carol Ann Duffy or Gillian Clarke, or as artifacts of oddity that require no recognition that this, too, is British poetry. The occasional Moniza Alvi poem finds its way into the classroom as well, where it can be used as part of a lesson to humanize English postcolonial history ("The boat docked at Liverpool" as Tariq stared at laundry on a line: "These are strange people, he thought / An Empire and all this washing" ("Arrival 1946").[6] Such perceptions need to be read through the eyes of ethnic diversity or they will be distanced and exploited as examples of Britain's self-admiring qualities of irony and the ability to laugh at itself—with pats on the back to the British values of order, perseverance, cleanliness, organization, predictability, and cultural hegemony. Jackie Kay's poetry also enters the literacy hour from time to time (especially in October, during Britain's Black History Month) to model the voice of an "other" as a way of driving home the treacly messages that poetry is a bearer of emotion and empathy and that one should not judge those who are different: "Where do you come from? / 'Here,' I said, 'Here. These parts'" ("In My Country").[7] The tone of defiance is sometimes mistaken for a plaintive response to childhood peer pressure if it is interpreted within a conventional paradigm of English poetry as a projection of the wish to conform and be like the others. "Jackie Kay is black and Scottish, but she is still English or British" might be the interpretive message, if one or two of her simpler poems are taught without context to convey an ideological social message (one hears Rodney King intoning, "Can't we just get along?!" in the background).

The poems of Jackie Kay, Moniza Alvi, Grace Nichols, John Agard—and those of many others, including Fred D'Aguiar, E. A. Markham,

James Berry, Mervyn Morris, David Dabydeen, Linton Kwesi Johnson, and Jean "Binta" Breeze—are essential to representing the vibrancy of contemporary British literature. Even so, they are not the whole story. There are many more excitingly diverse voices (some of whom are cited elsewhere in this book): Chris Abani, Patience Agbabi, Bunmi Ogunsiji, Andria Smith, Anthony Joseph, Akure Wall, Dorothea Smartt, Maud Sulter, Vanessa Richards, Mallissa Read, SuAndi, and Bernardine Evaristo, to list only a few. Some of them appear in recent seminal anthologies such as Lemn Sissay's *The Fire People* (cited earlier), *IC3: The Penguin Book of New Black Writing in Britain*, and *Bittersweet: Contemporary Black Women's Poetry*,[8] but even that good news is qualified. The mainstream press that published *IC3* has decided not to print a second edition—therefore, the collection, only released in 2000, is now out of print. For others on this list, the vagaries of publishing remain problematical. *I Love the Blackness of My People*, SuAndi's book where "Home" appears, remains unpublished after being described by the uninterested (white male) publisher as "too black."[9] Too black? Does that also imply not British enough? The answer appears to be Yes, to echo some of the ideas raised by Maria Helena Lima in her essay that appears in this book (chapter 3), "The Politics of Teaching Black *and* British."

In her M.A. thesis, Patience Agbabi wrote a parody of William Carlos Williams's "This Is Just To Say" to comment on the overall state of contemporary British poetry—the authenticating literary context where black British poetry resides, just as African American poetry is also part of American poetry. Agbabi implicitly calls for an increased range of all types of strong poetry within and outside of the classroom:

> I have gorged on
> the poems
> that were in
> *The Firebox*[10]
>
> and which
> you were probably
> saving
> for a SATS test
>
> Forgive me
> they were mellifluous
> so upbeat
> so controlled[11]

It will be necessary to widen public conceptions of British poetry (which surely can be more than "mellifluous," "upbeat," and "controlled") in order to validate in parallel the full range of black British poetry. As long as standards of approval for British poetry tend to be narrow and atavistic, the more experimental and bold black British poetry remains invisible and illegible as part of the British canon. It would be a great loss if this situation were not rectified, as contemporary black British poetry has the potential to move British poetry along into its future.

Should we be looking at "contemporary black British poetry" at all as a meaningful descriptor? This phrase undeniably names a category of poetry insofar as it refers to works written by a younger generation of poets who are British-born or British residents, who write from the perspective of their identities as poets who live in the United Kingdom, and who are black, but who may otherwise demonstrate as many differences as they do similarities. By sketching a span of poetic voices in this brief overview, I hope to inspire readers to seek out more of their works with pleasure and respect. I hope that current black British poetry will become more commonly recognized in its range of forms and styles as a significant part of the future of British poetry and poetry in English. It certainly exists and is making itself felt today. It would, however, be insufficiently persuasive simply to say, "This writing is here; so it should be read." Some sense of *why* the voices of black Britain have a vested importance for a fuller cultural and aesthetic understanding of British realities today must provide part of the support and justification for such a claim.

A number of critics have already begun to map this theoretical terrain. In *London Crossings: A Biography of Black Britain*, Mike Phillips devotes an entire chapter to the subject "Black British Writing—So What Is It?"[12] Phillips's question echoes Countee Cullen's 1925 sonnet: "Yet do I marvel at this curious thing: / To make a poet black, and bid him sing!" In Cullen, there is no specific reference to African American culture, only to the matter of race. The implicit questions are "What does it mean to be a black poet in any nation or culture?" and, following Phillips's lead, "Is there something that specifically sets black British poetry apart?" Regarding the aesthetic manifestations of racial identification for an *African American* poet, here is J. Saunders Redding's answer from his early critical study, *To Make A Poet Black*: "The literature of the Negro in America, motivated as it is by his very practical desire to adjust himself to an American environment, is 'literature of necessity.' "[13] The necessity, according to Redding, was the inevitability of the double voice, the need to maintain "two faces"—one that is intelligible to white culture and one that satisfies a black audience. We may do well to begin by asking, "Is the same true for today's black British poet?"

First, the African American connection is relevant for several reasons. In a reversal, where America's literary foundations and teaching are based on English cultural values and traditions, African American poets are often cited as having served as role models and voices of permission for many contemporary black British poets. Phillips traces the current concept of blackness in British culture to a model adapted from the American Civil Rights Movement, with its overlay of Caribbean-based pan-Africanism. As a result, according to Phillips, "we're stuck with a notion which has been partly constructed in Britain, but not for Britain . . . ."[14] It may be time for an adjustment as a new generation of young black poets begins to make a mark on its own terms, but identifications with the American Black Arts Movement and its long-term impact took hold for ideological as well as aesthetic reasons. That movement of the 1960s and 1970s presented a fusion between art and politics, writing and the musicality of oral traditions, attention to the dynamic relationship between the spoken and written word, awareness of the need for a sense of working collectively, and a search for an aesthetic practice that could have powerful social ramifications. These values continue to be evident, if not paramount, in much of the poetry and poetics of the African diaspora, including black British writing.

The need to borrow such models also was a practical matter. Until recently, black British writing was largely absent from British classrooms and libraries and difficult to locate in all but a few specialist bookshops. Caryl Phillips comments on his own experience:

> When I first realized that I wanted to write I looked to books by authors who were, both in terms of subject matter, and visage, in my ballpark. Given the fact that in the seventies there was not, in this country, what we might term a black British literary tradition, I looked to the United States and to a familiar roster of writers: Leroi Jones, or Amiri Baraka, Ralph Ellison, Richard Wright, James Baldwin, of course, and the poets Ted Joans, Nikki Giovanni, Don Lee, Sonia Sanchez and so on.[15]

SuAndi also struggled to find her poetic identity through examples offered in traditional English poetry and discusses both how that process failed and what saved her:

> Sixteen years ago I could quote Keats. He had been drummed into me parrot-fashion. I could quote him but he meant nothing to me. Like a hypochondriac I needed voices in my head. Voices to soothe me, to justify my struggle against so many odds. I wanted words that would center me as a Black woman. Sonia spoke to me. Not direct, as in face-to-face.

But reading her was like a conversation, a precious moment with a mentor, a wise-up session from a mature and *"oh-no-you-didn't"* older Sistah. People always ask one poet if another poet has influenced their work. I am always hesitant to give one name and anyway *to-be-under-the-influence* of anyone or anything ain't regarded as a good thing in this here world. But ask me who let me know it was OK to be a poet and speak out and I do not hesitate. My reply is always Sonia Sanchez.[16]

In trying to discover what black British writing is, Mike Phillips differentiates between immigrants of Caribbean and African heritage. He contrasts the earlier generation with the younger writers who have no firsthand experience of any homeland other than Britain. In spite of differences in geography, circumstances, and age, Phillips manages to identify some common strands among black British writers:

> First, there is a critical concern with identity and its relationship with a network of arguments about nationality and citizenship. This is accompanied by a focus on how the urban landscape shapes individual choices and outcomes, a consistent interest in excavating or describing the effects of migration on British society and a dominant interest in describing the language or motivation of black characters whose experience of growing up and living in Britain determines their identity.[17]

Such features inevitably link black British writing to what are increasingly likely to be some of our major cultural concerns in a postcolonial world, as Phillips suggests. Contemporary black British poetry may be seen in this light as a body of writing articulating an important dimension of current British experience—an experience worth promoting, preserving, sharing, and teaching. But what is in fact taking place in the current scene when it comes to promotions and publications?

Canons are most typically (and conservatively) preserved and dictated by the major instructional anthologies. Even today, the chief anthologies employed to teach post-Romantic British literature contain, at best, only a smattering of black British poetry. *The Columbia Anthology of British Poetry* includes not one black British poet, though it purports to chart the entire history of the genre from its genesis to the present. In the second volumes of both *The Norton Anthology of English Literature* and *The Longman Anthology of British Literature* (each over 2,000 pages long), the sole sample of a black British poet is Derek Walcott. In *The Oxford Anthology of Twentieth-Century British & Irish Poets*, the findings look more encouraging—James Berry, E. A. Markham, Grace Nichols, Linton Kwesi Johnson, David Dabydeen, Jean "Binta" Breeze, Benjamin

Zephaniah, and Jackie Kay—until we see from its table of contents that this anthology includes more than 120 twentieth-century British poets.[18]

It does not seem coincidental that of the major recent anthologies containing general representations of British poetry, some of the most generous samples of black British poetry are found in a volume called *Other: British and Irish Poetry Since 1970*. This is a significant but economical volume of a wide range of "others" who have resisted the pressure "to use some approximation to standard English, a koiné, nobody's native tongue," as the northerner Basil Bunting put it.[19] Bunting was one among many who reached out to American "others" with similarly alienated aesthetic positions, much the way black British poets were reaching out to those in the United States of America during and after the Black Arts Movement.[20] *Other: British and Irish Poetry Since 1970* contains poems by black Britons John Agard, Fred D'Aguiar, Amryl Johnson, Linton Kwesi Johnson, Grace Nichols, and Benjamin Zephaniah—an improved percentage, in a collection of fifty-five poets, over the volumes mentioned earlier, but still a skimpy representation compared to what could have been proffered in 1999. Its editors, Richard Caddel and Peter Quartermain, took as their charge to look to a changing British society, where the pretense of English standardization, as shown by its cultural products, is still maintained in some quarters despite all evidence that a standard Englishness never has existed, and certainly does not now.

In spite of the dizzying mobility of the twentieth century and James Clifford's assertion that " 'the exotic' is uncannily close" (as duly noted by Caddel and Quartermain in their introduction to *Other*), we live in an era where uniform visions of identity have crumbled, meaning that culture can no longer reasonably be identity's voice, mirror, or justification. We are presented in Caddel's and Quartermain's important volume with a compilation of distinctive poets with varied backgrounds and poetics. Apart from the Irish contributors, most would consider themselves British, but their poetry has been more or less marginalized for exploring such areas as vernacular language, the performative, the relationship between text and orality, the spatially inventive, the possibility of representing a unitary lyric subject, the ineffability of language, miscommunication—and, most of all, for looking closely at their own individual and sometimes alienated senses of the world, in contradistinction to homogenized and fictional visions of a wholly shared Englishness evident elsewhere.

The growth of such alternative or oppositional poetries in Britain became especially widespread in the 1970s and 1980s, not least due to the influence and presence of the second generation of migrant children of the African diaspora. This period coincides with the coming of age of a substantial group of young black poets some of whom knew no home other than Britain. Their poetic output during this shifting moment in British history (when poets from diverse ethnic backgrounds were searching for new meanings and greater artistic vitality) underscores how directly and crucially black British poetry has contributed to reinscriptions of the genre. This great wave included, among many other potential examples, Linton Kwesi Johnson's *Dread Beat and Blood* (Bogle L'Ouverture, 1975), Louise Bennett's *Selected Poems* (Sangsters, 1982), James Berry's *Bluefoot Traveller: An Anthology of West Indian Poets in Britain* (Limestone, 1976), and *Fractured Circles* (New Beacon Books, 1979), Jean "Binta" Breeze's *Riddym Ravings and Other Poems* (Race Today Publications, 1988), John Agard's *Mangoes and Bullets—Selected and New Poems* (Pluto Press, 1985), E. A. Markham's *Human Rites: Selected Poems 1970–1982* (Anvil Press, 1984), and Grace Nichols's *The Fat Black Woman's Poems* (Virago, 1984). Black British poets have been and continue to be central to the processes of revealing and commenting on the disintegration of the old imaginary of British cultural unity and purity. They are equally important in providing much of the means to repossess, revise, and reestablish the future voice of what Britain is in the process of becoming—echoing the often-quoted statement from Stuart Hall that he envies the sense of "ownership" shown by the younger generation. At the same time that they are providing "alternative" perspectives, they are—explicitly and emphatically—products of British culture.

In *Performing Blackness: Enactments of African-American Modernism*, Kimberly W. Benston looks to the fundamentally reconfiguring moments of African American modernism (the 1920s Renaissance, 1940s Bebop, and 1960s Black Arts Movement) as engendering a set of dynamic critical oppositions. Benston writes:

> [O]n the one hand, the work is measured against a privileged notion of "blackness" which is posited as external to both the Euro-American "mainstream" and, in a political sense, to the work itself; on the other hand, the work is tested for conformity to a universally applicable norm of "the literary" (a trope of cultural value in general) which is supposed to exist both in and outside any notion of "blackness."[21]

The audience's role, then, in both cases, is to determine the work's success or failure in relation to the selected norm—"blackness" or "the literary." A series of binaries spins itself out from either of these perspectives: "assimilationism versus nationalism, language versus self, form versus content, oral versus written, craft versus politics." Benston's solution is to sidestep "the conceptual do-si-do marked out by the secret partners of recent years, the Schools of Absolute Blackness and Chastened Universality" to embrace a more constructive platform: "that 'blackness' is not an inevitable object, but rather a motivated, constructed, corrosive, and productive process."[22] The tensions Benston identifies are some that we may find relevant today in our discussions of what black British poetry has been, is, or can be. In a similar manner, Beth-Sarah Wright links black British identity to African diasporic culture, which is "characterized by a fluidity and an advanced capacity to negotiate and shift in the face of change."[23] We see this afflatus exemplified in, among others, Linton Kwesi Johnson's classical anthemic poem "Inglan Is a Bitch." As in Benston's conceptualization, power in black culture is attached to agency. Indeed, Wright correctly identifies black British culture, again in a diasporic context, with a certain body of values, rites, and practices as inheritances that are historically enacted in differing times and places. These include performance, community, preservation of interpersonal memory through shared rites, a privileging of orality, the significance of historical narratives, and experiences of alienation, separation, dislocation, and exclusion.[24] The binaries dissolve in Wright's analyses, as they do in Benston's observations and Grace Nichols's *Fat Black Woman's Poems*. The oral/performative and the literary are viewed as mutually reinforcing of, rather than in opposition to, each other. A nonprescriptive range of poetic forms gains equal footing for the black British poet, whose art becomes a site for reclaiming the powers of identity and belonging that reinforce self and culture, past and present.

In spite of the general marginalization of black British poetry, as shown in the summary of literary anthologies, no group is more consistently excluded than those who are formally innovative (and the same is true of African American experimental poets). There is still an exceedingly limited range of conventional notions regarding what black British poetry should look and sound like and what it should be about. Such double marginalization reinforces racial and cultural stereotypes, creates a distorted view of black poets as not being involved in all areas of literary dialogue and influence, and effectively deprives black British poets from being seen as wielding total agency. We see this in Anthony Joseph's postmodern linguistic experimentation (certainly an "angry dog" and not an "urban griot"). Joseph is not included in *The Fire People* or *IC3* (though at age thirty-seven, he is of the same generation as those who are), and he is certainly not included in mainstream anthologies of either British poetry or world poetry in English. Nevertheless, he is a writer who articulates unmistakably the circumstances facing a black British poet who draws on modern and postmodern currents and does not appear to fit into any of the narrow molds of black (including black British) poetry:

> Black poetry or a poet that happens to be black? I prefer anti-essentialist ideas. My assumption is that the oral form of black poetry—the spoken word/performance poetry aspect is what most folks think it is. After all, how much black poetry is actually published in the U.K.? Besides the canonized ones, Walcott, Harris, Brathwaite, LKJ, Benjamin, how many black women poets are published by Faber? I'm talking major publishers. Not much. And much of what is, is in the tradition. But what we almost have now is a mini canon of black British writing. Hopefully there'll be a category for experimental work. But seriously, the spoken word is resilient and flexible, it even comes disguised as hip hop. Maybe some folks still think black poetry is dub poetry. Or maybe it's those odes to my Nubian princess poems you hear on "the circuit." I prefer to stay out of the arguments: "form is what happens." I just do the work. That's the benefit of exile.[25]

With that passage as a prologue of sorts, I would like to turn now, for a case in point, to *teragaton*, Anthony Joseph's fascinating collection.

Joseph's writing brings together the worlds of postcolonialism and post-Language Poetry experiments—in its allusions to Amiri Baraka, Wilson Harris, Viktor Shklovsky, Miles Davis, Dexter Gordon, Kamau Brathwaite, and Ted Joans. For Joseph, the present state in Britain is one of "conceptual colonialism."[26] Obviously, Joseph wills himself to depart from the shackles of linguistic repression, affirming that part of the role of poetry is to question and even attack the hierarchies of cultural and aesthetic control designed to keep out voices of diversity and dissension and maintain narrow hedgerows of propriety. While that aspiration is hardly a novel one in the twentieth century (where Joseph is in good company), his is not the mode of black British poetry that is commonly seen as exemplifying "the right kind" of its genre and producer. When the hegemony of language conflicts with our experience and stops making sense, there is a history to draw on of others who have employed countervailing tactics of subject and style; but those modes of experimentation are generally associated with white Euro-American modernism and postmodernism. Roi Kwabena (surely an "urban griot," as we see in a poem such as "Obeahman") agrees with the point made by Joseph: "It appears [that] to be a successful black poet in the U.K. one must also be of a particular persuasion."²⁷

Joseph's book's title, *teragaton* (suggesting an elision of *terra* and *interrogation*), conjures "a place" characterized in his introduction by "departures from sense, syntax-logic, conscious focus, preset matrices into an explosion/implosion of raw word and solid thought matter—a bulk of chaos containing the pre-selective text."²⁸ Poems such as "Blackdadamasonsong (for Ted Joans)," "De Moko Jumbie," and "Vervain With Kimono" demonstrate inventive use of fonts, typography, space, shape, and page. Such techniques highlight senses of freedom and immediacy, reinforcing his comments from the introduction. His poetry interrogates "preset matrices" and challenges the notion of "a pre-selective text," where themes and ideas have been determined and the poem unfolds as planned. Joseph's poetry aims instead to be the trace of its process of creation and offers an experience that cannot be had before or outside of the poem. His poetry uses quick-shifting mixtures of vernacular dictions where speakers often remain unidentified. He relies on aggressive and deliberately nonstandard uses of punctuation to problematize the dynamics of reader–poet control. The result in *teragaton* is an exuberant and thoughtful series of experiments with form, drawn from literary and extraliterary contexts.

For instance, the book contains a section called "teragatonic sampling," drawing from the classic modernist techniques of Dada cutups, collage, bricolage, and intertextuality, while gesturing to one of the central techniques of rap. The three multi-part and fragmentary poems comprising this section of the book contain brief flashes of emotions and events left unattached to a unitary subject, where it is not clear if events are "narrated" by the self or the other ("in new hat bt nobody notices"). There are clipped and plaintive literary allusions, as attempts to form a canon or cohort of one's own for this poet who must feel his isolation within black British poetic practice ("roi jones collected prose&plays"). There are self-reflexive speculations on the nature of writing as a place or site, on reader expectations, and on the potential for communication to take place at all. These moments are sometimes tinged with ironized sentimental longing ("is the word long, will intended readers understand"), then answered with unapologetic commitment to the difficulties of his poetic mission ("the word is the word/necessary"). Sights are seen and reported ("3. Jury sees photo of victim's skull") without signposts of agency or contextualizing markers, resulting in a heightened sense of menace reflecting contemporary urban culture. An authoritarian voice sporadically booms surreally from center page:

```
DO SPORT
NOT DRUGS
PAY TOLL
```

Looking at similar textures in the works of other black British poets like Joseph—for instance, in the intermingling of verbal, visual, and conceptual boldness found in the poetry of Andria Smith or Mallissa Read—we may discern how the category of contemporary black British poetry opens to new possibilities, breadth, and alternatives. Adding such a historical dimension may also help us to link the black British poets to the equally marginalized "alternative traditional of [British] others"—including Tom Pickard, Basil Bunting, Peter Finch, or Carlyle Reedy—with whom they have as much (or more) in common as with a John Agard, James Berry, or E. A. Markham. The "crisis of representation" experienced by Joseph conditions, to some extent, the creative lives of all poets working in the twentieth and twenty-first centuries, but the context Joseph invokes (aesthetically postmodern) does not tally with what a number of contemporary British critics of black British literature perceive as an almost exclusively social realist tradition in the African diaspora, including black Britain. For similar reasons, British poets working on the margins of representational expression may still be marginalized and excluded even from collections designed to introduce readers to new poetry (hence the need for anthologies like *Out of Everywhere*[29]—a fine collection of experimental poetry by women, though it contains no black writers—and *Other*). But the exclusionary impact of canon formation turns unacceptable and intolerable for a black British poet who is stereotyped with the expectation of being deeply invested in the performative (much of Joseph's work, e.g., explicitly engages literary dimensions of presentation and, while some of it would perform well, other aspects would be impossible to reproduce orally); in class- and race-based social interventions (Joseph's interest is not to represent such concerns directly, but rather to engender social and political impact by interrogating one's identity as a user of language in a particular time and place and in relation to repressive forces standing in the way of meaningful communication); and conveyed in techniques and imagery demonstrating double voicing, conflictual identities, and cultural collisions (instead of engaging these issues directly as themes in his poetry, Joseph and some other black British poets represent them through semantic rupture, syntactic fragmentation, and active breaking of communicative frames and patterns). In describing the project of this book, Joseph offered these illuminating insights:

> The title was something my dead mother whispered to me in a dream, but your idea is fascinating, something I hadn't seen. Incidentally, that's my mom and dad on their wedding day (on the cover). I'm in there too, in her belly, which is what the book was trying to say, that there's a hidden text, a core text. I wrote *teragaton* during a year long period of experimentation with the language of the unconscious. I was searching for some true text, some hidden, profound and honest text, at the same time I was conscious of rhythm and form when poems were assembled on the page, respectful of poetry. Most importantly was my first life in Trinidad, coming to England at 22, the cadence and motion of our speech, memory. My influences—some cubist poetry, William Carlos Williams, Pound, the Beats, Ginsberg, Black Mountain, Wilson Harris, Monk, Bukowski, Baraka, Dorothea Brande, Negritude, and then I discovered surrealism. And it is this that shapes that text. But most is hard to explain, poets must believe in magic too. I've always felt like I write in a vacuum, I'm still waiting to meet other black experimental poets. There's a shortage of 'em in London. I guess like everyone else, in my work I've tried to construct a self-sufficient universe of text to fill this vacuum. I mean, as James says, "the metaphysics of another world," a body of work with a sense of continuity and cohesion, a method, a science. Now, I feel it necessary to experiment even further with poetry. I like the idea of resonance, minimalism, something. We'll see. It's not often I get to talk text.[30]

Joseph's means and goals are entirely normative for a contemporary poet interested in decentering and reconceptualizing identity, examining one's personal and literary lineage across time and space, and interrogating language as a system of discourse—his poetry and thought would be right at home in *In the American Tree*[31] or a critical study such as Peter Quartermain's *Disjunctive Poetics*, which addresses such relevant topics as "Writing as Assemblage."[32] Joseph's phrase "to talk text" gestures to the relocation of conceptions of written language into the body and prefigures Patience Agbabi's sense of "word of mouth" (to be discussed later in this essay). His poetry, although perhaps not exhibiting some of the conventional surface markers, also shows many features associated with other poetries of black Britain and the African diaspora—connections to deceased elders as spirit guides, the importance of family, heritage and what one inherits, dispossession and the effort to create a functional world of one's own, and cultural and linguistic alienation. The focus here on the poetry of Joseph, an immigrant to and citizen of Britain, is meant to signify that such concerns belong rightfully to and are claimed by a black British poet.

There are fascinating examples of contemporary black British poems that aim to link the poet's personal history with the history of black people in Britain, and both to a larger diasporic community. These poems often are recuperative endeavors of cultural memory, revivifying forgotten or overlooked moments and figures, and reanimating them through the voice of the poet. Many of these projects are multimedia creations, incorporating poetry with art, music, photography, and film. One of our urban griots, Vanessa Richards, has undertaken a number of projects that fall into this category. She has created two important short films using diasporic imagery and utilizing personal and national histories. "Traveling Light" focuses on that necessary trait among African diasporic peoples: an ability to become comfortable in places where they may not have wished to travel. The film's voiceover recites: "We have traveled so far to call this place home, these people family," and ends: "People on the move, traveling light." One of the central themes of Richards's poetry is the exceptional ability to manage travel and change, to take root and thrive in foreign soil (in this connection, Beth-Sarah Wright's previously cited key ideas concerning the African diasporic consciousness may be recalled). Richards's film "Jazz Slave Ships Witness/I Burn" records an undertaking that the poet describes as "a remembering for the dead who are not dead."[33] The film commemorates a project based on the history of the English port Whitehaven and its role in the triangular slave-trading route, as depicted through the story of a young female griot, Mary Christian Grassett. Richards, an Afro-Canadian who spent eleven years (1992–2003) living and writing in London, has produced work that resonates with images and themes of the African diaspora. As an urban griot, she tells—and so preserves—the stories of wherever she is at the moment, connecting her own experiences to other diasporic tales and integrating herself in the process with the community in which she happens to be residing, even if it is a transitional location.

Richards's poem "Post-Caribbean Reds"[34] opens:

> I've become one of those transplanted tropical flowers
> that withers in English cold.
> Newly accustomed to a lifetime spent above the 54th parallel
> where the sky knows more shades of grey than blue,
> rain is never warm and trees are evergreen.
> A new world black soul
> that can't recall the reasons for a big city career.

In some respects, Richards is here adopting, quasi-ironically, the conventionalized black British female literary persona—a colorful creature from a warmer, brighter elsewhere who shrinks from the cold monotones of England. But in the phrase "I become one of those," the speaker acknowledges that she is transforming, taking on a culturally approved role by metamorphosing griot-like through this trope into the persona we have already encountered in Grace Nichols's poetry and elsewhere. The speaker has become a diasporic traveler. By establishing a relation to other black female immigrants, Richards frames the point of view as one of identification rather than affectation, for Richards has Caribbean as well as European roots. Her speaker may be a "new world black soul"; but she, too, has come to the center of the Empire from the far reaches of the Commonwealth. Later in the poem, we read: "Tell me again Tante, tell me again / of herbs, roots and history." From that moment, as if through the invoked spirit of the storytelling, elder-female prototype, the speaker embarks on a journey in memory to reproduce family stories superimposed over tales of her own time in the Caribbean and the United Kingdom. As an Afro-Canadian writing in London, Richards narrates a tale in a lyrical form that is immediate and personal, but also historical and touristic. In "Post-Caribbean Reds," we begin with an urban sophisticate who opts for the enticements of London and "a big city career," and finds herself identifying with a variant of the "fat black woman." Through that scene of displacement and connection, we are transported back to the site of the speaker's ancestral values: respect for the elders, privileging of oral culture, and a reliance on the remedies of the earth. One might surmise that—at least, in part—it was Richards's decade as a black poet writing in Britain that enabled her more fully to access another part of her cultural inheritance: her migratory roots. This legacy, too, is a dimension of black British poetry.

The reclamation of a sense of community and cultural heritage, which is diasporic in perspective and race-based, is also a major theme for SuAndi, who similarly draws together historical and personal materials to position herself as the locus of cultural memory resonating with the local, or urban, subject matter. SuAndi, a resident of Manchester, is an internationally celebrated performance poet and cultural activist of partly Nigerian origin. Having been awarded the honor of membership in the Order of the British Empire (an O.B.E.), she is widely known and admired for her involvement with community groups as well as for her incisive and increasingly ambitious theatrical productions. SuAndi's poetry levitates from the page to function similarly to dramatic monologues, often in a highly musical fashion, as she embodies a variety of current personae and historical characters, generally permutations of womanhood. Ultimately, her work is intended to provide a cultural portrait that expresses the breadth of shared experience conveyed by the intimate, personal detail. As described by Catherine Ugwu, "SuAndi provides a unique insight into British society and the diversity of the Black British experience. . . . SuAndi's works are a heightened form of writing, a form that enables her to combine linear narrative with the ability to concurrently expose layers of fact and symbol."[35]

SuAndi's literary motives are to be watchfully and socially alert and to be a corrective influence on society—an orientation that allies her with other poetic "angry dogs." To those ends, in two recent works, she has combined autobiographical information with the documentation of black British history. Her verse performance piece *The Story of M*[36] is an auto-biographical tribute to her mother, Margaret, and to the poet's own experience growing up in a mixed-race family in Manchester. This long poem describes with pride the details of SuAndi's British childhood, including the message that "if any of you think that all mixed/raced people/Grow up confused, without identity,/ Think again."[37] According to SuAndi:

> My work has the locality of my upbringing in the exotic climes of Manchester. No patois for me or the beat of my father's Nigeria nor the flat tones of my mother's Liverpool. The more indigenous poets I listened to, the more I realized that my voice sat in a different octave. Not for me descriptive verse of the countryside. In deep dells, many a brave bunny rabbit might dwell. I've got business that is more important. I can be comic, I intend to be, but my voices nearly always have a message that cry for respect. I am not a ranting civil rightist, (I don't rap either) nor does my work embody the narrative style of many African griots.[38]

SuAndi also wrote the libretto for the opera *Mary Seacole*. While it does not draw directly on facts of SuAndi's own life, the story of this Victorian era, Jamaican-born healer struck powerfully familiar emotional chords, SuAndi found, for its familiar patterns of exclusion based on race, class, and gender: "I had tried to 'get into her head,' as to what drove her forward against so many obstacles. Seacole epitomises so many Black folk and naturally Black women in particular. Did I write these words for her or for myself?" While Florence Nightingale remains well known, Mary Seacole is hardly remembered[39] (they did, in fact, meet, but there are reports that institutionalized racism prevented Seacole from being invited to join Nightingale's nursing team). SuAndi considers *The Story of M* and *Mary Seacole* to be linked insofar as they depict *herstory*—and represent SuAndi's commitment to inscribing, for the record, the lives of significant women. SuAndi's memorializing of Mary Seacole in the rarefied form of an opera performed at one of the major bastions of British culture (Covent Garden) represents a thrilling act of reification and a major contribution to the cultural milestones of contemporary black British poetry.

Reared in England and Wales and educated at Oxford, Patience Agbabi found aspects of her identity in the discovery of such ostensibly disparate cultural markers as Northern Soul and Chaucer. She honed her art at the Afro Style School run by Kwame Dawes at Spread the Word, and also at The Hard Edge Klub in Soho with its mainly white, working-class audience. She uses such traditional forms as sonnets and sestinas, which she shares with audiences in printed collections as well as on stage as a self-described performance poet. Agbabi denies any conflicts in what might be perceived as differing identities, believing that pre-inscribed roles and sets of influences are themselves the problem. She wrote in her M.A. thesis: "On the one hand we have 'silence': on the other 'Caribbean speech, jazz, blues and calypso.' Much contemporary poetry confounds these prototypes, e.g. not all 'page poets' are elitist and/or hard."[40] Accordingly, Agbabi would uphold Benston's and Wright's rejections of such limiting and artificial binaries as *performance* or *page poet, black* or *British*, and *high art* or *popular culture*. For Agbabi, such dichotomies are not only artificial; they are also destructive. She is a product of Oxbridge, regularly performs her rap-inflected sonnets publicly, and has already traveled some distance among British audiences toward cracking restrictive stereotypes and paradigms based on race, style, gender, or nationality. The confluence of forms, poetic values, and inter-textualities evident in Agbabi's works creates a fascinating mélange, and is a significant asset to the depth and range of current black British poetry.

Agbabi's M.A. thesis originally was titled "The Death of the Reader: Crisis in Contemporary Poetry." After first identifying a problem, she went on to provide a solution. She eventually changed her title to the less ominous "Word of Mouth: Deconstructing the 'p' words: 'performance,' 'page,' and 'poetry.'"[41] For Agbabi, the future of British poetry lies in its past and oral roots, but she aims to reanimate it by using her present-day cultural context, which includes her literary knowledge. Agbabi is committed to restoring the genre to its origins in sound and music while maintaining the discipline of structure and technique developed by conceptions of the poem as an artifact for the page. This is the "word of mouth" she aims for, a reminder that many of the pleasures of language lie in its production in and by the body (no coincidence that her forthcoming book is titled *Body Language*).

Agbabi cites a number of influential precursors who have refused the line of demarcation between page and performance in poetry: Chaucer (*The Canterbury Tales*), Browning (*Dramatis Personae*), Wordsworth (*Lyrical Ballads*), Eliot (*Four Quartets*), and Pound (*Cantos*). It is interesting that she reaches so far back into the history of British poetry for emotional and technical support. But why should there be an expectation that black performance poets would share a restricted range of common influences, or that the tradition of performance poetry springs from unitary roots? Lorenzo Thomas shows that there has been considerable cross-fertilization from a variety of sources in the development of African American performance poetry, including interchanges among the Beats, the Black Mountain Poets, and the Black Arts Movement.[42] Black performance poetry in the United States or the United Kingdom has not been produced by any one national, aesthetic, or ethnic tradition: we can look to the privileging of oral tradition in the African diaspora as having created hospitable terrain, just as we can also credit lyric poetry's oral roots. Other factors contributing to the development of performance poetry include the influence of black music, breakdowns in social stratification, questioning of views of art as either "popular" or "elite," increased concerns with community as a site of artistic activism for social benefit, the development of cultural centers in urban spaces, and public funding for a wider range of genres and styles of art. All of these developments apply to the work of Patience Agbabi.

A blending of factors from the African diaspora and present-day Britain has generated interest in and enthusiasm for poetry that is performed publicly as a popular form of entertainment. This is all the more reason that Agbabi should be able to freely acknowledge meaningful influences, whatever their source, when they are plainly within her realm of experience. From her own perspective, she has inherited the British poetic tradition and is adding to it her way, with contemporary touches such as rap-inflected sonnets and sestinas. As she puts it, "I liked the essay 'Tradition and the Individual Talent' a lot. It made me realize why not use the standard classics if I like them and can use them? I think it's a shame to make distinctions between R & B, Northern Soul and English classics—if they give you pleasure, go for it."[43] When Agbabi turns for inspiration to the British and Troubadour traditions, that choice represents her bona fide right as a poet who is British and has experienced the finest in British education.

Agbabi has been critical of the quality of some contemporary performance poetry by black as well as white poets, believing that a poem must be well written to perform well. The separation often seen between these media is echoed by Lorenzo Thomas: "To the extent that poetry readings have been perceived as entirely secondary to the existence of poems as printed texts, very little attention has been directed to possible impact of performance contexts on poetic composition."[44] Thomas is correct that this area represents a gap, and it is one that Agbabi is aiming to fill by refusing to allow poetry to split into "page" or "performance." She has said, "Writers of the African Diaspora shouldn't neglect form," but is equally interested in the impact on form of immediate feedback from an audience. Such didactic and aesthetic concerns influence the way that she teaches creative writing to college students. Agbabi tends to integrate a wider range of models than usual: "I do an exercise where I teach simultaneously the opening of *The Canterbury Tales*, the opening of *The Waste Land*, and Linton Kwesi Johnson's *Di Great Insohreckshan*, which all open with the month of April. These are three male models but with very diverse voices. This is always a revelation to my students." By such means, she is impacting the wider public through her performances, the literary strongholds through her printed collections, and the next generation of multiethnic British poets through her teaching. In keeping with her commitment to the value of British literary tradition, Agbabi also teaches an M.A. course on the sonnet. The sonnet has been a highly productive form for her, but hers are sonnets that extend the genre, once again demonstrating the important contribution black British poets are making in pushing British formal conventions forward. Regarding the sonnets, which continue in *Body Language*, Agbabi says, "I like it that the form gives me the opportunity to work out a problem, to deal with what could potentially feel like repression. This is where I'm reminded of what Chaucer did, all that freedom in form, and what that felt like for me to read."

Agbabi's goal is to reanimate audience interest in poetry by reaccessing the oral roots of the lyric tradition as a means of reclaiming the vitality of the genre. The opening poem of *Transformatrix*, "Prologue," is one of Agbabi's consistent crowd-pleasers in performances. An impeccably crafted poem (with Chaucerian echoes), it plays the dozens with her skills while revealing itself as a genuine lexical and conceptual tour de force on how poets play with the "word"

> till its meaning is in tatters
> till its meaning equals sound
> now write it down,
> letter by letter
> loop the loops

till you form a structure.
Do it again again again again again
Till it's a word picture.
Does this inspire?
Is your consciousness on fire?
Then let me take you higher.[45]

The speaker of this poem is a verbal diva to the British literary manor born, which she then remodels to suit herself in the present moment.

Recalling her early development, Agbabi says, "By age eight, I wanted to be a writer. I was read to early in life by my foster mother, especially nursery rhymes. I read *The Lion, the Witch and the Wardrobe*, *The Secret Garden*, those were my favorites. I loved *The Canterbury Tales*. When I was 16 I wrote a parody of the Prologue. The language of Chaucer fascinated me, the rhyming couplets, the irony, the idea of people telling stories in poetry. It was a major door opening in my head." Related to her early love of British literary tradition, Agbabi's sense of identity also emanated from her father's great respect for British education and aspirations for his daughter: "My father's educational encouragement made me feel less alien than some others did with white people." However, there were experiences that Agbabi encountered which resulted from various kinds of cultural collisions. She explains: "There are large differences between Nigerian and Caribbean culture. People would expect me to know about Caribbean culture just because I was black. I didn't, but thought maybe I should. That was part of the confusion of growing up as a black child in Britain."

Such encounters were mitigated by increasing stages of self-discovery, especially finding "a place" in poetry, and recognizing aspects of her diasporic heritage that actually enhanced her social status (as reflected autobiographically in her poetry): "I moved to North Wales at age 12, which was very disruptive. I'd figured things out where I was in England and then had to start again. It was a hard age to relocate anyway. The poem 'North(west)ern' is about that—how I discovered Northern Soul in the late seventies, how it really helped me to fit in. Because I was black, people looked at me as having special knowledge, having a place. Northern Soul was a very particular culture, peculiar to that time and place, with its own kind of clothes, clubs and dances. I carried that with me to Oxford." The poem that Agbabi cites (which will appear in *Body Language*) is a prime example of her amalgamation of forms and themes— it is a sonnet, a fundamentally musical form in origin, but with the culturally unexpected twist of focusing on a contemporary black-based musical genre:

> . . . . . I heard that tune
> named it in one. Soul. My heart was break
>
> dancing on the road to Wigan Casino,
> northern soul mecca where transatlantic bass
> beat blacker than blue in glittering mono.

The poem focuses on a pivotal moment in the speaker's developing identity. It closes with a turn reflecting the awakening of senses associated with the memory of powerful feelings (recollected in proper Wordsworthian tranquility):

> Then back, via Southport, Rhyl, to the time, place
> I bit the Big Apple. Black, impatient, young.
> A string of pips exploding on my tongue.

In Agbabi's poetry, there is an open embrace of what she sees as the best of all that is black and all that is British, including international imports and inflections.

Agbabi's interest in form has been evident from the time of her first collection, *R.A.W.*[46] (which stands for *r*hythm *a*nd *w*ord), where equal attention is paid to sound and logos. Her second book, *Transformatrix*, continues to display Agbabi's interest in form and rejection of the "page"/"performance" split that sometimes prevails in the current poetry climate, especially in relation to stereotypes applied to black British poets: "By the time I wrote 'Transformatrix,' I wanted to write more sonnets. I had written a few in my teens. The book *Transformatrix* has a sonnet at the end and a rap poem at the beginning. I knew the poem 'Transformatrix' would have a corset in it. I wanted to subvert the feminist vision of the sonnet as corset: I think constriction can give you freedom." Accordingly, the title poem, which closes the book, is a quasi-erotic fantasy—humorous with a bite—about writing in which the poet's muse is transformed into a literary dominatrix. In the final lines, the speaker assumes shared agency in a charged moment of multiple signifying: on the training of a young poet, on the delicate dynamics of control and submission specifically for this black British female poet, and on embodying a living art form as a freely complicit practitioner—with tradition, as a knowing mediator of the current moment, and uniquely as herself, as Patience Agbabi, who bestows vitality and meaning on the rules and authorities, just as much as they enable her true identity:

> . . . She trusses up
> words, lines, as a corset disciplines flesh.
> Without her, I'm nothing but without me
> she's tense, uptight, rigid as a full stop.[47]

How have concepts of black British poetry impacted Agbabi's search for her own style and approach? Her answer is direct: "When I was developing as a poet, I read and saw Merle Collins, Linton Kwesi Johnson. I don't speak patois, but there was pressure to write in a Black idiom adhering to stereotypically 'Black' content. There are people who grew up speaking and surrounded by Nigerian English like Akure Wall but that wasn't true for me." The same way she is using the constrictions of the sonnet form to find artistic freedom, Agbabi refused the binds of stereotypical "black" poetry, charted her own path, and has enjoyed splendid support from black and racially diverse audiences and readers.

There is no single cohesive genre of contemporary black British poetry, which is very much to the good. Some themes and techniques appear with frequency: music and song; the importance of family, cultural heritage, and memory; the body; love and relationships; current events; poetry as a political force; re-representations of history; community; pan-African identity; alienation and otherness; freedom from authoritarian domination; techniques of witness that "give voice" by allowing characters to speak in the poems (whether or not otherwise disempowered); narrative and storytelling; and double voicing, where private feelings are represented alongside the face one puts on externally. It is important to recall that until *Bittersweet* and *The Fire People* were published in 1998, few anthologies of black British poetry were widely available. Many in this generation of poets (now in their twenties, thirties, and forties), as well as their elders (also cited in this essay), have looked to Dudley Randall's *The Black Poets* and Arna Bontemps's *American Negro Poetry* and the like for inspiration while also reading the standard British canon, with varying levels of connection. It is a bittersweet irony that this new British poetry that exudes historical awareness and contemporary cultural vibrancy is a gift created by the descendants of colonized subjects. Looking forward to the future of British poetry, I find it impossible to imagine that this dazzling surge of black British writing will not continue to play a major formative role.

Notes

1. SuAndi, *I Love the Blackness of My People*, unpublished poetry collection, 17.
2. I have indicated throughout this essay the cross-dialogue between African American and black British poets, as well as the influence of the American Black Arts and Civil Rights Movements on the imaginations of black British poets. For that reason, my use of the term "angry dogs" is partly a nod of respect to the example of Cave Canem, whose name was selected this way: "When Toi Derricotte shared her dream of a retreat for African American poets with Cornelius Eady and his wife Sarah Micklem, they agreed to work together to make it a reality. In Pompeii, Italy, they found a fitting symbol for the safe space they hoped to create: the mosaic of a dog guarding the entry to the House of the Tragic Poet, with the inscription CAVE CANEM (Beware of the Dog)." (http://www.cavecanempoets.org/ pages/ about.html #history.)
3. I use the term "urban griots" descriptively to refer to a perceived social and aesthetic role and function applied to some black British poets, but also wish to recognize the important and seminal group by that name in the United Kingdom that started in 1997. One of the founding members of this group was Fatimah Kelleher, whose inspiration for Urban Griots came during an academic year abroad in Atlanta, where she "first became aware of the cultural importance [that] performance poetry was having on the 'nineties generation, and became enamoured with the heady fusion of literary scholarship, hip-hop militancy and New Age spirituality that had started its journey in the spoken word hubs of Chicago and New York. Collaborating with friends who also wished to see this movement gain momentum in the multi-cultural and rich literary traditions found in London, Urban Griots made its debut in Brixton's Bug Bar." (http://www.cityofwomen-a.si/2001/ fatimah_kelleher.html.) Here is another example of a black British poet inspired by a combination of factors in post–Black Arts Movement America, but who aimed to adapt the values and energy to a specifically urban English context. I cite Breis as an "urban griot" for his poetic mission, but he also is associated with this specific group.
4. Lemn Sissay, ed., *The Fire People: A Collection of Contemporary Black British Poets* (Edinburgh: The Payback Press, 1998), 8.
5. Grace Nichols, "The Fat Black Woman Goes Shopping," *The Fat Black Woman's Poems* (London: Virago, 1984).
6. See Moniza Alvi and P. Daniels, *Peacock Luggage* (Huddersfield: Smith/Doorstop Books, 1992).
7. Jackie Kay, *Other Lovers* (Newcastle upon Tyne: Bloodaxe Books, 1993), 24.
8. Karen McCarthy, ed., *Bittersweet: Contemporary Black Women's Poetry* (London: The Women's Press, 1998); Courttia Newland and Kadija Sesay, eds., *IC3: The Penguin Book of New Black Writing in Britain* (London: Hamish Hamilton, 2000).
9. Personal correspondence to Lauri Ramey, 1999.
10. *The Firebox: Poetry in Britain and Ireland after 1945*, edited by Sean O'Brien, was published by Picador in 1998 to much acclaim as a site of preservation of the great British tradition extending into the present.

The seventy-five featured poets include Ted Hughes, Philip Larkin, Peter N. F. Porter, Fleur Adcock, Seamus Heaney, Paul Muldoon, Sylvia Plath, R. S. Thomas, E. G. Morgan, Andrew Motion, Ciaran Carson, Eavan Boland, Kathleen Jamie, and Peter Reading.

11. Patience Agbabi, "Word of Mouth: Deconstructing the 'p' words: 'performance,' 'page' and 'poetry,' " unpublished M.A. thesis, University of Sussex, 2002, 15.

12. Mike Phillips, *London Crossings: A Biography of Black Britain* (London and New York: Continuum, 2001), 143–157.

13. J. Saunders Redding, *To Make a Poet Black* (Ithaca and London: Cornell University Press, 1988 [first published in 1939]), 3.

14. Phillips, *London Crossings,* 143.

15. Caryl Phillips. "Following On: The Legacy of Lamming and Selvon," *Wasafiri* 29 (Spring 1999): 34.

16. E-mail correspondence to Lauri Ramey, 1999.

17. Phillips, *London Crossings,* 156.

18. David Damrosch et al., eds., *The Longman Anthology of British Literature, Volume 2* (New York: Longman, 1999); Carl Woodring and James Shapiro, eds., *The Columbia Anthology of British Poets* (New York: Columbia University Press, 1995); E. Talbot Donaldson et al., eds., *The Norton Anthology of English Literature, Volume 2* (New York and London: W. W. Norton & Co., 1993); Keith Tuma, ed., *Anthology of Twentieth-Century British & Irish Poetry* (New York and Oxford: Oxford University Press, 2001).

19. Richard Caddel and Peter Quartermain, eds., *Other: British and Irish Poetry Since 1970* (Hanover and London: Wesleyan University Press, 1999), vviii. The quotation comes from Bunting's "The Use of Poetry," *Writing* 12 (Summer 1985): 42.

20. Interestingly, some major African American poets were first published in the United Kingdom during this period, in the Heritage Series of Black Poetry published by Paul Breman in London between 1962 and 1975. Several African American contributors have stated that they sought publication opportunities abroad because they felt the United Kingdom afforded greater aesthetic freedom to a black poet outside the ideological confines of the American Black Power Movement. Breman also published a landmark anthology that brought together a body of quite bold and innovative poetry from Africa, the United States of America, and Britain called *You Better Believe It: Black Verse in English* (Penguin, 1973). Contributors included Frank John, John La Rose, Kamau (then L. Edward) Brathwaite, Derek Walcott, Christopher Okigbo, and Amiri ("Ameer") Baraka.

21. Kimberly W. Benston, *Performing Blackness: Enactments of African-American Postmodernism* (London and New York: Routledge, 2000), 5.

22. Ibid., 6.

23. Beth-Sarah Wright. "Dub Poet Lekka Mi: An Exploration of Performance Poetry, Power and Identity Politics in Black Britain," *Black British Culture and Society: A Text Reader,* ed. Kwesi Owusu (London and New York: Routledge, 2000), 271.

24. Ibid., 271–288. My summary primarily relates to pages 271–274.

25. E-mail correspondence to Lauri Ramey, December 2003.
26. Anthony Joseph, *teragaton* (London: poisonenginepress, 1997), 16.
27. Personal correspondence to Lauri Ramey, October 1999.
28. Ibid., 15.
29. Maggie O'Sullivan, *Out of Everywhere: Linguistically Innovative Poetry by Women in North America and the U.K.* (London: Reality Street Editions, 1996).
30. E-mail correspondence to Lauri Ramey, December 2003.
31. Ron Silliman, *In the American Tree* (Orono: National Poetry Foundation, originally published in 1986 and reissued in 1999). This was one of the earliest and most important collections of the poetry and essays associated with the Language Poetry movement.
32. Peter Quartermain, *Disjunctive Poetics: From Gertrude Stein and Louis Zukofsky to Susan Howe* (Cambridge: Cambridge University Press, 1992).
33. Vanessa Richards, personal papers provided to Lauri Ramey, "Jazz Slave Ships Witness/I Burn."
34. "Post-Caribbean Reds" appears in McCarthy, ed., *Bittersweet*, 71.
35. Catherine Ugwu, *Let's Get It On: The Politics of Black Performance* (Seattle: Bay Press, 1995), 48.
36. SuAndi, *The Story of M*, published as an illustrated script in *4 For More*, ed. SuAndi (Manchester: artBlacklive, 2002), 1–18.
37. Ibid., 18.
38. E-mail correspondence to Lauri Ramey, December 2003. All quotations that follow in this section are from e-mail correspondence with Ramey, December 2003.
39. For further information on Mary Seacole, see Judith Bryan's incisive essay in this volume (chapter 4). Seacole's own autobiography, *The Wonderful Adventures of Mary Seacole in Many Lands*, now is also available.
40. Here Agbabi is picking up on an aphorism coined by Don Paterson, poetry editor at Picador: "*Read Poetry: It's Really Quite Hard.*" Agbabi notes that Paterson is signifying here on (former) Faber & Faber editor T. S. Eliot's statement in "The Metaphysical Poets" that "poets in our civilization . . . must be difficult." This information is on the first page of Agbabi's unpublished M.A. thesis "Word of Mouth" (full citation in note 11).
41. Agbabi, "Word of Mouth."
42. This is an important topic in Lorenzo Thomas's "Neon Griot: The Functional Role of Poetry Readings in the Black Arts Movement," *Close Listening and the Performed Word*, ed. Charles Bernstein (New York and Oxford: Oxford University Press, 1998); see especially, 307–317.
43. Unpublished interview with Patience Agbabi by Lauri Ramey, December 2, 2003, in Cardiff, Wales. All quotations that follow are from the same interview.
44. Thomas, "Neon Griot," 304.
45. Patience Agbabi, "Prologue," *Transformatrix* (Edinburgh: Payback Press, 2000), 9.
46. Agbabi, *R.A.W.* (London: Izon Amazon/Gecko Press, 1995).
47. Agbabi, *Transformatrix*, 78.

CHAPTER 8

THE SOCIOPOLITICS OF
BLACK BRITAIN IN THE WORK OF
BUCHI EMECHETA

Susan Yearwood

When I first came across fiction by Buchi Emecheta, I was already an undergraduate student of black literature at the University of East London in 1989. I was familiar with the works of Ama Ata Aidoo, Chinua Achebe, and Bessie Head and eager to advance my knowledge of postcolonial discourse from the African diaspora. Although I had studied works by contemporary writers of Caribbean parentage living in London (e.g., Joan Riley and Caryl Phillips), I had yet to enjoy the work of an African-born writer who wrote about the London experience.

Indeed, Buchi Emecheta has been writing in and about London, England, for almost thirty years. She has published fourteen novels as well as children's books. Born in Lagos, Nigeria, in 1944, she is of Ibuza parentage. She studied at a colonial Methodist high school for girls before becoming pregnant and moving with her then husband to London in 1962. She received an honours degree in Sociology from the University of London in 1974 and worked subsequently as a teacher, librarian, and community worker. She began to write with some success after her marriage ended. Her first novel, *In the Ditch*, was published in 1972; her second, *Second Class Citizen*, in 1974. Both novels are semi-autobiographical and depict the life of Adah, a Nigerian-born, single mother living in North London during the early 1960s.

What interests me about Emecheta, apart from her prolific literary output, is the sociopolitical dimension of her fiction. Much of Emecheta's fiction directly concerns the lives of women in or from West Africa. These women suffer tragic struggles against neo-colonialism—a particularized economic exploitation—and the patriarchy that is firmly entrenched in West African religious and ontological traditions. Emecheta's fiction maps the social trajectories of West African women on the continent and in Britain and reveals the political nature of mores and communities that shape a woman's destiny wherever she may live. Both *In the Ditch* and *Second Class Citizen* are studies of the exploitation and displacement of African women who, like their Caribbean contemporaries, migrated for economic reasons to Britain in the postwar era.

The most significant migrant influx from the Caribbean (now known as the "Windrush generation") had occurred earlier, in the late 1940s. By the early 1960s the succeeding masses were no more "clued up" on what was to happen to them once they touched Britain's shores than the earlier arrivants had been. As was the case with Emecheta's protagonist Adah, their knowledge of their adopted society was prescriptive and, to a certain extent, atavistic. Caribbean and African notions about social positioning were obfuscated by Britain's inherited color and class codes as well as by what V. S. Naipaul has referred to as "the Enigma of Arrival" (Donnell and Welsh 1996: 207, 261–262).

The title of Emecheta's first novel is metonymical and instructive: the ditch is the situation that Adah finds herself in after her marriage breaks up. Her husband denies his family in a court of law and burns her passport, wedding certificate, and the manuscript that she has been working on. She is forced to live with her children in the rat-infested room provided by an African landlord. The ditch is also Pussy Cat Mansions, the filthy tenements Adah and her family inhabit after they relocate to escape the first landlord's harassment. When eventually Adah lives on welfare, the ditch appears in many additional forms and symbols, most notably in terms of the continuum of political and social discontent with which Adah becomes familiar. We learn from the author's narrative that Adah is a determined woman whose initial confidence in her new home is nullified by the economic and cultural realities that inform her life.

The ditch itself is a feminized space, inhabited by Adah and the other women living at the Mansions. Their discontent is associated with their gender; Adah and the white women "in the ditch" battle within similar social constraints, which are, in the main, patriarchal, and encounter parallel discourtesies that inform their dialectic as women. Adah's gaze remains that of the Other among a group of unwaged, working-class white women and welfare officers. While not being quite the equivalent of the nineteenth-century hysteric (Kahane 1995), Adah is depicted as either enacting verbal asides to herself (1994: 8) or being passive within conversations with other women in her new surroundings. Throughout exchanges within which Adah experiences self-doubt or self-denigration, her utterances become more passive. During a conversation with her welfare officer, Adah is depicted as speaking on few occasions. Instead, she is represented by indirect speech that includes asides about the welfare officer's physical disparities, a deceptively objective eye that does much to mirror Adah's own self-doubt. Consequently, the feminized space that tells us of Adah's social positioning is also conscious of race and, according to Emecheta's narrative, named by it. Adah's outlook and vision are determined by her ideas about race and her new reality.

It is important here to look more closely at Emecheta's rendering of Adah's immutable space, the British social "ditch," especially as determining the basic ideas around this is essential to a better understanding of the political as well as cultural machinations that constructed that space and established its social efficacy. With Adah as a gendered, racialized representative of black migration, and with *black* designated as African and Caribbean rather than Asian, the English inner city, in this case London, becomes her cultural space, her political milieu. Adah, the Other, is symbolic. Her condition symbolizes what the state has deemed appropriate for black migrants. Her space also symbolizes what the migrant's immediate and preceding communities consider appropriate. If we suppose that the rat in Adah's first home in London is a metaphor for the fear of Otherness and of its dual forces—Homi Bhabha has called them determination and difference—we see Adah at the mercy of feelings that can be ephemeral yet self-defining, cultured yet irresponsibly volatile. The rat is her nemesis, in a sense, because Adah must, for a while, remain in the space assigned to her. Her first landlord is an agent provocateur, a withered token of displaced African patriarchy that tests Adah in her new role as migrant when he attempts to use witchcraft on her so that she will leave his property. Here ideas on gendered and cultural duality become clearer. The landlord becomes representative of an anachronism that places Adah's thinking on divergent planes. Adah is, as she herself perceives, neither a Londoner nor an African from Lagos, but she can see things through a neutralised dual perspective. In fact, she declares that the landlord's display would have appeared out of place in her home district—he is Yoruba, she is Igbo. The political import of the moment is the dual seeing and the Othered retentions; not one of the characters watches the landlord's exhibition with a culturally aware eye. White onlookers catch the landlord—in fully feathered regalia—in the act of terrorizing Adah; Adah, wearing a *lappa*, a traditional Nigerian dress, endures their gaze with him. The African migrants are no longer solely the protagonists, but the antagonized.

Adah has a choice after all and finds it in the feminized space of the moment. Her white co-tenant forces a change of events by contacting local government authorities while Adah maintains the visceral anonymity of the migrant and the passive utterances of the Othered; the protagonist utters asides to herself throughout the event and does not tell the authorities about her landlord's alarming display and his deranged harassment of her family. Therefore, Adah's immutable space is defined by her Otherness and the sociopolitical conditions that place her there. She begins, in the novel, as a working mother struggling to maintain a certain independent status quo for the sake of her young children and her sanity, but finding the task too difficult to follow through with, Adah accepts the financial offerings of the Welfare State, despite her earlier, ideological quest for dignified self-expression and economic autonomy.

The dole, or welfare, becomes a convenient, if wholly unrewarding, financial crutch for Adah. At the time of publication, critics saw Emecheta's trajectory for Adah as improbable; it represented an unbelievable step for someone of Adah's educational level and social position in Africa to take. Emecheta's reviewers were hostile to Adah's new social positioning and considered Adah's line of reasoning, her tolerance of poor childcare, and the threat of Social Services' intervention to be unacceptable. The authorial use, implied or otherwise, of the feminized space was glossed over as a political crutch, and the gendered message was missed as an urgent aspect of national social care.

Emecheta's response to such criticism was to write a prequel to describe how Adah found herself in such a position in the first place. The muted utterances of the Other become, in the prequel, strikingly politicized and more confident. While in *In the Ditch* Adah articulates the views concerning debilitating poverty and increasing dependence on social care as she moves into a particularized, feminized space, *Second Class Citizen* is concerned with the corrosive nature of Adah's relationship with her husband, Francis, and the isolation she encounters as a woman, subsequent to their separation. As the implied author, using Booth's post-structuralist definition of the interpretation of texts (Bal 1985: 120) implies, black Britain was in political and moral turmoil in the 1960s, with black men finding their masculinity challenged by the state's patriarchy and belittled within their disempowered new roles. Black women like Adah were challenged by the unsupportable degradation of their men and the prejudices these women encountered toward their own womanhood. As Barbara Christian noted, the likes of Francis only show the masculine attributes of "power and acquisition [as] phantom qualities" (1985: 185)—because these attributes are unrealistic for black men in this new and toxic environment.

Emecheta's third novel, *The Bride Price*, chronologically the first instalment of this trilogy, I shall not discuss fully here, but relate the fact that it recounts the social economics of Adah's existence as a West African woman under the system of patriarchy existing in Lagos. Again, Emecheta takes a step back in time to place Adah within a space that is recognizable to anyone familiar with the role of patriarchy and its part in determining female deviance. In *The Bride Price*, Adah is sold, in the guise of a dowry, to her husband by her family; and in *Second Class Citizen*, we find her struggling in her relationship with that husband. Francis is a struggling student who, though financially dependent on Adah, asserts his dominance by causing her mental and physical anguish. It was common at the time for young African men to educate themselves in Britain and harbor the notion of a return home with qualifications and economic security. Francis is not exceptional, but only representative of the dynamics of economic migration. He defines and restricts Adah's self-determination and social position, constructing for her a space as restrictive as the feminized space that articulates itself at Pussy Cat Mansions, the housing estate of Emecheta's first novel, *In the Ditch*.

Early in *Second Class Citizen*, Adah works in the civil service in Lagos and is economically sound enough to support her husband and his family. She therefore experiences a rude awakening when she finds such prospects out-of-bounds for her in London by virtue of her outsider social status. She begins her life in London as a "second-class citizen," following Francis in his quest for education and witnessing his thwarted masculinity in this new setting. As a recent black migrant, she is not thought to merit the social prestige she enjoyed in Lagos. Her race determines the housing income that is acceptable for herself and her family and, at first, she feels confined by the choices made by her husband in her absence. It is he who tells her that she is a second-class citizen in her new home and it is at this point in the novel that we can locate the shift in sociopolitics that dominates Adah's new thinking.

Francis is a determinant; his role in Adah's life is important, as it has been in Lagos. What appeared to amount to her economic autonomy and raised class status in Lagos was actually due to a predestined role determined by the adverse effects of patriarchy. The monolithic male head of family, represented by Francis in London, is a role delegated to Francis's parents in Lagos, and although this positioning kept her from being physically beaten by Francis, Adah remained bound by the social and political mores that defined her. Any recognition or acceptance of Adah's income dominance is corrected by Igbo social customs. In London, Francis's acceptance of the new world order and grudging ability to conform places Adah both outside and divergent from his thinking. Adah remains the person who brings in the money, which puts her on par with other black female economic migrants who shared her social status. However, as parental dominance is removed from his new social domain, so Francis identifies the role of second-class citizenship by focusing on its racial determinants in British society and enforcing its genderized dominance.

Francis, also a second-class citizen in his own lexicon, is unhappy in London with having to share a social status identical to that of his wife. Therefore, he must unsettle her, damage any sign of self-determinism or genderized autonomy, in order to place himself in line with the dominant status quo within British society. As he is not earning an income and his status, as defined by that society, precludes him from social parity with his white peers, he finds recompense in the notion of male-gendered didacticism and ruthless hegemony within his own household. He ritualizes his sense of self-determinism and his rightful status within this foreign, post-traditional society by beating his wife and possessing a white prostitute as a lover. Francis becomes both morally and culturally divisive and his role is perhaps metaphorically in keeping with the state's corrosive quality made clearer later in the narrative.

Black Britain is depicted as being morally and socially corrupt, determined by its deficiencies—poverty, racism, sexism—rather than by its strengths. Adah is subjugated and predictably muted by the perseverance of Francis, the abject personification of confused masculinity. His self-determination as a second-class citizen specifies her own meager options and is stultifying. Adah's response is to be reified as an independent mother with five children, a seemingly impossible juxtaposition, but one that enables her to locate the feminized space that becomes a major concern in Emecheta's writing. In parts of the narrative, the feminized space gives way to a reading of neurosis at its most fundamental; Adah loses interest in her appearance and hygiene and becomes increasingly cut off from the outside world physically and through her own utterances. The deepening of this neurosis is transitory yet reveals the gaps and fissures within what was the norm to provide a reading of abnormality, inarticulateness, and the move away from the autodidactic. Adah does not go totally mad but releases herself from personal responsibility and autonomy in the way that only the mad do, unconditionally. In *In the Ditch*, she stops herself from falling even deeper into a malaise by taking stock of her responsibilities and reasserting herself through a more vital appropriation of speech and the utterance.

The sociopolitical problems in Adah's life—including the hazards of patriarchy, poverty, motherhood, and self-determinism—continue to be central to the lives of the black female migrant from Africa and the Caribbean living in London and throughout Britain. Emecheta personalizes multiracial Britain's "irresistible rise" (Phillips and Phillips 1998) as contentious and invariably corrupted by the status quo—such as the inadequacies of the social welfare system in London during the 1960s—and in so doing relates the case histories that name our dilemma in contemporary Britain.

Works Cited

Bal, Meike. *Narratology.* Canada: University of Toronto Press, 1985.

Bhabha, Homi. *The Location of Culture.* London: Routledge, 1994.

Christian, Barbara. *Black Women Novelists: The Development of a Tradition, 1892–1976.* Connecticut: Greenwood Press, 1985.

Donnell, Alison and Sarah Lawson Welsh. *The Routledge Reader in Caribbean Literature.* London: Routledge, 1996.

Emecheta, Buchi. *Second Class Citizen.* Orig. pub. 1974. Oxford: Heinemann, rpt. 1994.

———. *In the Ditch.* Orig. pub. 1972. Oxford: Heinemann, rpt. 1994.

———. *The Bride Price.* New York: Braziller, 1976.

Kahane, Claire. *Passions of the Voice: Hysteria, Narrative, and the Figure of the Speaking Woman, 1850–1915.* Baltimore: Johns Hopkins University Press, 1995.

Phillips, Mike and Trevor Phillips. *Windrush: The Irresistible Rise of Multi-Racial Britain.* London: HarperCollins, 1998.

CHAPTER 9

DETERRITORIALIZATION, BLACK BRITISH WRITERS, AND THE CASE OF BEN OKRI

Jude Chudi Okpala

The quest for definition, beginning with the logocentric histories of the West, has always been engaged through politics of exclusion. Such politics marked Kadija George Sesay's argument at a Black British Writers Conference held at Howard University. In mapping the works of black British writers, she excluded Ben Okri and vigorously discussed Bernardine Evaristo's *Lara*. Unlike Okri, Evaristo was born in England. It would not be unreasonable to suppose that Sesay's definition—exclusion and inclusion—may have been founded on her degree of familiarity with these writers, and, as such, suggests what I choose to call eclectic hermeneutics, selective reading, which is the *bête noire* of the politics of exclusion. This exclusion, which, of course, follows the protocol of representation, operates at two levels. It is a form of "repression operated as a sentence to disappear"; it is also "an affirmation of non-existence, and, by implication, an admission that there is nothing to say about such, nothing to see, and nothing to know"[1] about Okri as black British writing. The protocol of representation that Sesay uses to identify black British writers who are born in England—that is, signifying on a black cultural ethos—is common in the writings of other black émigrés in Britain, including Okri. Although she seems to say that British-born black writers do not use the protocol to enact their longing to go home, there is in their pragmatic labels, however, an enactment of their consciousness of their home, of their participation in celebrating, like other black writers in England, their provenance and identity.

My focus is to present Okri as a black British writer, and I proceed in three parts: (1) An apologetic discourse on Okri's narratives, *The Famished*

Road and *Songs of Enchantment*; (2) A discussion of Okri's narrative as deterritorializing—as a border writing; (3) An examination of Okri as a British writer.

Okri: An Apologia

Defending Okri as a black British writer seems ironical. Okri describes himself as a Nigerian who lives in London and writes in English. This description subtly denies labeling, as it evokes exilic imperatives. "Is the exiled writer primarily concerned with preserving his national tradition or with opening up a new influence? What are the favorite topics of the exiled writer? Is he part of the avant-garde of an incipient 'world literature?' How different is the situation of the émigré who only began to write once he was abroad from that of the writer who had already established his literary credentials at home? Should the émigré writer strive toward literary/social integration in the new community? What is the nature of the creative process doomed to be ignored, given the condition of exile?"[2] These questions, though raised in the context of the political assault and process of displacement from home that go with exile, should as well be asked regarding Okri.

Perhaps, the Eurocentric interpretations that are given to his works might be traced to his self-definition and not to the implications and benefits of his exilic condition. For in discussing *The Famished Road* and *Songs of Enchantment*, critics use a predetermined aesthetics, namely that of "magic realism." An African literature discussion group of the University of California at Santa Barbara, through a world wide web, solicits articles that discuss "magic realism" in Okri's works. Critics congregate here, as the web explains, to discuss formal and thematic issues in Okri, "to make sense of [his] quick jumps between realistic and mythical events, his description of mythical events with realistic details or real events through mythical figures, his violation of the unity of time or place, his exploration of liminal spaces, his proliferation of characters who transform themselves, his uncanny imagination. . . ."[3] But that sort of reading forges a different accessibility to the text, at the price of immense misinterpretation and in the absence of a critical analysis of the historical and cultural context of the novels.

Identifying Okri's narrative as magic realism is anachronistic, a violent translation and displacement. Works are translated not only when they cross from one language to another; to cite John H. Miller, "A work is, in a sense, 'translated,' that is displaced, transported, carried across, even when it is read in its original language by someone who belongs to another country and another culture."[4] Reading Okri's works as magic realism does exactly that.

The term *magic realism* comes from art history—which has nothing to do with Nigerian *weltanschaung*—where it has been used to describe Arnold Bocklin's and Giorgio di Chirico's works. Further, magic realism might be said to be a departure from the classic Western "realist" novels (those of Honoré de Balzac, Henry James, Gustave Flaubert, George Eliot) whose omniscient narrators commented on and defined every thought of their characters—that is, a departure from a hegemonic Western point of view. Such a departure may be legitimate because the West is experiencing a crisis of identity with its so-called realist narratives, but it is not proper to extend the crisis, and hence magic realism, to all narratives that exemplify such a departure. As D. Emily Hicks notes, speaking of border writing, "this term [*magic realism*] obscures important issues such as narrative non-linearity, the decentered subject . . . [and it denies] the larger, broader understanding of reality that informs" the text.[5] It is pertinent to note that before magic realism became a tool for reading literature, Nigerian writers were already telling stories of spirit-children—living a life that is best described with Achebe's aesthetic of "flying without perching"—having no particular locus—of enchanted horizon, of the human's interface with the spirit world.

In an interview with Jean W. Ross, Okri claims that those things that are considered magical in his novels are simply realistic representations of Nigerian experience: "I'm looking at the world in *The Famished Road* from inside the African worldview, but without it being codified as such. That is just the way the world is seen: the dead really are not dead, the ancestors are still part of the living community. . . . So what seems like surrealism or fantastic writing actually is not fantastic writing, it's simply writing about the place in the spirit of the place. I'm not trying in the slightest to produce strange effects."[6]

To use magic realism in reading Okri novels simply depoliticizes and traduces them; it weakens and uproots their cultural difference from the West's own semblance. Even the title *The Famished Road* is an enactment of Nigerian ethos: "In the South-western Nigeria, there are special prayers said to the road asking it not to swallow up suppliants on their journey. In Soyinka's *Ibadan, The Road*, and *Death in the Dawn*, this prayer is used, and the name of his alter ego in *Ibadan*, Maren, is a contraction of such a prayer . . . : 'May you not walk when the road waits, famished.' "[7] The title suggests that the road has the capacity of swallowing a sojourner, or of interfering in the affairs of the people who tread on it. More important, the title evokes the formidable deity associated with *ani*, earth.

Azaro's journeys and Madam Koto's liminal presence, in *The Famished Road* and *Songs of Enchantment* respectively, cannot merely be viewed as imaginative excesses, but rather as salient representations of

Nigerian sensibility. In Madam Koto's case, it is a belief in witchcraft. She "is shown as highly resourceful, independent and ambitious. When she is first introduced in the narrative, her credentials are rapidly established by her wrestling with a drunken customer who tries to make trouble after being defeated at draughts in her bar. . . . The rumour mill turns out an elaborate and coherent understanding of Madame Koto's character" and is "based entirely on witchcraft" (Quayson 144). Many evils are attributed to her: people said that she had buried three husbands and seven children, that she was a witch who ate her babies when they were still in her womb; they said she was the real reason why the children in the area didn't grow, why they were always ill, why the men never got promotions, and why the women in the area suffered miscarriages; they said she had a charmed beard and that she plucked one hair out every day and dropped it into the palm-wine she sold; they said she belonged to a secret society that flies through the air at night. Okri's description of Madame Koto serves as a literary inscription of some of the attitudes toward strong-willed women in Nigerian society. In Yoruba, where Okri grew up, and in Igbo land, there is a process of demonization of women. "The first level of the process involves linking the marketplace, the very seat of women's commercial activities, to Eshu, the god of mischief" (Quayson 145). Even a woman's commercial success is linked to witchcraft. A witch is said to prosper through her liaison with the spirit. This idea is expressed in the assertion that Madame Koto uses her charmed beard to sell palm-wine.

Azaro, a spirit-child, *abiku*, is another means Okri uses to illustrate a Nigerian worldview. Okri is not the only person who uses the *abiku* (*ogbanje*) theme. Chinua Achebe uses it in *Things Fall Apart*, in the case of Ezinma; Buchi Emecheta uses it in *The Slave Girl*; John Pepper Clark uses the same theme in *The Masquerade*; Amos Tutuola, in his animist sensibility, does so in *The Palm-Wine Drinkard*. Soyinka, in *Aké*, uses Bukola as a resting place of the otherworldly spirits. Soyinka describes her as "one of the denizens of that other world where voices were caught, sieved, re-spun and cast back in diminishing copies."[8] These authors connect *abiku* to that which comes from an individual, but is not imprisoned in a corporeal self. The proliferation of this theme suggests how integral the concept of *abiku* is to Nigerian sensibility.

At the simplest level, Azaro represents a world with a continuity between the realistic and mystical realms of experience. In *The Famished Road*, Azaro observes, "In that land of the beginnings spirits mingled with the unborn. We could assume numerous forms. Many of us were birds. We knew no boundaries. . . . Our king was a wonderful personage who sometimes appeared in the form of a great rat. . . . He had been born uncountable times. . . . We are the strange ones, with half of our beings always in the spirit."[9] In *Songs of Enchantment*, Okri makes a similar claim, "Yes, the spirit-child is an unwilling adventurer into chaos and sunlight, into the dreams of the living and the dead."[10] In these texts, Okri introduces a character whose main and most striking quality is his duality and ability to transcend physical space and time. An interesting thing to note as well in the first passage (earlier) is the use of the plural first-person pronoun: *we*. The pronoun suggests that the *abiku* is not a single entity; *abiku* even has a king; in addition, the pronoun suggests that everyone participates in this being, and does not refer back to a single subject, but to a collective perception. What Azaro says in the beginning of *The Famished Road* signifies a collective worldview, signaling a unified vision of animist metaphysics. As Soyinka observes, "It is not . . . a question of difference between 'I' and 'We' but a deeper subsumption of the self into vision and experience."[11] Using such a strategy, Okri wants to show that Nigerians understand *abiku* as an integral part of their worldview, where all things are linked. It is this worldview that critics have to investigate to interpret Okri, a world filled with "gifted men and women known variously as *dibias*, medicine specialists, herbalists, and priests who in one way another have access to the parallel worlds of spirits and ancestors" (Maggi Phillips, Afrlit). Magic realism as a concept cannot capture the true essence of this world.

What does the magic of explaining the imbroglio is Okri's "The African Way":

> . . . The Way of compassion and fire and serenity; The Way of freedom and power and imaginative life; The Way that keeps the mind open to the existences beyond our earthly sphere, that keeps the spirit pure and primed to all the rich possibilities of living, that makes of their minds gateways through which all the thought-forms of primal creation can wander and take root and flower; The Way through which forgotten experiments in living can re-surface with fuller results even in insulated and innocent communities; The Way that makes it possible for them to understand the language of angels and gods, birds and trees, animals and spirits; The Way that makes them greet phenomena forever as a brother and a sister in mysterious reality; The Way that develops and keeps its secrets of transformation—hate into love, beast into man, man into illustrious ancestor, ancestor into god; The Way whose centre grows from divine love, whose roads are always open for messages from all the spheres to keep coming through; The Way that preaches attunement with all the higher worlds, that believes in forgiveness and generosity of spirit, always receptive, always listening, always kindling the understanding of signs,

like the potencies hidden in snail tracks along forbidden paths; The Way
that always, like a river, flows into and flows out of the myriad Ways of
the world. (*Songs of Enchantment* 159–160)

The African Way is a metaphysical trajectory that collapses the distinction between the spiritual and physical worlds, and transcends the ratio-
nalist epistemology of Western discourse. More important, the African
Way suggests a heteroglossic culture, where all differences are dissipated.
Accordingly, Okri's *abiku* is not merely a signifier of magical realism. As
Bill Hemminger argues, the figure of *abiku* becomes a trope for Okri's
more general commentary on the nature of being. In other words: to
some extent, the *abiku* may reside in everyone.[12]

Okri, however, does not use *abiku* without enacting foreign aesthetics. He believes in some kind of multiculturalism, a confluence of cultures. In "Among the Silent Stones," he asserts, "The fact is that in
nature all organic things of single strain have short histories. Obsessions
about purity of blood have wiped out empires . . . and our roots are fed
from diverse and forgotten places."[13] Okri's aesthetics could be grouped
among those Soyinka described as possessing " 'stylistic bridges.' "[14]
Okri adroitly juxtaposes Igbo animist metaphysics and European realism/
modernism. Many critics have written on his stylistic bridges. Charles
Nnolim argues that Okri's works belong to a new modernist and aesthetic Nigerian tradition;[15] Olatubosun Ogunsanwo holds that "Okri
develops a complex cross-cultural aesthetic from," mixing realism and
myth "to bring both genres into a productive crisis through mutual
intertextual parody";[16] Margaret Cezair-Thompson maintains, "Okri
presents the regenerative force of *re*placement, rather than the debilitating colonial legacy of *dis*placement, and therefore moves beyond the historical catalepsy which has marked so much postcolonial writing."[17] It
is not my intention to discuss the stylistics as noted by these critics. I see
a totally different form of stylistic bridging, which, in essence, is a concomitant progressive transformation and subtle decaying of both Igbo
culture and Britain's psyche. With that in mind, I consider Okri's texts
as examples of deterritorializing literature, as border literature.

Okri and Border Writing

According to Deleuze and Guattari, "border literature" is made up of
texts written by a minority in a major language.[18] Such a text "emphasizes the differences in reference codes between two or more cultures and

depicts, therefore, a kind of realism that approaches the experience of border crossers, those who live in a bilingual, bicultural, biconceptual reality."[19] Okri is Igbo; writing in English, he demonstrates bilingual reality: to write in English for him is to cross over to the West, or to preserve the West he received through colonial education while keeping, at the same time, his native concepts; he becomes, thus, a smuggler of Igbo concepts into English Language, and thereby disrupts the one way flow of Igbo or English semantic constructions; such a technique creates a "dialectical image," which refuses the violence in which the West dominates, and creates a "matrix of interaction" that can resist "symbolization."[20] Recognizing the ontological poverty of postcolonialism and postmodernism as representative labels for Okri, John C. Hawley suggests a montage: "postcolonial postmodernity," through which Okri challenges "the European master narratives of history . . . with alternative ontological system . . ." and employs aporetic dispositions.[21] Hawley's nomenclature seems like a stitching of old names and ideas; it addresses more philosophically, though, *abiku*'s intractable locality and consciousness.

Okri's *abiku* is a sign of this disposition, and, in itself, a border metaphor. Niyi Osundare's observation should be appropriate in this connection: "The morphological agglutination in Abiku . . . reflects the mystery child's fusion of two states of being and non-being. It creates a situation in which being born and dying become an integrated cycle. With the passage of time the sequence of occurrence becomes irrelevant as a + bi + ku one + born to die becomes synonymous with a + ku + bi, one + dead = (to be) born—a cyclical feat that makes Abiku truly ageless."[22] Okri employs this integration of spheres well. Discussing such a concept in English, he brings into English an only partially translatable concept. Noting that Okri lives in London would be significant here. He conducts his daily business in English, converses in the English language, and keeps silent, of course, his native concepts, like palm-wine, *ogwu*, and so on—except when he is among his fellow Igbo, who understand these concepts. But when he writes, he escapes the rigor of English language usage and employs a kind of polylingualism that challenges the centrality of English language. Take these passages from *The Famished Road*, where Azaro tells about his mother's sickness, for example:

When I woke up, Mum was sweating and quivering on the bed. Dad had bought malaria medicine and bitter roots which were marinated in yellow alcohol. Dad, noticing what was happening to me, snatched me from Mum's frightened embrace, and made me drink of the bitter dogonyaro, as a precaution. (53)

Another example occurs when Azaro recounts one of his spiritual encounters:

I was awoken by voices in the dark. I was on Mum's shoulder and I saw faces of women in the rain, faces lit up by lightning flash. . . . There was a man asleep on the chair. . . . On the center table, in front of him, there was a half-empty bottle of Ogogoro. (28)

In *Songs of Enchantment*, Okri reminisces on Western traditions, on the lost philosophies of Pythagoras, on powerful symphonies, while discussing some African (Igbo) mannerisms:

That night the Jackal-headed Masquerade, surrounded by its multiples and companions of hyenas and panthers, chanting with the voices of possessed men, wreaked an incredible violence on the forces of the wind and forest, slaughtering the spirits and the insurgent women, murdering the trees. . . . I saw the old man turn into a green vulture. . . . When the Jackal-headed Masquerade laughed three hundred children died in the country in secret ways, and many fathers went berserk. . . . I saw the blind old man that night, in a Black suit and Black shoes. He went around in his new guise, supervising the carnage inflicted on our area. . . . The old man inspected the evidence of his powers. He inspected the twisted forms of animals . . . the quivering maniacal rage of his followers and party supporters in their unholy bacchanalian possession. Their faces were covered with masks from whose tight nostrils they breathed in fumes. . . . The masks possessed the wearers with the image of menace carved on their dread-manufacturing features. The wearers became their masks, and the masks took on their own true life, enacting the violence of the blind old man's sorcerous dictates. (138–145)

These passages enact a stylistic bridge that is intercultural as well as interlingual: they are purveyors of "texts from one signifying form into another, the transporting of texts from one historical context to another, and the tracking of migration of meaning from one cultural space to another."[23] In addition, they represent forms of polylingual relationships and hybridity that figure centrally in the novels. In the first two passages, you have a simple relationship, where Okri introduces words that are untranslatable: *traduttore, traditore*. These words stand out, defying English signification; they aim at identifying the gap between mother tongue and English. What is *dogonyaro*? What is *ogogoro*? What is yellow alcohol?

Dogonyaro is a medication for malaria, and it is made by cooking the leaves of a particular tree. It is naturally bitter, but has the power to dissipate fever and stomach ache. *Ogogoro* is a homemade liquor derived from palm-wine; it is colorless and equivalent to Remy Martin, Courvoisier, and Hennessey. Although "yellow alcohol" is an English phrase, connoting a unity of two distinct ideas, the meaning of *ogogoro* cannot be deciphered by associating those two ideas. Here is an example where de Saussure's binary system of the signifier and the signified is cast overboard as a culturally insensitive theory. One may verify the reality of such a concept by empirically looking for a yellowish alcoholic drink; one can as well believe that such alcohol exists if one finds a yellowish alcoholic drink in a liquor store; but that is not what Okri's "yellow alcohol" is. Yellow alcohol is a medicine (*ogwu*) for malaria and fever. It is a medley of roots—not just any roots—and *ogogoro* or water; before this combination can be effective, it must be left for some days. During that time, the roots dissolve their bitter essence into the *ogogoro* solution, and thereby turn colorless *ogogoro* to yellow. In using such a representation as "yellow alcohol," Okri has migrated his native concept into an English vocabulary, while creating ideas that may seem alien and decontextualized to Igbo and non-Igbo readers alike. In this connection, Okri would appear imperceptible because he is locating himself vis-à-vis both English and Igbo consciousnesses; to quote Deleuze and Guattari, he is, indeed, creating a "collective assemblage of enunciation," a hyphenated discourse.[24]

This form of assemblage occurs in Okri's use of complex relationships, of which the third passage (earlier) provides an example. That passage relates the activity of Jackal-headed Masquerade and the blind old man and his entourage. These entities have supernatural powers; as you can see from the description, the blind man is a *dibia*, not unlike the one Okonkwo uses to cure Ezinma in *Things Fall Apart*. In *Songs of Enchantment*, the *dibia* is diabolic, just as they are sometimes in reality. In Igbo culture, masquerades represent spirits who may possess the dancers, giving them special knowledge, which they express through their disabling performance. The mask confers on the person wearing it the essence and powers of the spirit or ancestor it symbolizes. The wearers of masks are subject to constraints and taboos, which protect them from the dangerous powers of masks they don. Okri is not essentially imaginative in that passage; he uses Igbo cultural norms that are, of course, defiant and resistant as to English signification. Saying that the old man inspects the evidence of his power, Okri is suggesting that he examines his *ogwu*, talismanic elements that allow him to interfere with the flow of things, and he does: the old blind man does animate the spirit of the masks to revenge the violence done by the masquerade.

Okri is suggesting that the masquerade has committed a taboo in this performance, that the wearers of the masks do not represent the spirits and the ancestors properly.

At this juncture, I should note a phrase that stands out in the third quoted passage: "unholy bacchanalian possession." The phrase creates a dialogic rupture as it invokes Greek and Roman gods of wine and revelry. Okri uses that image to embed a picture of recklessness and impropriety. "By embedding and implicating one generation's story in the folds of another's, [Okri's] text compels the reader to think in terms of modes, as well as levels . . . to ask, What are the enabling and disabling narrative conditions on which . . . [the] African novel in English depends? Is there a mother tongue in the text? How [do we] identify the tension, the stress points, the violence that results when the colonial language and its literary conventions and cultural assumptions encounter the indigenous Igbo modes and strategies and the value they convey?"[25] By invoking Bacchus, Okri seems to deterritorialize the concept, that is, to displace and recreate it. Tagging European language onto a European concept and using it to explain the Igbo worldview decontextualizes the concept because it has migrated to another cultural space; and using the Igbo worldview to contextualize a bacchanalian frenzy indigenizes it. In brief, then, this function of indigenizing results from a stylistic ensemble of traditions. In this connection, Okri's novels are on a continuum: they do not present native ideas and concepts as static, but as agents of change that (themselves) undergo change.

Okri and Black British Literature

Okri's participation in recreating Western concepts through polylingualism suggests a heterogeneity of being, as well as refigures and reimagines geographies, community, and identity. As Okri observed, "We are all mixtures. . . . Those who think that the homogenizing forces of the world will not turn their valued spaces into little deserts without mystery deserve to see the coming of the storm" (*A Way of Being Free* 100–102). Based on his observation, can we classify Okri as one thing or another and, so, reduce him to a desert? Is he an African writer, a British writer, or a black British writer? Are Olaudah Equiano and Phillis Wheatley black British authors?

Equiano and Wheatley were Africans. They were exported from Africa as slaves. In this economic and brutal transaction, they thrived and wrote. Today, Africans, African Americans, Americans, and Britons claim them as their own literary figures, not because they were indigenes, but because their literary expression followed the traditions that make up the protocol of aesthetic representation for these nations; however, the works of Equiano and Wheatley are a traffic of cultures, ruptures of any one-dimensional epistême. For them, identity requires definition outside the boundary, where ethnicity is both significant and insignificant.

Like them, though not as a commodity, Okri came out of Africa. He traveled to London in 1961 when he was three years old, having been born in 1959 in Lagos, Nigeria. In 1966, he was sent back to Nigeria, where he continued his education. What was education in Nigeria then, if not British? An educated Nigerian, in those days, knew the streets of London because London was like a neighboring town. Some Nigerians assumed some degree of Englishness, speaking the Queen's English, practicing an imported etiquette that suggested their proximity to the British Queen and the outlandishness of native Nigerian manners and sensibility. In this circumstance, a typical Nigerian was English. Okri may not classify himself as such, however, because he was in Nigeria when it was in the throes of a civil war that was in part attributable to the negative excrescence of foreign legislation. By the time he turned eighteen, he moved once again to England, which was at that time a second home for self-exiled Nigerians.

In simple parlance, Okri exhibits the poetics of "errantry," to use Édouard Glissant's term. "Errantry . . . does not proceed from renunciation nor from frustration regarding a supposedly deteriorated (deterritorialized) situation of origin; it is not a resolute act of rejection or an uncontrolled impulse of abandonment. . . . That is very much the image of the rhizome, prompting the knowledge that identity is no longer completely with the root but also in Relation."[26] Having lived in London and having read scores of works of Western literature from his father's library, Okri activates in his works perspectives that combine indigenous Nigerian beliefs and Western models. He forges a relationship between Africa (Igbo) and the West. His use of stream-of-consciousness narration and of the off-centering and reaggregating of identities are modernist strategies and could be associated with mainstream English literary expression. The modernist technique is more apparent in *The Landscape Within* and "When the Light Returns," where Okri develops "a sense of Renaissance perspectival space" and the psychology that goes with it"[27] than in *The Famished Road*, where Azaro travels between dreams. In *Flowers and Shadow*, he re-creates *Romeo and Juliet*. He uses English literary paradigm; his use of Igbo concepts is just a means of "coming home," of negotiating his identity in a metropolitan, diasporic environment. As Paul Edwards and David Dabydeen note, we see the same technique of "coming home" in Equiano, Gronniosaw, Sancho, and Wheatley, who are seen and taught as black British writers. Based on this double consciousness, which is here, an "empowering motor, not . . . an angst-filled otherness machine,"[28] it would not be absurd to call Okri a black British writer. For, given the history of Africa, to take Britain out of Okri is to take Nigeria out of him. Nigeria and Britain share a discursive field in his world, and that is also the political implication of Okri's narrative aesthetics; he challenges the moribund "totalitarianism of any monolingual intent."[29]

Conclusion

As we negotiate borders and their contents, we should consider the emerging voices—within these borders—which complicate the philosophy that establishes borders in the first place; we should also consider the millennial concept of space, where last names can no longer represent accurate citizenship, where literature has become a means of "crossing boundaries and charting new territories in defiance of the classic canonic enclosures."[30] No matter his native exigencies, Okri inscribes a double consciousness that is characteristic of black British writers. We may even say that his narrative is a colossus astride Africa and the West, leaving each transformed by the other.

Notes

1. Michel Foucault, *The History of Sexuality*, trans. Richard Hurley (New York: Vintage Book, 1990), 4.
2. John Glad, ed., *Literature in Exile* (Durham: Duke University Press, 1990), xi–xii.
3. Subsequent references to this AFRLIT Discussion will be given in the text of the essay henceforth as "Afrlit." The Internet address for the AFRLIT Discussion on Okri is http://www.uweb.ucsb.edu/%7Erbb0/academic/projects/okri/discussion.html.
4. John H. Miller, *Topographies* (Stanford: Stanford University Press, 1995), 316.
5. Emily D. Hicks, "Deterritorialization and Border Writing," *Ethics/Aesthetics*, ed. Robert Merril (Washington D. C.: Maisonneuve Press, 1988), 47–48.
6. Jean W. Ross, "CA Interview," *Contemporary Authors: A Bio-Bibliographic Guide to Current Writers in Fiction, General Nonfiction, Journalism, Drama, Motion Pictures, Television, and Other Fields*, ed. Donna Olendorf, vol. 138 (Detroit: Gale Research, 1993), 337–338.
7. Ato Quayson, *Strategic Transformations in Nigerian Writing* (Oxford: James Currey, 1997), 121–122. Subsequent references to this source are given in the text of this essay.

8. Wole Soyinka, *Akè* (New York: Vintage Books, 1981), 16.
9. Ben Okri, *The Famished Road* (London: Anchor Books, 1991), 3. Page references to Okri's novels are henceforth cited in the text of this essay.
10. Ben Okri, *Songs of Enchantment* (London: Doubleday, 1993), 4. Page references to Okri's novels are henceforth cited in the text of this essay.
11. Cited in Biodun Jeyifo's "Introduction," to *Art, Dialogue, and Outrage: Essays on Literature and Culture.* By Wole Soyinka (New York: Pantheon Book, 1988), xiv.
12. Bill Hemminger, "The Way of the Spirit," *Research in African Literatures*, 32, 1 (2001): 69.
13. Ben Okri, *A Way of Being Free* (London: Phoenix House, 1997), 100. Henceforth, page references appear in the text of this essay.
14. Wole Soyinka, *Art, Dialogue, and Outrage: Essays on Literature and Culture* (New York: Pantheon Book, 1988), 125.
15. Charles E. Nnolim, "Ben Okri: Writer as Artist," *Approaches to the African Novel: Essays in Analysis* (Port Harcourt, Nigeria: Saros International Publishers, 1992, 173–189).
16. Olatubosun Ogunsanwo, "Intertextuality and Post-Colonial Literature in Ben Okri's *The Famished Road*," *Research in African Literature* 26, 1 (1995): 30–39.
17. Margaret Cezair-Thompson, "Beyond the Postcolonial Novel: Ben Okri's *The Famished Road* and Its 'Abiku' Traveller," *The Journal of Commonwealth Literature* 31, 2 (1996): 34.
18. Gilles Deleuze and Felix Guattari, "What Is a Minor Literature?" *Falling into Theory*, ed. David H. Richter, (New York: Longman, 1996), 167.
19. Hicks, "Deterritorialization and Border Writing," 53.
20. Ibid., 54.
21. John C. Hawley, "Ben Okri's Spirit-Child: Abiku Migration and Postmodernity," *Research in African Literatures* 26, 1 (1995): 35.
22. Niyi Osundare, "The Poem as a Mytho-Linguistic Event: A Study of Soyinka's 'Abiku,' " *African Literature Today* 16 (1988): 95–96.
23. Bella Brodzki, "History, Cultural Memory, and the Task of Translation in T. Obinkaram Echewa's *I Saw the Sky Catch Fire*," *PMLA* 114, 2 (1999): 208.
24. Deleuze and Guattari, "What Is a Minor Literature," 169.
25. Brodzki, "History, Cultural Memory, and the Task of Translation," 209.
26. Édouard Glissant, *Poetics of Relation*, trans. Betsy Wing (Ann Arbor: The University of Michigan Press, 1997), 18.
27. T. J. Cribb, "Transformations in the Fiction of Ben Okri," *From Commonwealth to Post-Colonial*, ed. Anna Rutherford (Sydney, Australia: Dangaroo Press, 1992), 145.
28. Edna Aizenberg, " 'I Walked with 'Zombie': The Pleasures and Perils of Postcolonial Hybridity," *World Literature Today* 73, 3 (1999): 465.
29. Glissant, *Poetics of Relation*, 19.
30. Edward Said, "Figures, Configurations, Transformations," *From Commonwealth to Post-colonial*, ed. Rutherford (Sydney, Australia: Dangaroo Press, 1992), 15.

Works Cited

"On-Going Discussion on The Famished Road." March and April 1996. AFR-LIT Discussion. 3rd March 2000. http://www.uweb.ucsb.edu/ %7Erbb0/ academic/projects/okri/discussion.html<http://www.uweb.ucsb.edu/ %7Erbb0/academic/projects/okri/discussion.html>

Aizenberg, Edna. " 'I Walked with Zombie': The Pleasures and Perils of Postcolonial Hybridity." *World Literature Today*, 73, 3 (1999): 461–466.

Brodzki, Bella. "History, Cultural Memory, and the Task of Translation in T. Obinkaram Echewa's *I Saw the Sky Catch Fire*." *PMLA*, 114, 2 (1999): 207–220.

Cezair-Thompson, Margaret. "Beyond the Postcolonial Novel: Ben Okri's The Famished Road and Its 'Abiku' Traveller." *The Journal of Commonwealth Literature*, 31, 2 (1996): 33–45.

Cribb, T. J. "Transformations in the Fiction of Ben Okri." In *From Commonwealth to Post-Colonial*. Anna Rutherford, ed. Sydney: Dangaroo Press, 1992. 145–151.

Deleuze, Gilles and Felix Guattari. "What Is a Minor Literature?" In *Falling into Theory*. David H. Richter, ed. New York: Longman, 1996. 167–174.

Edwards, Paul Geoffrey and David Dabydeen. *Black Writers in Britain, 1760–1890*. Edinburgh: Edinburgh University Press, 1991.

Foucault, Michel. *The History of Sexuality*. Trans. Richard Hurley. New York: Vintage Book, 1990.

Glad, John, ed. *Literature in Exile*. Durham: Duke University Press, 1990.

Glissant, Édouard. *Poetics of Relation*. Trans. Betsy Wing. Ann Arbor: The University of Michigan Press, 1997.

Hawley, John C. "Ben Okri's Spirit-Child: Abiku Migration and Postmodernity." *Research in African Literatures*, 26, 1 (1995): 30–39.

Hemminger, Bill. "The Way of the Spirit." *Research in African Literatures*, 32, 1 (2001): 66–82.

Hicks, Emily D. "Deterritorialization and Border Writing." In *Ethics/Aesthetics*. Robert Merril, ed. Washington D. C.: Maisonneuve Press, 1988.

Jeyifo, Biodun. Introduction. *Art, Dialogue, and Outrage: Essays on Literature and Culture*. By Wole Soyinka. New York: Pantheon Book, 1988.

Miller, John H. *Topographies*. Stanford: Stanford University Press, 1995.

Nnolim, Charles, E. "Ben Okri: Writer as Artist." *Approaches to the African Novel: Essays in Analysis*. Port Harcourt, Nigeria: Saros International Publishers, 1992. 173–189.

Ogunsanwo, Olatubosun. "Intertextuality and Post-Colonial Literature in Ben Okri's *The Famished Road*." *Research in African Literatures*, 26, 1 (1995): 30–39.

Okri, Ben. *A Way of Being Free*. London: Phoenix House, 1997.

———. *Songs of Enchantment*. London: Doubleday, 1993.

———. *The Famished Road*. London: Anchor Books, 1991.

Osundare, Niyi, "The Poem as a Mytho-Linguistic Event: A Study of Soyinka's 'Abiku.' " *African Literature Today*, 16 (1988): 91–102.

Quayson, Ato. *Strategic Transformations in Nigerian Writing*. Oxford: James Currey, 1997.

Ross, Jean W. "CA Interview." In *Contemporary Authors: A Bio-Bibliographic Guide to Current Writers in Fiction, General Nonfiction, Journalism, Drama, Motion Pictures, Television, and Other Fields.* Donna Olendorf, ed. Vol. 138. Detroit: Gale Research, 1993. 337–341.

Said, Edward. "Figures, Configurations, Transformations." In *From Commonwealth to Post-Colonial.* Anna Rutherford, ed. Sydney: Dangaroo Press, 1992. 3–17.

Soyinka, Wole. *Art, Dialogue, and Outrage: Essays on Literature and Culture.* New York: Pantheon Book, 1988.

———. *Akè.* New York: Vintage Books, 1981.

CHAPTER 10

THE BLACK MAN AND THE DARK LADY: THE IMAGINARY AFRICAN IN EARLY MODERN AND MODERN BRITISH WRITERS

Alinda J. Sumers

I owe the concept of the imaginary in art to Yoko Ono, whose works I have never seen and can only imagine.[1] The depth of affection between John and Yoko, as well as their persecuted lives, qualifies them as the ideal imaginary English black couple, when that term is understood as responding to artistic intertextuality and as the expression of the cultural other among us.[2] They represent the postmodern version of the Black Man and the Dark Lady, elusive figures of the English imagination from the Renaissance to our own time.

In the seventeenth century, the keystone of my argument may be found. Robert Burton's *Anatomy of Melancholy* opens with a poem dedicated to the melancholic figure infected with a preponderance of black bile, which makes his humor pensive, philosophical, scholarly, and often depressed. In the drama, the malcontented figure makes his appearance, like Hamlet, dressed all in black,[3] so the audience will make no mistake that this is—according to Burton—the "black man" of the Renaissance imagination:

> But see the madman rage downright
> With furious looks, a ghastly sight.
> Naked in chains bound doth he lie,
> And roars amain, he knows not why.
> Observe him; for as in a glass,
> Thine angry portraiture it was.
> His picture keep still in thy presence;
> 'Twixt him and thee there's no difference.[4]

Burton thus introduces the attitude associated with the black or melancholic figure: a tortured persona, angry, a slave in chains—either mental or physical.

In Shakespeare's sonnets, the poet's muse, some say, is a man—his patron, the Earl of Southampton. Others hold that Shakespeare's muse is a woman—the Dark Lady of sonnets that begin as follows: "In the old age black was not counted fair" (#127); "My mistress' eyes are nothing like the sun" (#130); "When my love swears that she is made of truth, / I do believe her, though I know she lies" (#138); "Two loves I have of comfort and despair" (#144).

That Shakespeare's persona enjoys a love–hate relationship with his ideal is not disputed; he admires her above the conventionally pale beauties of the Italian Renaissance lyric tradition and substitutes for Petrarch's Laura and Dante's Beatrice a woman closer to Sir Philip Sidney's Stella, whose dark eyes hold the potential terror of a real touch. Shakespeare's dark beauty is a real woman, with an unpainted face and curly hair. In the sonnets he teases her, flatters her, and worships her. When she chooses another lover, perhaps his friend, he turns on her and calls her his evil angel, "a woman colour'd ill" (#144). When she betrays him he mourns, "For I have sworn thee fair, and thought thee bright, / Who art as black as hell, as dark as night" (#147). We meet her again in Cleopatra, the darling and duplicitous Egyptian. We see her in little Athenian Hermia, whose angry lover disparages her as an Ethiop in *A Midsummer Night's Dream*.

Shakespeare's Caliban, portrayed by Richard Burton's film version as complete with fins and a tail, has been more recently portrayed as a Caribbean-born black slave. His mother, Sycorax the witch, is also represented as an African. In the modern stage versions, Prospero becomes the hated colonizer who eventually says of Caliban, "This thing of darkness I / Acknowledge mine" (5.2.278–279). By that he means, perhaps, that Caliban is his slave, whose anger he created; or, perhaps, he means his own evil, colonizing black heart.[5] Of course, Shakespeare's *Othello, the Moor of Venice* posits a black prince as his hero, one who is beautiful, powerful, tragic, and, like his other heroes, flawed. In the case of Othello, his disease of epilepsy is described as a contemporary form of melancholy.[6]

Aphra Behn's 1688 *Oroonoko* presents a political portrait of the Jacobite court in exile and intends to flatter the deposed King James II by comparing him to her noble hero, a black prince whose African heritage is matched with Behn's description of his European features:[7]

His face was . . . of perfect ebony, or polished jet. His eyes were the most awful . . . and very piercing, the white of 'em being like snow, as were his teeth. His nose was rising and Roman, instead of African . . . . The whole proportion and air of his face was so noble and exactly formed, that bating [excepting] his color, there could be nothing in nature more beautiful, agreeable, and handsome. (2175)

Although Behn claimed to have lived in Surinam,[8] her portrait of Oroonoko imagines a black King James II whose second queen, Mary of Modena, may have provided the model for Oroonoko's consort, Imoinda, whom Behn describes as the "black Venus" and as the "fair queen of night" (2175). This signifying upon the words "black Venus," "fair," and "night" points back to Shakespeare's Dark Lady, who is also irresistible, dark, and fair (or fickle, therefore foul) as well as to Shakespeare's Othello. Indeed, the parallels between Othello's murder of Desdemona and Oroonoko's sacrifice of his wife, the pregnant Imoinda are, perhaps, intended in Behn's text to remember the dispossession of the little Prince of Wales, who had been born to Queen Mary just before the exile into France. The horrible martyrdom of Oroonoko at the end of the novel glances at the symbolic martyrdom of the Catholic James II by the English Protestant nationalist movement. Behn appropriates for Oroonoko imaginary African qualities that she encodes as belonging especially to the lost paradise of the English royal court.

Rasselas, Prince of Abyssinia, written in the eighteenth century, is Dr. Samuel Johnson's wise African who rises to the level of the heroic ideal. The prince and his sister Nekayah undertake their pilgrimage to Cairo (read London), leaving the "happy valley" of the country family life in Egypt, only to find that people everywhere are much the same. Their cultural difference of outlook, however, allows Johnson to satirize newfangled philosophical ideals of his day.

In the nineteenth century, the black muse became associated with the poetic act of inspiration. For example, Coleridge's figure of the imagination is represented by the African (specifically Abyssinian) maid in "Kubla Khan," singing of Mount Abora. This figure, obviously modeled upon Botticelli's painting of the "Birth of Venus" (which depicts Aphrodite rising from the sea), echoes other Florentine representations and is reflected again in the twentieth century in James Joyce's *Portrait of the Artist as a Young Man*, where a young Irish girl, his inspiration, rises from a seaside pool. While Joyce's figure of the imagination is not black, exactly, the tradition of the Irish as black is obvious to us from eighteenth-century novels where, for example, the dark and mysterious Heathcliff in *Wuthering Heights* stands for the melancholic torment of the Romantic imagination.

This admiration for the imaginary African—the longing for the darker half of self, for exotic, warm, and passionate children of the sun who suffer at the hands of the puritanical north—is echoed later in William Blake's poems "Little Black Boy" and "Visions of the Daughters of Albion." The latter poem is an allegory eulogizing the fate of the slave Oothoon (read America) at the hands of the Colonizer Bromion (read British slaver).[9] Listen to Bromion proclaim his superiority:

> Thy soft American plains are mine, and mine thy north & south:
> Stampt with my signet are the swarthy children of the sun.
> (Inscription to Plate 1, lines 20–21, 66)

This abolitionist poem calls for Theotormon (read British Parliament and other wishy-washy British reform groups) to rescue Oothoon, but Theotormon ignores Oothoon's plea because she is not "Pure" (read white), and tragedy results. Theotormon, the melancholic, like Hamlet, who cannot act upon his abolitionist convictions, represents the English nation who cannot hear the wails of Oothoon, but every morning "sits / Upon the margind [sic] ocean conversing with shadows dire" (inscription to Plate 8, lines 11–12, 71). The immobilized quality of the English in regard to the African plight during the era of the slave trade was legendary.

The satiric attitude toward the British puritanical mercantile classes resurfaces in the poetry of Lord Byron, who ridicules the English in *Don Juan* for idealizing Italy, Spain, and Tunisia: "Happy the nations of the moral north! Where all is virtue, and the winter season / Sends sin, without a rag on, shivering forth" (canto 1, stanza 64, lines 505–507, 631), Byron writes—implying that the northern climes do not foster the depth of passion, the ability to access the feelings, and the sympathies proper to poetry. Is Byron's hero Don Juan—"A little curly-headed, good-for-nothing, / And mischief-making monkey from his birth" (canto 1, stanza 25, lines 192–193, 625)—not a black man? Likewise, Elizabeth Barrett Browning's little Italian heroine, Aurora Leigh, says that England's "frosty cliffs / Looked cold" when she arrives on an alien shore. Later, she meets the melancholic, dark figure of her caretaker aunt, who is clad in the "black garb" of mourning, and tightly braids the "copious curls" of the little girl's hair (book 1, line 314, 1182; and line 385, 1183). Not surprisingly, "The Italian child / For all her blue eyes," complains the aunt, "Thrives ill in England" and has become so "pale" that "she will die" (book 1, lines 495–498, 1186). The shifting values associated with dark or pale images remind us of the warmth of the southern countries, from Italy to Africa, all associated with inseparable ethnic otherness. These shifting valences demonstrate, also, that the typical English literary melancholic is not always depicted as a man.

Aurora Leigh presents the enslaved captive as a child, while John Ruskin's prose description of J. M. W. Turner's nineteenth-century painting entitled "The Slave Ship" exhibited in 1840 describes the imaginary horror of the African slave trade which, technically abolished, was still going on. In the following quotation, Ruskin (the great art critic) describes the painted canvas

> . . . as a sunset on the Atlantic after . . . the torture of the storm. . . . [T]he fire of the sunset falls along the trough of the sea, dyeing it with an awful but glorious light, the intense and lurid splendor which burns like gold and bathes like blood. Along this fiery path and valley the tossing waves . . . divided lift themselves in dark, indefinite, fantastic forms, each casting a ghastly shadow . . . . Purple and blue, the lurid shadows of the hollow breakers are cast upon the mist of night . . . advancing like the shadow of death upon the guilty ship . . . amidst the lightning of the sea, its thin masts written upon the sky in lines of blood, girded with condemnation in that fearful hue which signs the sky with horror . . . and, cast far along the desolate heave of the sepulchral waves, incarnadines the multitudinous sea. (*Modern Painters*, vol. 1, part 2, section 5, chap. 3, 1429)

The phrase "incarnadines the multitudinous sea" is an allusion to a passage in Shakespeare's *Macbeth* (act 2, scene 2) just after the character of the same name kills King Duncan, the honorable and just ruler of Scotland. These words would have been instantly recognized by Ruskin's elite Victorian public, although modern readers might not now so easily recognize the source of the allusion. Ruskin relates the intense horror of the painted, blood-red sea as a depiction of nature's sympathetic grave for some of the murdered inhabitants of the slave ship who have, perhaps, been tossed overboard. Ruskin's reaction to the plight of Turner's imaginary painted captives illuminates as well the passionate feeling and empathy that many British writers have for the black experience of captivity and suffering during the Middle Passage—when black people were stolen from their homes in Africa and transported in traders to Liverpool and Bristol and, from there, over the culpable and deep waters of the Atlantic.

Although much of British literature has not been written by black writers *per se*, an imaginary African man and woman—refugees from the (Mesopotamian) garden of Adam and Eve—populate the literature as lost ideals from which hypocritical Western societies in all eras have fallen away.[10] These are the figures who undertook, according to Rousseau, the social contract, and for whom, in the eighteenth century, the social love of the formal abolitionist movement was founded. England, as the black

American poet Phillis Wheatley had observed, did not really understand Niobe's tears. Nor could English writers understand the double consciousness of an Olaudah Equiano, for the figure of the black in British literature was, by and large, imaginary.

The hopelessly imaginary nature of black consciousness in British literature is perhaps most fittingly expressed by the West Indian writer Derek Walcott, who comments in his celebrated poem "A Far Cry from Africa,"

> Where shall I turn, divided to the vein?
> . . . how choose
> Between this Africa and the English tongue I love?
> . . .
>
> How can I turn from Africa and live?

Walcott is caught between two inherited cultural voices. One voice echoes the freighted mind of the melancholic black man of the Burtonian tradition. The other voice echoes the enigmatic Shakespearean Dark Lady who represents freedom from poetic convention.

Can the tradition of imaginary reading—or misprision—be corrected by the young black British writers of the postmodern generation? One may only anticipate that their literary voices shall overcome the angry cries of the poet who worshiped the Dark Lady, of the malcontented Black Man of Renaissance dramatic tradition, and of the men and women writers who anticipated our emotional investment in the abolitionist British past.

Notes

1. In a televised interview shown in America on PBS in 1999, Yoko Ono discussed how she and John Lennon met at one of her art gallery showings. Regarding one canvas, which was blank, with nail and hammer hanging beside it, Yoko remarked that her art was at times "imaginary." Thus, one might surmise, to place a nail in the canvas with the hammer might make an artistic, if imaginary, statement. Apparently, this was what John was preparing to do at the moment she noticed him.

2. If I read Anthony Gerard Barthelemy correctly, "several centuries of prejudice" have lumped together "at the simplest level . . . the other, the non-English, the non-Christian." See *Black Face, Maligned Race: The Representation of Blacks in English Drama from Shakespeare to Southerne* (Baton Rouge: Louisiana State University Press, 1987), 17. See, also, Joan Lord Hall, *Othello: A Guide to the Play* (Westport, Connecticut: Greenwood Press, 1999), 18–19, n. 19. Ania Loomba argues, "imperialism was eventually to place natives of Asia, Africa,

and the Americas in similar positions of inferiority vis-à-vis Europe." See " 'Delicious Traffick': Alterity and Exchange on Early Modern Stages," *Shakespeare Survey* 52 (1999): 201.

3. Gertrude urges Hamlet to "cast thy nighted [black] color off" (1.2.68). Citations from Shakespeare's works are to *The Complete Works of Shakespeare*, ed. David Bevington (New York: Longman, 1997). Eric P. Levy assumes that Hamlet wears black, connecting the costume to melancholia, and offers a short bibliography relating Hamlet to melancholia and the theory of humors in " 'Defeated Joy': Melancholy and *Eudaemonia* in *Hamlet*," *The Upstart Crow: A Shakespeare Journal* 18 (1998): 95, 107, n. 2.

4. Robert Burton, *The Anatomy of Melancholy: What It is, with All the Kinds, Symptoms, Prognostickes & Severall Cures of It*, ed. Holbrook Jackson (London: Dutton. New York: J. M. Dent, 1932. Rpt. First Vintage Brooks, 1977). See "The Argument of the Frontispiece," stanzas 7, 8.

5. The 1997 production of *The Tempest* at the Shakespeare Theatre in Washington, D.C., featured Chad Coleman, a black actor, in the role of Caliban. Stephen Orgel's "Shakespeare and the Cannibals," *Cannibals, Witches, and Divorce: Estranging the Renaissance*, ed. Marjorie Garber (Baltimore: Johns Hopkins University Press, 1987), 40–66, has become the departure point for all modern conversations about Shakespeare's *The Tempest*. Jyotsna G. Singh also considers *The Tempest* in a postcolonial context in "Caliban Versus Miranda: Race and Gender Conflicts in Postcolonial Rewritings of *The Tempest*," *Feminist Readings of Early Modern Culture*, ed. Valerie Traub, M. Lindsay Kaplan, and Dympna Callaghan (London: Cambridge University Press, 1996), 101–209. Singh comments that "the political message" of Aimé Césaire's modern variation also attempts to "promote 'black consciousness' and rewrite the script of colonial history provided by Shakespeare's 'brave new world' " (205). See also, Eric Cheyfitz, *The Poetics of Imperialism: Translation and Colonization from the Tempest to Tarzan* (Philadelphia: University of Pennsylvania Press, 1997), 108–109. Compare Tee Kim Tong's "The South Seas Tempest in the Renaissance" with Eugene P. Wright's "Columbus, Shakespeare and the Brave New World, "*The Mutual Encounter of East and West, 1492–1992*, ed. Peter Milward (Sophia University, Tokyo, Japan: The Renaissance Institute, 1992), 89–91, 116–117.

6. See Robert Kinsman's article "Folly, Melancholy, and Madness: A Study in Shifting Styles of Medical Analysis and Treatment, 1450–1675," in *The Darker Vision of the Renaissance: Beyond the Fields of Reason* (Berkeley: University of California Press, 1974), 273–320. Kinsman affirms the link between black bile and the melancholic temperament in documents by authors ranging from Galen to Burton. Ben Johnson's dramatic theory of the "comedy of humours" relies upon Renaissance commonplaces regarding the link between the conventional stage malcontent and his preponderance of black bile. Kinsman notes that associations of madness with the physical symptoms of frenzy were manifested according to contemporary accounts in "their casting about of eyes, their wagging of the head, . . . their 'grinding and gnashing togethers [*sic*] of the teeth' " (201). These are as well symptoms modern directors and audiences associate with Othello's epileptic fit of

"ecstasy" (4.1. 34–81). See, e.g., Sir Laurence Olivier's 1932 film performance in black face. Compare this with Laurence Fishburne's portrayal of Othello in the 1996 film version produced by Kenneth Branagh. Jack D'Amico contends in *The Moor in English Renaissance Drama* (Tampa: University of South Florida Press, 1991), 187, that Olivier's performance gives us a mentally unstable Othello, while Fishburne "plays Othello without any obvious character flaw." However, I must argue that Othello's illness, like Hamlet's madness, is a symptom not of a flaw, but of the melancholia that afflicts an othered personality.

7. On Oroonoko's resemblance to the "perfect Restoration man" represented by King James II, see George Guffey's "Aphra Behn's *Oroonoko*: Occasion and Accomplishment," *Two English Novelists: Aphra Behn and Anthony Trollope* (Los Angeles: William Andrews Clark Memorial Library, University of California, 1975), 29–41. Laura Brown compares Oroonoko to the martyred King Charles II of the earlier civil war era in *Ends of Empire: Women and Ideology in Early Eighteenth-Century English Literature* (Ithaca: Cornell University Press, 1993), 56–63.

8. George Guffey cites Bernbaum as having first questioned the "close connections between George Warren's *Impartial Description of Surinam* and Mrs. Behn's Novel" (29). Warren's account was published in 1667, a year before the publication of *Oroonoko* (40). This would argue that her personal account of having lived in that land was a convenient fiction.

9. On the abolitionist conversation carried on by "The Little Black Boy" and "Visions of the Daughters of Albion," see David Bindman's "Blake's Vision of Slavery Revisited" and Anne K. Mellor's "Sex, Violence, and Slavery: Blake and Wollstonecraft," *Huntington Library Quarterly* 58, 3–4 (1996): 373–382 and 366–370, respectively. All subsequent literary quotations are selections from *The Norton Anthology of English Literature*, 7th ed., volumes 1 and 2 (New York: W. W. Norton, 2000).

10. Henri Baudet's *Paradise on Earth: Some Thoughts on European Images of Non-European Man*, trans. Elizabeth Wentholt (New Haven and London: Yale University Press, 1965), 26–49, considers that the myth tended to privilege the "red Indian" over "the Negro," although the "claims of the *bon nègre* were more venerable," because they were "based on a tradition dating back to the manger of Bethlehem and on Europe's respect and predilection for the legendary Christian kingdom of Ethiopia" (29).

CHAPTER 11
A BLACK BRITON'S VIEW OF BLACK BRITISH LITERATURE AND SCHOLARSHIP

Tracey Walters

[T]he landing of the *SS Empire Windrush* at Tilbury Docks on 21 June 1948 began a process which has steadily and radically transformed Britain, and brought about the changed landscape we witnessed.

Empire Windrush was the first ship bringing home the people of Empire from their peripheral margins to the metropolitan centre itself.

—Onyekachi Wambu[1]

Because of the increasing popularity of "Postcolonial," "Transatlantic," and "Diasporic" studies, black British literature, once marginalized if not entirely ignored, is today a burgeoning field that is beginning to receive serious critical attention from scholars on both sides of the Atlantic. In light of the past Windrush celebrations in England (celebrations that embraced the cultural, social, and political contributions that blacks made to British life and culture, both before and after the 1940s–1950s *SS Empire Windrush* era), British readers and critics are also beginning to examine black British literature. This essay presents a view of black British literature from the perspective of a black Briton who resides in the United States. It does not, however, seek to provide an in-depth critical analysis of black British literature itself. Instead, my discussion focuses on my earliest experience with British literature (while I was growing up in England), on my graduate experience of and exposure to black British literature in the United States, on my personal sense of the crucial issues for scholarly and teaching attention, and on what most certainly would be the cultural and social implications of *my* teaching black British literature in this country, especially as it relates to

African American scholarship and my experience of the American academy.

In 1996 I read an article by Fred D'Aguiar titled "Have You Been Here Long? Black Poetry in Britain."[2] Since 1994, like D'Aguiar, I had asked myself this same question. My earliest exposure to black British literature occurred after I left England in 1986. I grew up in a small suburb outside of London called Letchworth in Hertfordshire. As a child, I was not exposed to black British literature. In school we read no books written by black authors, and I did not question this. In fact, I never really thought about blacks writing books. Additionally, I did not define other black people as essentially British. Most of my elders and playmates were Caribbean immigrants, and so I was taught to celebrate the achievements of great Jamaican heroes such as Marcus Garvey and Bob Marley. Outside of these individuals and some sports figures, I was unaware that blacks in Britain had contributed to the culture in important ways.

I grew up during the 1970s at the height of what is known as the Caribbean Artists Movement, a movement similar to the Black Arts Movement here in America. In *There Ain't No Black in The Union Jack*, cultural critic Paul Gilroy contrasts the similarities between the Black Arts Movement in America and an analogous campaign in England. Unbeknownst to me, dub poets and writers such as Linton Kwesi Johnson, John La Rose, Grace Nichols, Jawiattika Blacksheep, Levi Tefari, and many others were sounding their literary voices and tapping their various rhythms onto British soil during those years. It was not, however, until I left England, came to the United States, and completed my undergraduate degree and first year of graduate study at Howard University that I was exposed to black British writers as such.

When I began my education at Howard, I was mainly interested in African American and Caribbean literature. However, as I began to read and examine texts, I realized these narratives did not reflect my life experiences. At least with Caribbean literature I was able to recognize cultural traits I had encountered in my own life, but the experiences narrated in Caribbean fiction and poetry were still somewhat different from my own. When I approached several professors and asked for help in locating some specifically black British texts, I was referred immediately to texts written by Paul Gilroy and Stuart Hall. After reading Gilroy and Hall I was encouraged somewhat, but ultimately disappointed because these writers did not focus directly on black British *literary* scholarship. Fortunately, though, while taking courses in eighteenth-century British literature and a course in the Black Arts Movement

(United States of America), I began, at last, to find reading materials to satisfy my thirst for writing that was black *and* British, and to utilize their bibliographies and find other texts relative to this suddenly vital interest of mine. Texts that were most instrumental to my education included: Houston Baker's and Manthia Diawara's *Black British Cultural Studies* (1996), Gretchen Holbrook Gerzina's *Black London: Life Before Emancipation* (1995), Margaret Busby's anthology *Daughters of Africa* (1992), Vincent Carretta's *Unchained Voices* (1996), and Paul Gilroy's *There Ain't No Black in the Union Jack* (1987), and *Small Acts* (1993). Most of these books were being published while I was doing my graduate work at Howard.

Over the years, while I *have* been able to engage in research, my work in this field has been somewhat arduous. Here, in America, it has been difficult to pursue serious research because it is hard to access the primary texts, not to mention secondary sources of information. However, the *MLA Bibliography* and the Internet have been vital, if sketchy, resources—the problem with the former being that it only lists scholarly books and articles; with the latter, that its posted data is ephemeral. In London, and in other parts of England, the search for materials is a little easier. Again, because of the 1998–1999 *Windrush* Celebration and the many books about the *Windrush* generation of immigrants to the United Kingdom, people in the publishing business and the media have begun to pay more attention to British blacks. However, local libraries, colleges, and bookstores do not always have substantial holdings or materials about black British literature. Oftentimes, when there are materials available, the items are classified under the rubric of "Commonwealth literature" and therefore can be hard to identify as specifically about life in Britain itself. While researching in England can be difficult unless you are in London, or in other major urban areas with large black populations, fortunately, there are a few bookstores in England that specialize in and carry large selections of black British literature. New Beacon Books, for example, which was established by the black British poet John La Rose, is a good resource to know about. However, those specialized stores, reportedly, sell more books written by popular African American writers—such as Alice Walker, Toni Morrison, or Richard Wright—than by black British writers. This is not to suggest that people in England do not read texts written by black British artists. Indeed, just as America has its Terry McMillans and E. Lynn Harrises, England has its cadre of pop writers such as Victor Headley, who wrote *Yardie*, and Yvette Richards, author of *Single Black Female*. These writers are published by a young, black-owned publishing company, The X Press. Caribbean-born British writers like Caryl Phillips, Jackie Kay, E. R. Braithwaite, Beryl Gilroy, and a handful of others also bask in relative fame, but British-born writers like Courttia Newland and Dorothea Smartt do not enjoy the same broad-based reading audience nor the critical attention they deserve. This is partly because the British reading public has not quite realized that there are many black British writers worth reading and, of course, because black British writers are often overshadowed by American writers.

A critical issue that the scholar of black British literature must be aware of is the difficulty that arises in defining black British literature. Black British literature is not easily definable for several reasons. Unlike the case in the United States of America, where black literature is just another name for African American literature, in England, one would not necessarily define "black British literature" as that which is written by a person of African descent who resides in England. Rather, black British literature has been defined, variously, as literature written by people of African descent who were both born and reared in England, literature written and published by expatriate writers from Africa and the Caribbean who published on both sides of the Atlantic (e.g., V. S. Naipaul or Christine Qunta), literature composed by authors who did not necessarily establish literary careers in England but published in England, and, lastly, literature written by people who are simply dark in color, such as East Indians, Pakistanis, Bangladeshis, and other Asians, Near Easterners, and North Africans. The complexities in defining the literature have been raised by one of the few literary critics writing on this subject, David Dabydeen. In his introduction to *A Reader's Guide to West Indian And Black British Literature*, Dabydeen notes the problem of trying to define black British literature:

> Black British literature refers to that created and published in Britain, largely for a British audience, by Black writers either born in Britain or who have spent a major portion of their lives in Britain. But what of the term "black"? Does *black* denote color of skin or quality of mind? If the former, what does skin colour have to do with the act of literary creation? If the latter, what is "black" about black? And what are the literary forms peculiar to "black" expression?[3]

Clearly, then, this matter of defining black British literature is a concern for many and needs to be addressed. The social significance of nomenclature and classification are a major part of the story.

Black British literature is also hard to define because some of the writers themselves might not necessarily classify their work as "British," or might rather seek inclusion in the Caribbean, the African, or some other more precisely identified literary canon. Some black Britons are dealing with the same issues of double-consciousness and identity that American blacks encounter. Therefore, as cultural critic Stuart Hall has contended, "the new cultural politics is operating on new and quite distinct ground—specifically contestation over what it means to be 'British.' "[4] In an interview with graphic artist Sonia Boyce, Manthia Diawara turns the conversation to what it means to be a black British artist. In response to Diawara's question about identity, Boyce notes that she identifies herself as a black woman artist. "That's not necessarily *who* I am, but *what* I am . . . . Within the last few years, I've been pushing up against this idea, trying to find other avenues that aren't to do with identity, even though people still try to place you under that blanket."[5] Boyce's response bespeaks the problematic nature of being a black British artist while retaining the freedom to express individual creative impulses.

The questions of identity and of defining oneself within the larger society are also relevant to the scholarly concerns raised by black Americans. The shared experience of African Americans and of Afro-British people forges a link between the two cultures and, therefore, serves as a strong framework for teaching black British literature in America and showing its relationship to African American discourse. Steadily, African American scholars have begun examining the literature of the African diaspora as the broader cultural and historical context for an appreciation of African American literature. However, much hard work remains to be done to expose teachers and scholars of mainstream American literature to the theory and practice of diasporic writing, particularly because even those academics with a vested interest in the future of black literary scholarship in America give the project of main-streaming African American literature a higher priority. Because black literary culture manifests itself in a different manner in England, it would be entirely remiss to teach Colonial (African) American authors and ignore the important trend-setting contributions of abolitionist writers like James Albert Ukawsaw Gronniosaw, Francis Williams, and Phillis Wheatley—whose works belong very definitely to the British body of literature. Likewise, we should not contemplate the American Black Arts Movement without examining its connections to the contemporaneous British Black Arts Movement, which was as powerful worldwide and included writers of both Caribbean and African provenance. And more recently, when we recollect the contributions made by a Toni Morrison or a John A. Williams, we should also bear in mind the sophisticated artistic accomplishments of a Jean "Binta" Breeze, a Caryl Phillips, or a Fred D'Aguiar. And, as teachers of contemporary black diasporic literature, we should not focus exclusively on writers of poetry and fiction, but also on such pathbreaking intellectuals (black and British) as David Dabydeen, Hazel Carby, Ferdinand Dennis, Naseem Khan, Catherine Ugwu, Buchi Emecheta, and the many others who work as historians, critics, and cultural interpreters within the field. Indeed, within the American academy we must learn that it is important to study black British literature both inside and outside the margins of Caribbean, African, and even contemporary British literature courses. This has not yet happened because the achievements of black Britons still are not recognized, nor so respected, as they should be. In *Cultures in Babylon: Black Britain and African America*, Hazel Carby writes about the difficulty she faced in the 1970s when she tried to publish her book *The Empire Strikes Back: Race and Racism in Seventies Britain*. Carby notes,

> The irrational rationale of publishing companies was patiently explained to this obviously ignorant European: the majority of Americans were totally unaware of the existence of black communities in the UK; those few who might be interested in such a phenomenon would be African American; but African Americans did not constitute a sufficient reading public to warrant the publication of *Empire* in the USA.[6]

Sadly, to some degree things still have not changed. People remain unaware of the relevance or significance of black British discourse. But there appears to be hope.

Conferences and courses on black British literature both here and in England, which are just beginning to be inaugurated at universities and other cultural institutions, make it clear that people are beginning to acknowledge the field. Book-length studies on black British literature and culture such as James Walvin's *Black Ivory: A History of British Slavery* (1993), Vivienne Francis's *With Hope in Their Eyes* (1998), Jeffrey Green's *Black Edwardians: Black People in Britain 1901–1914* (1998), Ferdinand Dennis's and Naseem Khan's *Voices of the Crossing: The Impact of Britain on Writers from Asia, the Caribbean and Africa* (1999), Onyekachi Wambu's *Empire Windrush: Fifty Years of Writing about Black Britain* (1999), *IC3: The Penguin Book of New Black Writing in Britain* (2000), and so forth, and summer programs dedicated to black culture and history, such as the Black Roots Summer Program offered by the University of Liverpool, prove that many desire to know more and to embrace black British literature and culture as an authentic field of academic study. While there is a long way to go, the progress is rapid, steady, and promising. It's going to be hard keeping up with it. It seems likely that soon black British literature will assume a featured place in the literary chronicle of the African diaspora, that widespread efflorescence of creativity that has been, we now recognize, world-transforming.

Notes

1. Onyekachi Wambu, ed., *Empire Windrush: Fifty Years of Writing about Black Britain* (London: Orion Books, 1999), 20.
2. Fred D'Aguiar, "Have You Been Here Long? Black Poetry in Britain," *New British Poetries: The Scope of the Possible*, ed. Robert Hampson and Barry Peters (Manchester, England: Manchester University Press, 1993), 51–71.
3. David Dabydeen and Nana Wilson-Tagoe, eds., *A Reader's Guide to West Indian and Black British Literature* (London: Rutherford Press, 1987), 10.
4. Stuart Hall, "New Ethnicities," *Black British Cultural Studies: A Reader*, ed. Houston A. Baker, Jr., Manthia Diawara, and Ruth H. Lindeborg (Chicago: University of Chicago Press, 1996), 170.
5. Boyce's interview with Diawara, "The Art of Identity: A Conversation," *Black British Cultural Studies: A Reader*, ed. Baker et al., 308.
6. Hazel Carby, *Cultures in Babylon: Black Britain and African America* (London: Verso, 1999), vii.

Works Cited

Baker, Houston A. Jr., Manthia Diawara, and Ruth H. Lindeborg, eds. *Black British Cultural Studies: A Reader*. Chicago: University of Chicago Press, 1996.

Busby, Margaret. *Daughters of Africa: An International Anthology of Words and Writings by Women of African Descent From the Ancient Egyptian to the Present*. New York: Ballantine Books, 1992.

Carby, Hazel. *Cultures in Babylon: Black Britain and African America*. London: Verso, 1999.

Carretta, Vincent, ed. *Unchained Voices: An Anthology of Black Authors in the English-Speaking World of the 18th Century*. Kentucky: The University Press of Kentucky, 1996.

Dabydeen, David and Nana Wilson-Tagoe. *A Reader's Guide to West Indian and Black British Literature*. London: Rutherford Press, 1987.

D'Aguiar, Fred. "Have You Been Here Long? Black Poetry in Britain." *New British Poetries: The Scope of the Possible*. Robert Hampson and Barry Peters, eds. England: Manchester University Press, 1993. 51–71.

Dennis, Ferdinand and Naseem Khan, eds. *Voices of the Crossing: The Impact of Britain on Writers from Asia, The Caribbean and Africa*. London: Serpent's Tail, 1999.

Diawara, Manthia. "The Art of Identity: A Conversation." *Black British Cultural Studies: A Reader.* Houston A. Baker, Manthia Diawara, and Ruth H. Lindeborg, eds. Chicago: University of Chicago Press, 1996. 306–313.

Francis, Vivienne. *With Hope in Their Eyes.* London: The X Press, 1998.

Gerzina, Gretchen Holbrook. *Black London: Life Before Emancipation.* New Jersey: Rutgers University Press, 1995.

Gilroy, Paul. *Small Acts: Thoughts on the Politics of Black Cultures.* London: Serpent's Tail, 1993.

———. *There Ain't No Black in the Union Jack: The Cultural Politics of Race and Nation.* London: Routledge, 1987.

Green, Jeffrey. *Black Edwardians: Black People in Britain 1901–1914.* London: Frank Cass Publishers, 1998.

Hall, Stuart. "New Ethnicities." *Black British Cultural Studies: A Reader.* Houston A. Baker, Jr., Manthia Diawara, and Ruth H. Lindeborg, eds. Chicago: University of Chicago Press, 1996. 163–172.

Headley, Victor. *Yardie.* London: The X Press, 1992.

Newland, Courttia and Kadija Sesay. *IC3: The Penguin Book of New Black Writing in Britain.* London: Hamish Hamilton, 2000.

Richards, Yvette. *Single Black Female.* London: The X Press, 1994.

Ugwu, Catherine. " 'To be Real': The Dissident Forms of Black Expressive Culture." *Let's Get It On: The Politics of Black Performance.* London: Bay Press, 1995. 12–33.

Walvin, James. *Black Ivory: A History of British Slavery.* London: Fontana Press, 1993.

Wambu, Onyekachi, ed. *Empire Windrush: Fifty Years of Writing about Black Britain.* London: Orion Books, 1999.

CONTRIBUTORS' NOTES

R. Victoria Arana is Professor of English at Howard University. Her scholarship appears in *Literature and Psychology, BMa: The Sonia Sanchez Literary Review, African American Review, Callaloo, Dictionary of Literary Biography, Encyclopedia of Life Writing, Genre, Delos, Biography: An Interdisciplinary Journal, A/B Autobiography Studies, Language and Style: An International Journal, Langston Hughes Review,* and other scholarly publications. She organized groundbreaking international conferences on The Achievement of Chinua Achebe, Black British Writers, and Black Travel Writing.

Judith Bryan won the 1997 SAGA prize for new Black British novelists for her first novel, *Bernard and the Cloth Monkey* (Flamingo/HarperCollins), and was awarded a London Arts Board Writer's Bursary to work on her second novel. She has also published short stories, for example, in *Afrobeat* (New Black British Fiction).

Ann Kelly is Graduate Professor of English at Howard University, where she has revised and developed a number of British literature courses that foreground the "Africanist presence." She has published two books on Jonathan Swift, as well as a number of articles on a variety of subjects, including Jonson's *Masque of Blackness,* in *SEL, PMLA, CLAJ, ELH,* among others.

Maria Helena Lima is a Brazilian who is an Associate Professor of English at SUNY-Geneseo. She has published on Jamaica Kincaid, Michelle Cliff, and Merle Collins in *Genre, ARIEL,* and *Callaloo.* "Negotiating Black British/ Caribbean Identities: The Fiction of Andrea Levy" will appear in Kadija George Sesay's edited volume, *Write Black British: A Literary Criticism Anthology* (Hansib Books, 2004). She is currently working on a book of interviews, *Black Britons Writing.*

Jude Chudi Okpala is a theorist. He teaches both English Language and Literature and Philosophy at Howard Community College and Howard University. Among his publications is *The Visible Man* (1995); he has also published on Achebe and is currently working on Nigerian diasporic writers.

Lauri Ramey is Associate Professor of English at California State University, Los Angeles. Her articles and reviews on creative writing, and African American, American and black British literature have appeared in journals including *Black Renaissance/ Renaissance Noire, Journal of the American Academy of Religion, Wasafiri, Facture, Humanitas, BMa: The Sonia Sanchez Literary Review* and *Textual Practice.* She is co-editor (with Aldon Lynn Nielsen) of *Every Goodbye Ain't Gone.*

Kadija George Sesay graduated from Birmingham University in England in West African Studies. She has edited *Six Plays by Black and Asian Women Writers* and *IC3: The Penguin Book of New Black Writing in Britain* (with Courttia Newland), and is the publisher of *Sable LitMag*. She is a George Bell Fellow and a 2001–2002 Vilar Fellow in Performance Arts Management from the Kennedy Center of Performing Arts (Washington, D.C.). She is currently editing *Write Black British: A Literary Criticism Anthology* (Hansib Books, 2004).

Alinda J. Sumers, Associate Professor of English at Howard University, specializes in Renaissance studies. She has published on John Milton in *Praise Disjoined: Changing Patterns of Salvation in Seventeenth-Century English Literature* (1991) and *A Fine Tuning: Studies of the Religious Poetry of Herbert and Milton, A Festschrift* (1989). Her essay "The Armchair Traveler in the Renaissance: John Pory's 1600 Edition of Leo Africanus's 'Geographical History of Africa' " appears in *BMa: The Sonia Sanchez Literary Review* (Fall 2003).

Tracey L. Walters is an Assistant Professor of Literature at the State University of New York where she holds a joint appointment in Africana Studies and the Department of English. She has published articles on black British literature and is currently completing a manuscript on black women writers and their appropriation of Greco-Roman mythological narratives.

Chris Weedon teaches in the Centre for Critical and Cultural Theory at Cardiff University in Wales. She has published widely on feminism, cultural theory, cultural politics, and women's writing. Her books include *Feminist Practice and Poststructuralist Theory, Cultural Politics: Class, Gender, Race and the Postmodern World* (with Glenn Jordan), *Postwar Women's Writing in German, Feminism, Theory and the Politics of Difference* and *Identity and Culture: Narratives of Difference and Belonging*.

Susan Yearwood is a Ph.D. student at Sheffield Hallam University in England studying creative writing and representations of madness in black literature. Her articles and reviews have appeared in *BMa: The Sonia Sanchez Literary Review, The Voice, New Nation,* and *Pride*. Her short stories have been published in *Mizz* and *Playing Sidney Poitier*, and a memoir appeared in *IC3: The Penguin Book of New Black Writing in Britain*. She is currently writing her first novel.

Printed in the United Kingdom by
Lightning Source UK Ltd., Milton Keynes
139217UK00001B/5/P